THE COMPLETE IDIOT'S GUIDE TO

Paying for College

by Ken Clark, CFP

ALPHA

A member of Penguin Group (USA) Inc.

To everyone fighting an uphill battle to educate themselves or someone else—it's worth it!

ALPHA BOOKS

Published by the Penguin Group

Penguin Group (USA) Inc., 375 Hudson Street, New York, New York 10014, USA

Penguin Group (Canada), 90 Eglinton Avenue East, Suite 700, Toronto, Ontario M4P 2Y3, Canada (a division of Pearson Penguin Canada Inc.)

Penguin Books Ltd., 80 Strand, London WC2R 0RL, England

Penguin Ireland, 25 St. Stephen's Green, Dublin 2, Ireland (a division of Penguin Books Ltd.)

Penguin Group (Australia), 250 Camberwell Road, Camberwell, Victoria 3124, Australia (a division of Pearson Australia Group Pty. Ltd.)

Penguin Books India Pvt. Ltd., 11 Community Centre, Panchsheel Park, New Delhi—110 017, India

Penguin Group (NZ), 67 Apollo Drive, Rosedale, North Shore, Auckland 1311, New Zealand (a division of Pearson New Zealand Ltd.)

Penguin Books (South Africa) (Pty.) Ltd., 24 Sturdee Avenue, Rosebank, Johannesburg 2196, South Africa

Penguin Books Ltd., Registered Offices: 80 Strand, London WC2R 0RL, England

Copyright © 2010 by Ken Clark, CFP

International Standard Book Number: 978-1-61564-031-7
Library of Congress Catalog Card Number: 2010903637

15   14   8 7 6 5 4

Interpretation of the printing code: The rightmost number of the first series of numbers is the year of the book's printing; the rightmost number of the second series of numbers is the number of the book's printing. For example, a printing code of 10-1 shows that the first printing occurred in 2010.

Printed in the United States of America

Note: This publication contains the opinions and ideas of its author. It is intended to provide helpful and informative material on the subject matter covered. It is sold with the understanding that the author and publisher are not engaged in rendering professional services in the book. If the reader requires personal assistance or advice, a competent professional should be consulted.

The author and publisher specifically disclaim any responsibility for any liability, loss, or risk, personal or otherwise, which is incurred as a consequence, directly or indirectly, of the use and application of any of the contents of this book.

Most Alpha books are available at special quantity discounts for bulk purchases for sales promotions, premiums, fund-raising, or educational use. Special books, or book excerpts, can also be created to fit specific needs.

For details, write: Special Markets, Alpha Books, 375 Hudson Street, New York, NY 10014.

Publisher: *Marie Butler-Knight*
Associate Publisher: *Mike Sanders*
Senior Managing Editor: *Billy Fields*
Executive Editor: *Randy Ladenheim-Gil*
Development Editor: *Lynn Northrup*
Senior Production Editor: *Janette Lynn*

Copy Editor: *Megan Wade*
Cover Designer: *Rebecca Batchelor*
Book Designers: *William Thomas, Rebecca Batchelor*
Indexer: *Tonya Heard*
Layout: *Ayanna Lacey*
Proofreader: *Laura Caddell*

Contents

Introduction

Titanic was meant to be the ocean liner by which all others were measured. Not only did it represent the height of seagoing luxury for its day, but its designers also believed that its seaworthiness was unparalleled. In short, this masterpiece of planning, design, and execution was believed to be unsinkable. Of course, it only took one oversized chunk of ice to prove that theory catastrophically wrong.

During my years as a financial planner, I've seen few things sink as many households' finances as the failure to be strategic in planning and paying for a college education. Some fail to plan for their own educational expenses, which results in iceberg-size student loans they spend decades paying off. Others fail to plan for their children's costs, which ends up ripping a gaping hole in their otherwise impervious retirement plans. Tragically, some fail to plan for both, which leaves them treading financial water for the rest of their lives.

Of course, many of these households attempted to be responsible, socking away money for future costs. But by the time college was actually in sight, they realized that it was not going to be nearly enough. Between sky-rocketing tuition, underperforming investments, and a lousy economy, they realized too late that there was not enough time to play catch-up. Unfortunately, they also lacked the skills and knowledge to take evasive and creative maneuvers to help them dodge impending financial doom.

That brings me to what this book is meant to be: a captain's manual to guiding your finances safely through the financially treacherous waters of the college experience. More than anything else, it is designed to helping current students and their families do some last-minute maneuvering to avoid ending up on the rocks or going down with the ship.

How to Use This Book

You'll find all the best need-to-know information conveniently arranged into five parts. While I think you'd do yourself a favor if you read this guide from start to finish, you're free to jump around (heck, it's your book). If you have a burning need for knowledge in a certain area, feel free to flip straight to that section.

Part 1, Getting a Grip on College Costs, gives you a buffet of tips and tricks that savvy students are using to lower the real costs associated with attending school. Not only will we put things like tuition, room, and board under the microscope, but we'll also dissect hidden costs such as travel and medical expenses. We'll round out this part by taking a look at how to tap your savings wisely to minimize taxes and penalties. By the end of this section, it's very possible that you'll have lowered the cost of a year of college by anywhere from 10 to 50 percent.

Part 2, Strategies for Borrowing, takes the mystery out of borrowing and repaying student loans. Considering that borrowing might be a nonnegotiable fact for many who cannot or will not compromise on where they get their education, mastering the lending lifelines and loopholes is essential. Not only will these chapters touch on which programs you should consider and tips for maximizing your loan package, but we'll also cover legal ways to reduce or even eliminate your repayment period.

Part 3, Free Money for College, covers some of the best, as well as some of the least-known, programs for getting a free education. Chances are, between the scholarships, grants, tax breaks, and free tuition programs covered in this part, you'll be paying a lot less than most people attending the same school.

Part 4, Best-Kept Funding Secrets, will give you an insider's guide to some of the most overlooked sources for college funds. It's not uncommon for parents or students utilizing one or more of these programs to pay little or nothing for a college degree. Of course, because these programs require a student or his parent to hustle a bit more than just filling out a scholarship application, we'll give you the inside track on exactly what you need to do to make these programs work for you.

Part 5, Thinking Outside the Box, rounds out the book by examining the logic behind some radical approaches to a college education. We'll take a look at the financial merit of nontraditional and online educations, utilizing community colleges to save tens of thousands of dollars, some of the biggest mistakes typical parents or students make, and the merits of putting your kids to work to help diffuse the cost.

I've also included six appendixes to give you everything you need on a practical level to put the advice contained in this book into action. You'll find a Glossary that defines unfamiliar words and terms; a College Cash Strategy Worksheet on which to track your progress as you work your way through the chapters; a helpful list of resources to pursue different funding opportunities; a directory of financial aid programs organized by state; a list of my favorite scholarship programs with their contact info; and a state-by-state list of Section 529 plans.

Bonus Features

Kind of like a tutor who helps ensure that you pass your calculus exam, this book comes with some built-in extras. These sidebars give you definitions as well as cautions and pointers that are immediately usable in your attempt to pay for college:

DEFINITION

Like a first-year freshman in Latin 101, the language of college funding can give you a panic attack. To keep you from feeling like a dunce, I've included some basic definitions of the terms that trip most people up.

CHEAT SHEET

You've only got one chance to pass the college funding test, so I've included these "must know" tidbits that will keep your finances on the honor roll.

FLUNK-PROOF FINANCES

There are some common mistakes that can set you back a pretty penny. Pay close attention to these warnings and red flags to avoid getting tripped up.

WORLD WIDE WISDOM

These resources from the Web and other experts can help ensure that you ace one of life's biggest financial tests.

Acknowledgments

As always, I'd like to thank my amazingly patient and wise editors at Penguin/Alpha Books, Randy Ladenheim-Gil and Lynn Northrup.

To my agent, Bob Diforio at D4EO Literary Agency. I'll never be able to thank you enough for the ongoing education you've provided.

Thanks to the marketing and publicity gurus who have helped me make a career out of writing, Gardi Wilks and Patty Henek at Wilks PR and Dawn Werk at Alpha Books.

Thanks to the gang at About.com (especially Melissa Phipps), who truly gave me my big break in writing about saving for college of all things! Likewise, thanks to my friends at Investopedia.com (especially Sean Joyner), who continue to provide such fun writing opportunities.

Thanks to my close friends at the University of Phoenix, including Steve Elder, Beth Langevin, Dana Padilla, Autumn Hemphill, Yvette Palmer, Leah Duchanoy,

Kimberly Westbrook, Christie White, Christy Oberste, Alicia Banks, Stacy Perkins, Ted Kitchens, Randy McCormick, Felicia Johnson, and all the Little Rock faculty and staff. I've never seen a group of people who believe so much in the power of an education and care so much for the future of their students.

Thanks to Dr. Brenda Sullivan, one of the best bosses, friends, and teachers I've ever had. I hope, "just this one time," you know what a gift you've been to so many people and how proud we all are to know you.

Thanks to my parents and grandparents, who were generous enough to foot the bill for my college education; and to my in-laws, who were kind enough to do the same for my wife!

Thanks to Drew, Price, Ryan, and Spencer. Few things in life make me happier than your individual thirst for knowledge. Your desire to understand makes you the smartest people I know and my pride in you goes beyond measure.

But most of all, thanks to my wife Michele. If it wasn't for getting stuck in a car with you on a scavenger hunt, college might have been a total waste. Your lessons in grace and your heart for hurting people have shaped me more than anything I ever learned in school.

Trademarks

All terms mentioned in this book that are known to be or are suspected of being trademarks or service marks have been appropriately capitalized. Alpha Books and Penguin Group (USA) Inc. cannot attest to the accuracy of this information. Use of a term in this book should not be regarded as affecting the validity of any trademark or service mark.

Getting a Grip on College Costs

Motivational speaker Robert Ringer once said something very appropriate for people staring down the price tag of a college education. According to Ringer, "Reality isn't the way you wish things to be, nor the way they appear to be, but the way they actually are." In other words, reality is reality.

No truer words could be spoken when it comes to tackling the high costs of college, as I'm sure you're coming to understand. College is going to cost a lot of money, and all the wishing, hoping, and dreaming in the world is not going to pay those bills. But luckily, by the end of this book, you will be.

But to reach that financial finish line, you're going to have to figure out where you're starting from today. That's what this part is all about—helping you determine what those costs really will be, understanding how you can trim them, and strategizing how to use whatever assets you have at your disposal.

The Math Behind College Costs

In This Chapter

- Creating a college cash strategy
- Why you need a game plan
- Direct costs: tuition, room, board, and books
- Uncovering hidden or indirect costs

The first day of college can be a little overwhelming for many students. They're sleeping in a new bed and their campus may be the size of a small town. But that feeling usually fades quickly under a landslide of new friends and adventures, with most students happily embracing the college lifestyle.

But for some students, as well as many parents, the joy of being a student or watching your child set sail for college is often met by an even bigger problem than finding the right classroom or dealing with a roommate who snores. In the midst of being a student, or running a household, you've got to simultaneously figure out how to come up with thousands, even tens of thousands, of dollars to pay for it all. In fact, this hurdle can feel so high that many otherwise talented and thriving students put their academic dreams on hold because the money just doesn't seem to materialize.

If you're reading this right now, there's a good chance you recognize the stressed-out and overwhelmed feelings of which I speak. You've probably watched college costs climb 5 to 10 percent a year, while your income and savings have been knocked around by one of the worst recessions in decades. You've also probably put off dealing with the high price of college, promising yourself that you'd eventually get around to dealing with it.

No doubt, this is that time. College costs for you or your child are right around the corner and reality has set in. You've got to do something and do it quick, or a college education is not going to happen. That's where this book comes in; it's going to help you systemically deal with the challenge of paying for college. But before discussing more complex issues like financial aid or where to stick your money until it's needed, I need to start with the basics and determine what college is really going to cost you.

Your College Cash Strategy

Much of the advice and strategies you'll be reading about in this book revolve around the short worksheet in Appendix B. My College Cash Strategy Worksheet, as I like to call it, has three sections to help you quantify your goals, create a hit list of dated action steps you need to take, and track your progress.

For this first chapter, we'll be using portions of the first section, "Unique Costs and Resources." Take a second to peek at it now and bookmark the page so you can flip back and forth easily. I also strongly recommend that you make a copy of the work-sheet to work from (instead of writing in the book), so you can rework the numbers as your situation changes.

Determining Your College Costs

The first time you pay for a college education is not unlike the first time you buy a car. You usually do a lot of shopping and comparison before making the final decision of which car to buy. As part of the process, you might test drive different models, do research on the Internet, and read the reviews published by the most popular car magazines. Then, when you have your heart set on a winner, you sit down at the table with the salesperson to draw up the paperwork. Like clockwork, the price starts going up. By the time sales tax, document fees, and that mysterious undercoating are added, that $10,999 car is suddenly $15,000.

CHEAT SHEET

One of the easiest ways to guarantee your success in planning and paying for college is to find one or two other people who are willing to walk through this book at the same time you do. If you can find a friend, visit the forums at CollegeSavings.About.com to find a group meeting in your local area.

The cost of a year in college isn't much different, except instead of sales tax and an extended warranty, you have things like room, board, books, and student health fees. In the end, the tab for a year of college often ends up being thousands more than you expected.

Now don't get me wrong—I really don't think that most colleges are trying to wring every last dime out of you like some car dealerships do. However, countless students and parents set their hearts on a diploma from a certain college, only to realize that it costs a lot more than the advertised annual tuition rate. Of course, this leaves them in a lousy position, where they're playing financial catch-up in a panicked state.

The Direct Costs of College

The direct costs of college, which you'll read more about in Chapter 2, are those that are related *directly* to the cost of acquiring your education. The most common include tuition, room, board, and books. Unfortunately, the term *direct* has nothing to do with these costs being clearly communicated. Many students and parents find that these costs are hard to get a handle on and change frequently throughout the college experience.

In anticipation of the cost confusion and angry phone calls, most universities have begun publishing a *total cost of attendance* for their schools that attempts to take into account all the unknown variables of attending college. Although this is very noble of them, the total cost for attendance at a school is not set in stone and can vary wildly from student to student. In other words, you should not rely on it because you could be in for some sticker shock.

DEFINITION

Total cost of attendance is an estimate, usually provided by each individual college, of what a year of attendance will cost at that school. In addition to tuition, a total cost of attendance estimate attempts to include other costs such as room, board, and books.

Thus, the first step in figuring out *how* you'll pay for college is to determine *what* you will have to pay for college. There is no point in stressing out, scraping together, or borrowing significantly more money than you need. On the flipside, failure to plan for enough funding can leave you up collegiate creek without a paddle.

In choosing not to trust a school's total cost of attendance and instead estimating it for yourself, it is crucial to understand all the pieces that go into calculating the final bill. The cost of "tuition" you see on a school's website, which can look pretty sizable all by itself, is only one piece of the puzzle. To put the whole thing together, you're going to need to grab the first page of the College Cash Strategy Worksheet from Appendix B and begin filling in numbers for the categories we cover next.

Tuition

The term *tuition* represents the actual cost of the education someone receives. It pays for the teachers, the buildings, the school's administration, and the thousands of alumni fundraising letters you'll get after you graduate. It *does not* include things like a dorm room, the student cafeteria, the cost of books, and other student fees.

Typically, tuition is expressed in a cost per unit, such as $250 per unit. This means that a single three-unit, semester-long class might cost $750. Similarly, a student taking five, three-unit classes in a semester would be paying $3,750 in tuition (15 units × $250 per unit).

Estimate the cost of tuition in your first year of attendance and enter it on the first line of the College Cash Strategy Worksheet. Of course, this estimate depends on whether you know where you're going to college. If you or your student has been accepted or is currently enrolled, all you need to do is visit the school's website or give them a call. Be sure that you use the tuition number for the entire year of attendance, not just one semester.

FLUNK-PROOF FINANCES

Many schools offer a flat-rate tuition fee for each semester, which covers a range of units, such as 12–18. In other words, for a set fee such as $5,000 for the semester, a student could take up to 18 units without having to pay anything additional. If your school charges a flat-rate tuition fee, you're leaving money on the table by not taking as close to the maximum units as your sanity can bear.

Room

Room refers to a student's cost of housing and can vary for different students at the same campus. Depending on the college and the cost of living in the surrounding area, room and board can actually run a student or parent more than the cost of tuition itself. In fact, room and board may be the easiest or hardest portion of your college costs to control.

Typically, the costs associated with room fall into one of two categories: on-campus and off-campus housing. If a student lives on-campus, he will most likely be in a dorm or campus-run apartment complex. If he lives off-campus, he could live anywhere from a beach-front condo to the backseat of his car.

You'll typically have no problem finding the cost of on-campus housing on a school's website because the school controls the cost of housing. Off-campus housing is a different story, though, because prices are essentially set by local landlords.

If you think there's a good chance you'll be paying for a rocking bachelor or bachelorette pad off-campus, you're going to need to do some homework and make an educated guess about the *average* housing costs around the college. You should first call the school and see if it can give you a feel for what off-campus students are paying on a monthly basis. Then, you should get online and visit sites like Craigslist.com or the local newspaper's online classifieds and look at the "Roommates Wanted" sections to see what a local room goes for.

Next, you need to multiply your monthly estimate by either 9 months for on-campus housing or 12 months for off-campus and then enter this total amount on your College Cash Strategy Worksheet. The reason that off-campus is multiplied by 12 is that most landlords require a student to pay for the whole year, even if the student comes home for summer or winter breaks.

WORLD WIDE WISDOM

It's not surprising that many schools bury their tuition information deep in their websites. They know that if you saw that before the pictures of happy students and the campus landmarks, you might start running in the other direction. Generally, if you're having a hard time finding the tuition prices for a school, you can find it under the "Admissions" section of the website, buried in either the "Financial Aid" or "Financial Information" section.

Board

Board is a fancy term for "food" and can also range in cost from very predictable to "anybody's guess," depending on whether the student eats some or all of her meals in the on-campus cafeterias and restaurants. On one end of the spectrum are full meal plans provided by the school. These can be very pricey, but they allow students to eat as much as they can for one set price. If you're worried about your student coming home "all skin and bones," this might be the plan for you.

DEFINITION

Room refers to the on- or off-campus cost of putting a roof over your head, while **board** generally refers to the cost of feeding a student.

In the middle are modified or partial plans that allow the students to eat a certain meal (such as dinner only) or a predetermined number of meals per month (such as 15 meals) in the school's cafeteria or restaurants. This is a popular option, especially for younger, cooking-impaired students who are living off-campus. It helps to ensure that they don't just eat macaroni and cheese for the next four years of their lives.

Of course, students who are preparing all their own food or getting regular pizza deliveries can end up saving or spending a ton depending on their shopping habits. Students or parents expecting this situation should allow themselves some wiggle room in their budgets to learn how to shop wisely during the first year of college.

So what is an appropriate number to fill in on your worksheet for board? If you're going to be on the full meal plan, just use that number (or double it if it is priced per semester). If you're going to use the modified or partial plan, you'll need to enter that number, plus an estimate for the meals the student is buying on her own. If you're going to skip the school cafeteria, then you'll need to estimate the entire thing yourself.

As a rule of thumb, students shopping for themselves can expect to spend about $3 for each breakfast, $5 for each lunch, and $7 for each dinner. If your student is completely feeding herself, this amounts to roughly $450 per month.

Books

If you've felt cheated out of any blood pressure–raising experiences this year, a trip to a college bookstore can make up for lost time. For those of us used to buying our books cheaply on Amazon.com or at the local warehouse store, the idea of paying $100 or more for *one book* leads to words my editor wouldn't let me publish in here. In fact, a brand-spanking-new textbook can easily exceed $150 to $200. If you're lucky enough to get to the bookstore before the mad rush, you may find some "gently used" versions of the same textbook discounted by 25 to 50 percent. This means that a student taking five classes can easily spend anywhere from $350 to $1,000 for books *per semester*!

Of course, many new college students find hope in the fact that college bookstores often buy back books from students. Some students even foolishly pay for their books on their credit card, hoping to get the amount refunded after the semester is over. But as many veteran students will tell you, the likelihood of this happening is pretty low and is affected by things like textbook updates, future class offerings, and the number of other students also wanting to sell back their books.

In trying to accurately estimate this cost, a parent or student can safely guess that they'll incur an average of $125 in textbooks for every class they take during the year. If you think you're going to realistically be paying for five classes in both the fall and spring terms, you should plan on spending at least $1,250 on books per year (5 classes × 2 semesters × $125 per book).

More and more schools are opting for electronic textbooks, which saves both money and the environment. Typically, these e-texts are 50 percent of the cost of regular books, making the costs much more bearable. By choosing a school that has embraced the e-textbook revolution, you can easily save $500 or more per year.

The Hidden Costs

As we'll talk about more in Chapter 3, college has more hidden or "indirect" costs than a student has dirty laundry at Thanksgiving break. This can include major expenses such as travel if a student goes to school far away from friends and family, to minor costs that can pile up, such as student government and Greek life fees.

It's typical for almost every student to have at least $250 or more of these hidden costs per semester. However, students who will travel home frequently, participate in extracurricular activities, or have additional fees associated with their specific field of study can easily spend an additional $1,000 or more per semester.

On your College Cash Strategy Worksheet, you'll find a line for each one of the following expenses. Although they don't require as much explanation on my part, they do require some honest analysis on yours. Being overly optimistic about these expenses can easily lead to a substantial underestimation of your costs:

- **Annual travel costs**—If there is one expense that ends up costing thousands more than people plan for, this is it. Whether you're driving your car halfway across your state or flying all the way across the country, these are real costs that can't be ignored. To fill in this line properly on your worksheet, you need to pull out your calculator and figure out how much it will cost to move to college (whether across town or across the country). If someone is going to help in the move, you'll also need to account for them traveling back and forth. Lastly, you'll need to account for the holidays—will your student be coming home at Thanksgiving, Christmas, spring break, parents' costs of attending a parents weekend, etc.? Add up all those costs and put them on the appropriate line.

FLUNK-PROOF FINANCES

When it comes to the holidays, traveling home can be cheaper than staying on campus, considering some colleges actually charge students an extra $10 to $50 per night to stay on campus over the holidays. Before you decide to skip the plane ticket home, make sure you're not going to pay more by sticking around town.

- **Leisure travel costs**—If spring break in Florida, a semester in Italy, or regular road trips are part of your college dreams, then you're going to need to account for these as well.

- **Medical costs**—When a student stays on his parents' health insurance, there are not usually any surprise expenses. But students who drop off their parents' plans for one reason or another can incur some hefty bills. In fact, many schools are now requiring students to either show proof of insurance or buy a policy offered by the school, which can easily run $500 to $1,000 per year.

- **Campus and student activity fees**—Many schools charge a student government or association fee, simply for being a student. This catch-all fee can include things such as intramural sports and on-campus social events. However, it often does not include things like sporting events, yearbooks, and other campus perks. If you're going to want those things, you'll need to budget for them separately. A phone call to your college's activities office should get you the amount, but $50 to $100 per semester is a safe bet.

- **Greek life or club expenses or dues**—Fraternities and sororities are not quite as popular as they once were nationwide, but some schools' social lives are still dominated by Greek life. Naturally, if an *Animal House* is part of your future, you can expect some vet bills along with it. Typical dues for a fraternity can run from $100 to $250 per semester, not including the parties and other activities. Of course, if you live in a frat or sorority house, you can pay $2,000 or more per semester, but this also replaces much of your other room and board costs.

- **Technology**—A lot has changed since my days at Pepperdine University nearly 15 years ago. Back then, everyone jockeyed for a slot in the one computer lab to be able to type and print their papers. Nowadays, laptops seem virtually mandatory at most schools. If you don't already own one that will last you the duration of college, you can expect to spend $750 to $2,500 for a laptop and printer combo with all the right software, plus another $100 a year for things like printer cartridges and paper.

CHEAT SHEET

In an effort to ensure that all students are up to technological speed, more and more schools are including the price of a new laptop in the cost of freshman year. Although a school's ability to buy in bulk can save some families money, it may be an unnecessary expense for others who already have a working computer. Be sure to check your school's technology policies prior to enrolling.

- **Furnishings**—Whether you're moving into a dorm on the other side of the country or an apartment across town, it's likely you're going to need some new furnishings. Will you need to purchase a bed, bookshelves, a few lamps, or one of those mini-fridges? If you can't think of anything, I'd recommend you at least stick $250 in here per year to cover miscellaneous costs.

- **Clothes**—If you or your student is planning on studying on the beach or enjoying the perks of living near the ski slopes, there is a good chance some new clothes will be in your future as well. While you probably have a much better handle on your expenses in this area, you should budget at least $500 if you're going to experience a dramatic climate change.

- **Lost income**—This might seem like an odd expense to have to account for, but it can put you between a rock and a hard place in an instant. If a student who has been a financial contributor to your household is no longer working, this is money that may have to be made up for from other sources or cut out of the family budget. If it cannot be cut from the family budget, you need to include it in your College Cash Strategy Worksheet and make sure your funding plan makes up for this somehow.

The Least You Need to Know

- Until you understand what college is going to cost, figuring out how to pay for it is pointless.

- Developing a college cash strategy will help you figure out what college will really cost and what resources you'll have to tackle your costs.

- Direct costs (tuition, room, board, and books) represent the biggest portion of your college costs and the amounts that you'll have to fight the hardest to contain.

- Hidden or indirect costs can be substantial and can sneak up on you unless you identify and deal with them.

Lowering Your Direct Costs

In This Chapter

- Tips and tricks to cut tuition
- Reducing your room rates
- Three meals a day on a budget
- Avoid textbook sticker shock

There's an old saying that the best defense is a good offense. In other words, don't sit around and wait for your adversary to find you. Instead, take the fight to your adversary. In doing so, you have a better chance in winning the battle on your terms. Nowhere is this truer than with the substantial direct costs associated with college, such as tuition, room, board, and books.

If you sit back and accept these costs as a foregone conclusion, then that is exactly what they will be. You'll be slapped with the full cost, and you'll have no choice but to accept it and scramble to pay the tab. But, if you decide to not accept your financial fate, choosing instead to be proactive, you can cut thousands of dollars out of your tuition bill.

As with many things in this book, taking a hatchet to the direct costs of college requires some forethought and planning. If you wait until the last minute to make the cuts, you'll have far fewer opportunities and less overall leverage with the people who want your money.

Lowering Tuition Costs

As with all college costs, the tuition you pay is not set in stone. Understanding this, as well as understanding why, can help you to shave thousands off your tuition bills.

The reason tuition costs are highly flexible is because classroom instruction is a largely intangible cost. In other words, the cost of adding one more student to a class is very low for a college, especially if the instructors are not compensated based on the number of students they teach. That means that whatever you pay, even if it is a discounted amount, represents positive cash flow to a college or university. And because many institutions are generally strapped for cash, it behooves them to take every student they can fit, even at an often-reduced rate.

CHEAT SHEET

Many students feel torn about pursuing one major over another course of study, especially because sampling a few classes can cost thousands of dollars. *Auditing* a class is a great way around this and a cheap way to get a feel for a subject area without committing to all the costs. When a student audits a class, he pays a substantially reduced fee to participate in the class without receiving any official credit for it. Most campuses will let students audit a couple of full-length classes during their academic careers.

How easy is it to get your tuition costs lowered? Let me put it this way: you don't need to play tennis with the college president or be all chummy with a large donor to get a sweet deal on tuition. You simply need to know how to ask and have a valid reason. If you do, there's a good chance you'll get a discount.

Because the techniques listed are not sure things and can result in huge variances in your college costs, we're not going to include them in your College Cash Strategy Worksheet for now. If you manage to swing a deal on tuition, you can go back and rework your numbers to account for it.

Asking for the Discount

Discounts are one of the great missed financial opportunities of life. Whether it is on your lawn service or the next car you buy, there's a good chance you can save some of your silver by knowing how to play the game. You see, most businesses are happy to let even their best customers pay full price for their goods or services, as long as their customers don't seem to mind (as evidenced by them going somewhere else). But, those same businesses need to keep their doors open and would rather give their customers a discount to keep them than to lose them at full price. Typically, if a customer makes it clear that she either needs a discount or is going to go elsewhere, prices start dropping.

Colleges—especially smaller and less competitive colleges—often exhibit these characteristics. If you've been accepted, it means that college wants you as a student. You need to realize that the school is not just doing you a favor, but you're the kind of student who fits its reputation and business model. The school thought a lot about who it was going to admit and decided that it wants you there. That also means that it will jump through some reasonable hoops to attract and keep you.

CHEAT SHEET

Many private colleges offer a substantial discount for siblings attending the same school in the same academic year, ranging from $1,000 per student to over $5,000. If you're going to be putting multiple children through college, you should consider sending them to the same school to take advantage of this discount, as well as potential savings on travel, room, and board.

With that in mind, it's important to not be shy about asking a college for a discount if you don't otherwise qualify for one. The easiest way to do this is to send a letter to your school's financial aid office, explaining your financial situation, your need for a discount, and the possibility that you might not be able to attend under the current prices.

It should read something like this:

Dear Financial Aid Administrator,

I'm very excited about the prospects of attending _____ College. I have dreamed of attending such a school for a long time.

Unfortunately, due to a number of extenuating circumstances including _____ [the economy, job loss, other children in school, a recent divorce, and so on], it is unlikely that I will be able to afford the current tuition rate of $_____, even after the existing financial aid packages we've been offered.

Please understand that I am not rejecting my current financial package. I do believe, however, that if the cost of tuition was lowered somewhat, attendance would be financially feasible for our family.

Again, I really had my hopes set on attending _____ College and hope that there is something that can be done to further lower the cost. If you have any additional ideas or suggestions, please let me know.

Thank you in advance for your assistance.

This letter should be sent as soon as you receive your financial aid package from the school, unless your aid package covers the majority of the costs of college, in which case you might not want to burn any bridges. Further, it should be re-sent every year after freshman year because your chances of success will greatly increase during the middle years (sophomore and junior years) of college since graduation rates do matter to schools.

Working for Your College

One of the best-kept secrets in higher education is the tuition discount that the employees of most universities or colleges receive. Depending on the school, these discounts can range from small (10 to 20 percent) to huge (50 to 100 percent). I can speak from experience, with *all* the tuition on my second Master's degree being waived at one of the schools I teach for.

In fact, most schools actually extend tuition discounts or waivers to the spouses and children of employees. That spells opportunity for a parent who isn't in love with his current job and might be able to get a new job at his child's college or university. While employee tuition discounts won't remove all the costs (you still have to pay for room, board, books, and so on), they can represent a huge drop in the bucket.

> **WORLD WIDE WISDOM**
>
> The tuition discount policy for many colleges can be found on the human resources page of the college's website, which is also where you'll find that school's job openings.

Taking AP or IB Classes

If college is right around the corner, this option might be out of reach for you. But for those of you who have a year or more to go until college, you should really consider trying to squeeze in some advanced placement (AP) or international baccalaureate (IB) classes into your high school class schedule.

These classes, which are offered as part of the normal course load at many high schools, allow students to take part in college-level work. At the end of the year, the students have the option of taking an exam to demonstrate their mastery over the material. If they score high enough, they might very well be permitted to skip certain classes in college.

I have known students who have skipped *an entire year* of college by taking these exams, savings tens of thousands of dollars in tuition. But even taking just one AP course and scoring well on the subsequent exam could potentially save a few thousand dollars in tuition.

Unfortunately, not all colleges recognize one or both of these programs, so double-check to ensure that your school of choice accepts these AP or IB exam scores. For more information, visit www.IBO.org and www.CollegeBoard.com.

Taking CLEP Exams

The College Level Examination Program (CLEP) allows people to "test out" of certain subjects based on their existing knowledge, even if they have not taken classes in a certain area. For example, someone who is bilingual in Spanish can take the CLEP and skip her school's foreign language requirement.

Currently, 34 CLEP exams are offered through www.CollegeBoard.com, ranging in subject area from business to history to foreign languages. The CLEP exams aren't free, so you shouldn't take them if you don't feel like you have a good handle on the subject. But for those who do, it can save thousands.

Loading Up on Alternative Classes

Bumping off some of your lower-level, non-major classes on your holidays, mid-semester breaks, and summer vacation can save you some big bucks, especially when the classes are in an alternative format. Sometimes these classes are offered by your primary college; other times they're offered by other schools or community colleges. Just be sure to check with your school's registrar to make sure they'll transfer in and meet your degree requirements before committing to a class.

Some types of alternative classes to consider that can equate to discounted tuition include:

- **Intensives**—These short, impacted classes are often offered right before or after a semester starts, as well as over spring break and other holidays. They generally require a student to be in class 4 to 8 hours per day for 7 to 14 days. For example, I took a two-week intensive class on pre-Colombian civilization at my college, which earned me three credits at half the tuition rate and without a semester of room and board.

- **Community college**—We'll talk more about the joys of community college in Chapter 21, but for now just realize that you can take care of many of your general education classes (GEs) at a community college. At my alma mater, we were required to take four credits of physical education, presumably to help work off the beer and pizza. There was no way I was going to pay more than $500 a credit for someone to yell at me while I ran laps around a track. Instead, I took a golf class at my local community college for $15 in tuition.

- **Self-study and directed-study courses**—Many colleges allow students to take self-study and directed-study courses, often at a discount from regular classroom prices. These courses, which might be offered completely online or might include a few class meetings with a professor, allow students to study at their own pace. Again, these are great to utilize over breaks, when you don't have to pay for room and board on top of tuition.

> **CHEAT SHEET**
>
> More and more colleges are offering some credit for "life and work experience," meaning that if you spent time in the work force or received extensive technical training, you should ask about the possibility of having this count as college credit. Of course, there are strict rules on what counts and how many credits can be earned, but anything you can get approved will help lower your overall cost.

Other Tuition Tricks and Discounts

In addition to the tuition trimming tricks mentioned thus far, there are a number of other tricks and discounts that some parents have pulled off from time to time. As the old saying goes, it never hurts to ask, so consider making a call or dropping an e-mail and giving these techniques a try:

- **Travel discounts**—Some colleges actually offer a discount or tuition credit for students traveling long distances to attend school. For example, Point Loma Nazarene in San Diego offers a $1,200 annual tuition credit to students traveling from Hawaii.

- **Religious and nonprofit discounts**—Many smaller private colleges offer discounts to the children of missionaries, pastors, and other religious or nonprofit workers. If you or someone in your family is associated with a denomination or organization that has affiliated colleges, you'll definitely want to check on the possibility of a discount.

- **Prepaying tuition**—Not to be confused with prepaid tuition plans designed to be savings vehicles, making an actual offer to pay an entire semester or year's tuition upfront can earn you a small discount. Some parents have successfully shaved up to 5 percent off their total tuition bills by contacting the student accounts department at their school and seeing if they're interested in a little extra cash flow. Of course, if you have to put the tuition on a credit card or can earn more than the discount on your own, skip it.

- **Barter tuition**—Colleges, just like any other business, need parking lots paved, websites built, and mice exterminated. Because cash is king, some schools would happily trade tuition for the services you can provide them. If you own a small business or offer a professional service, take a good hard look at your prospective colleges' needs and send them a letter offering a swap of tuition for services.

Lowering Your Room and Board Costs

Living at home is, of course, the slam-dunk option for lowering your room and board costs, unless your parents are charging you an arm and a leg or your student is eating you out of house and home. If living at home is not an option for one reason or another, you can still do a number of things to substantially lower your room and board costs. Some options are easy but come with the potential for headaches, while others can be relatively painless but require a lot of preparation and planning. All of them, though, have the potential to save you thousands, so consider picking one and trying to make it happen.

Going Off-Campus

For the most part, choosing to live off-campus can save you a significant amount of money, usually 10 to 20 percent off the cost of living in a dorm. The major drawback to living off-campus is that the quality of the accommodations and the predictability of the situation become a lot more erratic. For example, when you're living on-campus, you know exactly what you're going to pay, can expect a certain standard of quality, and have some recourse if things aren't going right.

FLUNK-PROOF FINANCES

Without a parent there to look over their shoulder, many students find themselves stuck in very restrictive leases. Before you or your child signs a lease for an off-campus property, consider faxing it to someone more experienced who can look for any red flags such as penalties for breaking the lease, rent increases, and restrictions against subleasing.

Living off-campus, however, you have to deal with issues ranging from grumpy landlords to neighbors who hate college students to delayed repairs. Further, you have to deal with the fact that most landlords aren't looking for tenants for just the 9 months that college is typically in session, but an entire 12-month lease period.

If you are going to try to cut costs by leasing off-campus, be sure to follow these tips:

- **Do your homework**—Before you start looking at rental properties, check with your campus housing office for recommendations on where to search and what to avoid. Be sure to ask if there are any local landlords (who often own multiple properties) that you should stay away from.

- **Ask for a nine-month lease**—If at all possible, ask for a nine-month lease on the property if you're not going to stick around during the summer break. If a nine-month lease is not possible, check to see whether your landlord will let you sublease your property to another student who needs a room for the summer.

- **Take pictures**—Landlords in college towns are famous for sticking it to students on the security deposit. Much of this arises from the fact that students are notorious for damaging property, and most students leave town long before the security deposit has to be returned (usually 30 days). By taking pictures of the property prior to when you move in and again when you move out, you'll have a strong case against a landlord who is strong-arming your deposit.

- **Ask about a prepayment discount**—Because many students receive a substantial refund on their financial aid check that should be used for living expenses, consider negotiating a prepayment discount with your landlord. Offer to pay two or three months at once in return for a discounted rate for those months.

CHEAT SHEET

If you have a love (or at least a strong tolerance) for children, consider swapping nanny duties for free room and board. In a similar fashion, consider serving as a part-time caregiver for a special needs or elderly adult in return for some food and shelter. The easiest way to find one of these great gigs is to contact your local preschools, nursing homes, or regional center for people with disabilities and let them know you're looking for such a living situation.

Finding a Roommate

One of the quickest and easiest ways to cut your costs is to take on additional room-mates. Whether you have a room to rent or are willing to go so far as sharing a room with someone, the cost savings can be gigantic.

For example, in college, my wife shared a room with one of her close friends while everyone else in their house had their own rooms. She paid $350 per month to split a large master bedroom with a private bath, while the four other women each paid $500 for a private room with one shared bath. Over the course of 12 months, that put an extra $1,800 in her pocket.

Here are some tips on finding a good roommate, whether you are renting out an empty room or looking to split a room with someone else:

- **Put the word out**—The best way to find a good roommate is to put the word out to people you know and trust. Because birds of a feather tend to flock together, the people you know and like often know similar people who might be looking for a living situation.

- **Know where to advertise**—Although Craigslist is a great place to get a feel for local rental rates, it's not a great place to find a roommate. Talk about a total crapshoot! If you don't come up with any candidates from your circle of friends, consider posting ads in places where you might find more studi-ous and subdued students, such as church bulletin boards and your school's nuclear engineering department.

- **Ask for their credit report**—Instead of you paying to run their credit report, ask a potential roommate to pull one of their free copies from www. AnnualCreditReport.com and review it for a history of not paying their bills. Choose only roommates who don't have a history of leaving people and companies empty-handed.

- **Ask the "nightmare" questions**—Most college students have at least one story about living with a nightmare roommate. To cut this off at the pass, ask any potential roommate the questions that really matter to you. Does he smoke or drink? Is he a night owl? Does he have any pets? Does he snore?

- **Add him to the lease**—If your landlord allows you to sublease, try to get your new roomie added to your lease. Otherwise, the risk associated with him staying in the house is all on you. If you can get him added to the lease, then the risk has partially shifted to your landlord.

- **Ask for a deposit**—If at all possible, get your new roomie to split the security deposit with you, even if you've already paid it. If nothing else, take the money and put it in a savings account at your local bank. That way, your roommate has incentive to help maintain and protect your living space.

- **Trust your gut**—It seems that the vast majority of times someone tells me about a bad roommate, they also tell me that they had some initial concerns and should have listened to their gut. So if the red flags go up on a potential roommate, you're probably better off to wait for someone better.

FLUNK-PROOF FINANCES

Few things can sour a living situation faster than when valuables go missing. When it happens, it's usually not a roommate, but one of their guests who developed a case of sticky fingers. To protect yourself and your living arrangement, consider adding a lock and key to your bedroom door and leaving your most precious valuables safely at home.

Becoming a Residential Advisor

Not everyone wanting to do this will get a chance, but being a residential advisor can be a great deal for those who get their foot in the door. Most campuses with dorms employ students as residential advisors (RAs) who live in and oversee a dorm full of other students. In general, their job is to help keep the fun to a mild roar and alert the campus to any issues that need to be addressed. In return, they get free or discounted housing.

Many schools actually employ two RAs per dorm, with one usually being an older, more experienced advisor and the other being a sort of apprentice. With very few exceptions, these advisors are upper classmen, with juniors and seniors getting priority.

To become an RA, a student has to submit an application well ahead of the coming semester or year, as well as have a spotless academic and behavioral record. Students hoping for such a position should stay as far away from trouble as possible, while looking for opportunities to volunteer and demonstrate responsibility elsewhere on campus.

Keeping Meal Plans from Eating You Alive

The cost effectiveness of meal plans varies widely from campus to campus, as does the quality of food that is available. Because food quality and cost generally go hand-in-hand, you can reasonably expect colleges with great cafeterias to cost more than those where there's a large amount of mystery meat on the menu. In general, though, you can expect a full meal plan (three meals a day) to cost between $400 and $500 per month. This does not include providing your student with money for snacks or late-night pizza.

CHEAT SHEET

While being an RA is one of the juiciest jobs on campus, it's not the only one that offers benefits. Students willing to work in the student cafeteria often eat for free, saving as much as $400 to $500 per month. Likewise, students working in the campus bookstore often receive discounts on their textbook purchases.

For students who will be without a kitchen, the use of the school's cafeterias might be your only option. But that doesn't mean you should opt for the standard meal plan. In reality, a meal plan that covers two meals per day is often a much better use of your money because many students never visit the cafeteria for breakfast (they're either running late for class or sleeping in). If this is your student, you can probably save $50 to $100 per month by sending her some extra large boxes of cereal and opting for the two-meals-per-day plan.

For students living off-campus, however, the ability to save (or waste) money is greatly increased. Students who take the time to shop wisely, plan their meals ahead of time to maximize leftovers, and even share meals with roommates, can cut their food costs down to $250 per month. Further, in the months where they're eating light or are off campus more than usual, you're not wasting money on the school's meal plan.

Two types of students are ideal for opting out of your school's meal plan altogether—both of which need to have access to a refrigerator and/or a kitchen to save money while staying healthy. This, of course, can be a challenge, because most dorm room fridges are pretty tight on space and most campuses don't allow any type of cooking or heating element in their standard rooms.

That aside, the first type of student who can reap some savings is the undiscerning, "quantity over quality" type eater. These students can be taught to prepare cheap, easy, and nutritious meals like pasta, chicken, and sandwiches. The other type is the picky, finicky eater, who will do fine on salads, fresh fruits, vegetables, and other light fare. Vegetarians and vegans might fall into this category as well, especially since they may be venturing off campus to find the freshest items anyway. Both of these types of students should have no problem saving money over most schools' standard meal plans by shopping at the store and utilizing coupons.

Cutting Costs on Books

Saving money on books can be absolutely hit-and-miss, depending on which classes your student is taking, which textbook and edition an instructor is requiring, and whether other students have recently taken that class. But, when it is a hit instead of a miss, it's a homerun. Don't get discouraged if you end up paying full price for books for one or more semesters. Keep looking for savings opportunities because they will come along. Every semester, follow these tips, and savings should eventually materialize:

- **Get your class schedule as early as possible**—By registering early and getting your schedule as soon as possible, you'll be able to start searching for used books before everyone else. The early bird gets the worm!

- **Advertise your need**—Once you know which classes you're taking, which will usually be before the bookstore even opens for the semester, you can begin putting out feelers for secondhand books. Post some flyers on the school bulletin boards announcing the books you're looking for and the price you're willing to pay. Do the same on your school's online message boards. Chances are that you'll find a used book for even cheaper than what the school's bookstore has to offer.

- **Go online**—Check eBay, Amazon.com, and other online marketplaces for copies of your book. Heck, with an online auction, you might even get the books you need for as little as $10 to $20 each, plus shipping.

- **Consider renting**—As hard as it is for some of us old fogies to imagine, you can actually rent textbooks nowadays. Websites like Chegg.com, CampusBookRentals.com, and BookRenter.com all rent textbooks at about

one-third the cost of buying them new. If you do a little searching
Internet, you can find some coupon codes to get them even cheape

- **Consider sharing**—If you and your roommate or a friend are taking the
  same classes, especially ones that require you to purchase multiple books,
  consider splitting the cost on just one copy and sharing. Voila, your textbook
  costs have been cut in half!

- **Be first in line**—If you haven't been able to find a book through one of these
  other methods, be sure you're near the front of the line when your campus
  bookstore opens for the semester. Most campuses stock a limited supply of
  used books, and they go like hotcakes.

- **Be first in line, again**—When it comes time to sell your books back to your
  campus bookstore, you'll want to be first in line again because your bookstore
  will only likely buy back a portion of what it originally sold. If the store tries
  to lowball you on your book's value, consider posting some flyers around
  campus and trying to sell it directly to another student.

Don't avoid buying a cheap, older version of a textbook just because the class demands
a newer edition. Often, the changes in these textbooks are minimal, with 100 percent
of the crucial information staying the same. To find out how much a textbook has
changed and whether an older version will do the trick, visit the publisher's website
and look for the revision notes for the newer book.

The Least You Need to Know

- Write a formal letter asking your school for an additional discount due to financial hardship, every year that you attend.
- Use community college, intensive courses, CLEP tests, and advanced placement
  classes to get some general education requirements out of the way.
- Lower your room and board costs by moving off-campus, avoiding high-priced
  or unused meal plans, taking on an extra roommate, or even becoming a
  residential advisor (RA).
- Only buy your textbooks from the campus bookstore as a last resort.

Lowering Your Indirect Costs

Chapter

3

In This Chapter

- Keeping tech costs under control
- Saving 10 percent or more on travel costs
- Avoiding surprise medical bills
- Falling in love without breaking the bank
- Factoring in inflation

I live for pin the tail on the donkey and piñatas. In fact, they're the only things that sustain me through the mind-numbing joy that comes from sitting through a Barney or Teletubbies birthday party for little kids. It's the whole idea of the thing—that somehow, blindfolding someone who only learned to walk a few years ago, spinning them in circles, and giving them a sharp thumbtack or a large stick to swing around is a good idea. I'm not sure that half of the pint-size contestants could successfully complete the task under normal circumstances, much less after three spins and a blindfold.

Money and the college brain are not much different. Whether it is not blowing all their food money in the first week of the month or managing their financial aid refund wisely, the task is hard enough for a young adult. Add in the chaos of classes, a roommate who refuses to shower, and rebuilding a social life from scratch, and it's not hard to imagine why some students end up missing the financial mark by a country mile. By being deliberate about addressing hidden expenses from the get-go, you'll ensure that your wallet doesn't end up getting whacked around like a piñata.

Hacking the High Price of Technology

In the college world, the pressure to party is nothing like the pressure to have the right technology. It's not uncommon for parents to get calls from students during the second week of school informing them that the family computer that went off with them to college just won't cut it. For the next four years of college, and even their future, to not be wasted, they're going to need the newest laptop with all the bells and whistles. Oh yeah, and while you're at it, they're going to need a new iPod, too.

Don't give in to the pressure. While technology is definitely a part of the modern college experience, most students end up spending way more money than they need on something that might not survive the college experience. The trick is to find out exactly what you need before you step foot on campus, evaluate what you already have, and then take advantage of special deals for students to lower your costs.

CHEAT SHEET

Over the last few years, I've noticed that an increasing number of students spend only about $10 on their technology needs for four years of college. How in the world do they do it? More and more students are purchasing USB thumb drives that cost between $10 and $20 and can store more papers than one person could ever write. They simply clip these small hard drives to their key chains and then use the free computers available on campus to do their work.

Getting the Best Deals on Technology

The easiest way to waste money on technology is to decide that you need something today and that you don't have time to shop around. For those willing to wait and do their homework, saving $250 to $500 on a computer and software is a no-brainer. In fact, I want you to go ahead and add $250 in savings to the Technology line in the "Calculate Estimated Direct and Indirect Cost Savings" section of your College Cash Strategy Worksheet (see Appendix B).

Here are my top tips for keeping your cash in your pocket:

- **Avoid your campus tech shop**—Ever wonder how they can get away with charging you $10 for a hot dog when you go to a baseball game? It's because they know they've got you. Really, where else are you going to go? To some degree, the same is true with many campus technology stores. Although they offer some good deals, they never offer those screaming deals that will save you a lot of money. They know they don't need to because all of the students who didn't plan ahead will be in there in a panic, buying whatever they can get their hands on.

- **Scour the Sunday paper**—Really, when it comes down to it, the best deals for school-related technology needs can be found in your local Sunday paper. Just find the glossy inserts for your local "big box" retailers. Look through there and find a computer that fits your needs, do a quick online search to figure out if you're getting a deal and to look for any negative reviews, and then head to the store committed to buying that computer (not the much pricier one they'll inevitably try to sell you). One of the best Internet sites for technology reviews is CNet.com. Before you buy a computer for college, check CNet to see whether its reviewers give it their stamp of approval.

- **Buy bundled software**—Here's the skinny: you're going to need Microsoft Office (Word, PowerPoint, and Excel) at almost every college and for almost every major. Alternative programs like Microsoft Works, Corel WordPerfect, or any of the standard Mac programs just won't cut it. Ideally, the computer you buy should come preloaded with fully licensed (not trial versions) of these programs. If you buy them individually, you might spend hundreds of dollars, but if you get them preinstalled on your computer, you might not spend a dime extra.

- **Develop brand-name blindness**—Like any other product, brand-name technology usually costs more. In reality, though, for what most students are going to do at the college level (with the exception of needing Microsoft Office), non–brand-name computers and software are more than sufficient. This is especially true with Macs (don't get me wrong, this book was written on a Mac), which are all the rage with college students. A good non–brand-name laptop shouldn't run you more than $600 to $800, while a brand name or MAC can easily run over $1,000.

- **Look for open box specials**—Most large electronics stores have a special section where they tuck away products that have been returned, but for one reason or another cannot be sold as brand new. These products still have their full warranties and might have never been used, but because the seal is broken on the box, they're selling at a 10 to 50 percent discount. If you can't find the rack of "open box specials," just ask a salesperson.

- **Utilize student discounts**—If you are attending school in an area where there is a shortage of large electronics stores, or if you need to purchase any software including Microsoft Office, try to swing a student discount. To do this, either visit the link provided by your college or go directly to the manufacturer's website and look for a student or education link. As an example of how large the savings can be, I recently bought a student version of a $1,000 graphics program for about $350. That's a whole lot of savings.

Are Laptops Really Mandatory?

You'll constantly hear from other students, as well as from your own kids (who hear it from other students), that laptops are mandatory for college. So are they?

Laptops, which can run you a pretty penny, might be mandatory if you're getting a Ph.D. in coolness, but they're definitely not mandatory for graduating at the top of your class. Remember, some of America's greatest minds went to college when typewriters were still considered high tech. Yet, they managed to get a quality education.

As someone who teaches college on a regular basis, I can tell you that a laptop is by no means mandatory. In fact, I find that it is actually detrimental to many students' educations. Time and again, I and other professors catch students on Facebook, watching YouTube, or working on other assignments from other classes. Ironically, when they actually sit to write a paper with their fancy laptop, they're usually doing it in their dorm room, where you'd keep a less sexy desktop computer anyway.

Don't get me wrong, 24/7 access to a computer is essential. But, if you have a functioning desktop computer at home that can be taken to school, there is absolutely no reason to buy a laptop.

FLUNK-PROOF FINANCES

In mid-2009, student Joel Tenenbaum lost a lawsuit against the Recording Industry Association of America (RIAA) for illegally downloading music to his computer while at college. The fine was a staggering $675,000 for just 30 songs. It goes without saying that students need to be aware that irresponsible use of technology could cost them their financial futures.

Buying Your Technology, Once

Between accidental spills, unexpected bumps and bruises, and intentional techno-abductions, there is a good chance that the electronics you send to college with your student might not come home in one piece—or come home at all. In fact, laptop theft is so commonplace at larger campuses that many experts are now recommending that students purchase a harder-to-steal desktop.

Considering the potential for theft and damages, regularly replacing technology can end up being a recurring hidden cost that will bleed you dry. With that in mind, here are some key tips to making sure you only buy "it" once:

- **Don't leave technology unattended**—Most technology that gets stolen or damaged has typically been left unattended by the person it matters to most. In fact, many campuses are specifically targeted by small-time thieves who simply hang around coffee shops or libraries, waiting for a student to get up and take a potty break. Simply keeping a close eye on valuables will save you from paying for them more than once!

- **Get a cable lock**—One of the easiest ways to keep a laptop or desktop from growing a set of legs is to buy a $20 cable lock. In fact, virtually all laptops come with a built-in receptor for these locks, which look and function much like a bike lock. Although it won't keep a determined thief with a set of cable cutters from stealing a computer, it will keep the casual thief from grabbing a laptop while everyone's back is turned in the dorm or a library study room.

- **Check your homeowner's policy**—Many homeowner's policies cover students against theft and damage while they're at college. If a loss occurs, this can be the cheapest route to replacing your technology.

- **Buy the protection plan**—In *The Complete Idiot's Guide to Boosting Your Financial IQ* (Alpha Books, 2009), I share my disdain for the extended warranties pushed on you by the clerks at your local electronics store. Under normal conditions, they are generally a poor investment and will never get used. Under college conditions, however, they might be your best friend if you don't have a homeowner's policy. This is especially true if you can find one that covers accidental breakage or even theft.

Travel Expenses

It goes without saying that the easiest way to cut down on travel expenses is to go to school near where you currently live. Of course, this is not possible or desirable for many people, especially those who have an opportunity to go to a top-tier college or one that specializes in a certain area of study.

The to and fro of higher education can drain your bank account as quickly as any other hidden cost, especially for homesick students and parents who haven't seen their babies in 3 or 4 months. Two round-trip plane tickets per semester, plus those wonderful baggage fees, airport parking, taxis, and so on, can easily cost over $1,000 per semester.

Like virtually every other expense, the biggest strategy for curbing travel expenses is to plan ahead. This is especially true because 90 percent of the nation's students will all be trying to buy airline tickets for the same small travel window every year, with the cheap seats and the smart alternatives being snapped up quickly.

As a rule of thumb, embracing the tips in this section will save you at least 10 percent off your estimated travel costs. So as with technology, you'll need to add these savings to the second page of your College Cash Strategy Worksheet. To do this, simply multiply your estimated travel costs by 10 percent and then add this to the travel savings line in the "Calculate Estimated Direct and Indirect Cost Savings" section.

WORLD WIDE WISDOM

One of the best ways to save big on travel, technology, and other college necessities is to purchase a Student Advantage card. These cards cost anywhere from about $15 to $25 per year, but they earn discounts that pay for the card on the first purchase. For example, at the time of this writing, someone with a Student Advantage card could receive a 10 to 15 percent discount on airfare, rail, and bus tickets from a number of top U.S. carriers. Visit www.StudentAdvantage.com to learn more.

Rethinking High-Priced Airfare

Okay, sometimes you've just got to fly. But when you're trying to save money, especially if you're traveling within the country, flying can be costly and time-consuming. Trains and buses often get you there in comparable time—especially when you account for airline security and sitting on the runway—sometimes at 50 to 75 percent less than full-airfare tickets.

The two dominant players in this arena are Amtrak's train service and Greyhound's bus service, both of which offer discounts to students and military and do not charge baggage fees like the airlines do. Of course, you're not the first one to figure this out, so saving money is all about getting your reservations in early, before the price-gouging begins for those last available seats.

If you have to fly, the worst thing you can do is try to stay loyal to one airline. Even if that is the airline your main frequent flyer account is with, saving $50 to $100 on a ticket easily outweighs any mileage benefits. Smart travelers use ticket aggregators like Orbitz.com, Travelocity.com, and Kayak.com, which compare tickets from multiple airlines on multiple dates. To save even more, use the "Search for Nearby Airports" feature, which can save you big bucks if you're willing to drive just a tad.

Travel Off-Peak

The cheapest seats on any mode of transportation are going to be during off-peak hours. Your goal in booking transportation for your student is to go as off-peak as possible. Consider trying to travel during the following windows of time:

- **Get on E-Saver lists**—Most airlines, bus companies, and railways offer some great last-minute travel deals by way of "E-Saver" type e-mail lists. These lists are quick and free to sign up for and can offer you big savings if your travel plans are flexible.

- **Tuesdays, Wednesdays, and Saturdays**—With some holiday exceptions, the cheapest time to book tickets for any mode of transportation is going to be Tuesdays, Wednesdays, and Saturdays.

- **Early morning or late night**—Most leisure travelers don't have any interest in waking up at the crack of dawn to catch a flight or trying to get their kids to sleep on an overnight bus ride. Naturally, these will be some of the cheapest times to move about the country.

- **Travel on the holiday**—Surprisingly, if you're purchasing a ticket for the holidays, the actual day of the holiday itself can be one of your cheapest options. That's because everyone else is scrambling to arrive or leave on either side of the holiday.

- **Take the bump**—When my wife and I were newly married and without screaming kids, we used to volunteer to "get bumped" every time we'd check in for a flight in the event the airline had oversold the seats. In one single trip, the two of us racked up over $1,000 in free flight vouchers thanks to our flexibility to take a later flight. Whenever anyone in your family travels for any reason, try to make sure your plans are flexible enough for them to take a bump. It could pay for your whole year of collegiate travel.

Taking a Car to College

Many parents secretly rejoiced the day their kids got their driver's licenses, even though they'd never let on that this was the case. The reason for this hidden exuberance is that the days of playing taxi driver for teens had suddenly lessened or even come to an end. Of course, for teenagers, the day they received their licenses meant that they had a lot more freedom to go where they wanted, when they wanted.

Not surprisingly, many students refuse to even consider the idea of going to college without a car. Yet, taking a car to college can be a surprisingly pricey affair that parents need to think through. Aside from the additional mileage your student might rack up and the excessive freedom it can provide them, there are a number of other key points to consider. Be sure you get answers to these questions before your student drives off into the sunset:

- **Out of state costs**—If your student is taking his car out of state, will he need to get it registered? Will it be subject to smog-testing requirements that might require repairs? Will your insurance go up, or will you be required to buy another policy for that state? These costs alone can easily run you hundreds of dollars, especially for states like California that have exorbitant registration fees.

- **On-campus parking**—Many campuses are already overcrowded with student vehicles and aren't in a rush to build more parking spots. Getting a spot on-campus can require a pricey parking pass, monthly garage parking fees, and/or a fair share of parking tickets for students who perpetually run late for class. Find out what these fees and the campus policies are before you send a car off to college.

- **Gas and repair prices**—Especially if you're going from small town America to Metropolis, you might be surprised at how much more gas and repairs can cost you. It's not uncommon for gas to cost a full dollar per gallon more in some parts of the country, which can easily add up to hundreds of extra dollars over your current gas bills, each semester.

The Overseas Experience

Spending some time overseas can be a life-changing experience for many students. It also can be ridiculously costly because you have to add in the costs of foreign travel on top of your existing costs of college tuition.

That's not to say that you shouldn't indulge and see the world while you're young and free. It just means you need to be as strategic about it as you are your other expenses:

- **Follow the dollar**—A "strong dollar" makes for cheap travels and extended stays in foreign countries. You can significantly reduce your cost by choosing to live and study in a country where the dollar is strong versus the local currency. For example, in recent years the dollar has had roughly 125 to 150 percent of its domestic buying power in much of eastern Europe and South America.

- **Go for the whole year**—Although a semester overseas might sound just perfect, you're likely to experience less out-of-pocket costs by going for the entire year. Doing so lets you commit to longer-term lodgings there, while not having to commit to or break a lease here. Additionally, you won't be in a rush to see the sights there and can take advantage of off-peak and non-tourist seasons in your host country.

- **Sell your skills**—There's a reasonably strong demand for people with strong skills in a variety of areas to do things like teach English, act as tour guides, and provide child care in other parts of the world, especially in Asia. Getting a part-time gig can pay fairly well and might even come with free room and board, even for those without a college degree. All that it takes is a warm personality and a willingness to help people. Check out websites such as TeachAbroad.com and TravelAbroad.com for more details.

CHEAT SHEET

Would you be interested in traveling the world for little or no cost? What about getting some of your student loans forgiven for making a difference while you trot the glob? If so, the Peace Corps might be one of the best options for cash-strapped students. The Peace Corps offers travel opportunities to all over the world for 2- and 4-year degree holders. By simply holding off on that semester overseas until right after you graduate, you can keep thousands of dollars from evaporating.

Don't Let Spring Break Break the Bank

There's no doubt that one of the best parts of college for many students is the adventures, the road trips, and the all-night parties. These extra-curricular activities are not for every student, but a ridiculous number of successful students do blow off some steam a couple times per year without totally sinking their grades. One of the biggest outlets is of course spring break, which can end up breaking the bank if students aren't careful.

The biggest problem with spring break—one that I see over and over again—is that students do not set aside money in advance for their spring flings. Naturally, this leads many students to whip out their newly issued credit cards, along with a mentality of "you're only in college once." Sadly, because much of the expenses are going on a credit card, most students spend even more frivolously than if they had only a fixed amount of cash in the bank that they needed to make stretch.

So to keep spring break from breaking the bank, smart students (or their parents) set aside money in advance in an all-purpose "travel" account. This money can be used for spring break, coming home on the holidays, or traveling overseas. But, by deciding in advance to put $50 or $100 per month into this account, it creates some natural boundaries that a student is more inclined to stay within.

Medical Expenses

Let me just preface this whole section by saying, *I hate medical expenses.* Not just because I don't like paying them, but also because they can be the equivalent of a nuclear bomb being dropped on someone's finances. Everything's going just fine, you're cruising campus on the new moped you bought, and then a headfirst dive over your bike's handlebars sends you to the ER. There you conveniently find out that your insurance doesn't cover what you thought it did, and $10,000 in medical bills later, you're filing bankruptcy and wondering what the heck happened to your life.

College in particular places your personal finances straight in the path of oncoming traffic for a number of reasons. Whether it's the close and often less-than-sanitary quarters of the college environment, the likelihood of a student taking unnecessary risks, or the fact that your adult child might not be covered like she used to be, you have plenty you need to watch out for.

Keeping Your Kids Insured

If you have kids going off to college, or you're a student who is currently on mom or dad's health insurance, don't assume that it'll be there when you need it. Insurance company and state rules vary on how long adult students must be covered, who is actually considered a student, and what expenses are not covered. Because it can vary so much by insurance company and state, call your insurance company (if you have insurance) and get answers to the following questions:

1. Does my insurance cover my college student?

2. Until what age will a *dependent* college student be covered?

3. What is your definition of a student? Does she have to be full-time, part-time, at an accredited school, and so on?

4. How long of a break can my student take from school before she loses coverage?

5. Do I need to supply any documentation to ensure that she remains covered under my plan?

6. If she goes to school in _____ [insert city/state], will she still be fully covered, or is this outside of my network?

7. Does my insurance cover "transport" services if she's ill or injured away from home and needs to be moved back here?

DEFINITION

The term **dependent student** can be confusing for parents—specifically, whether an adult child who is working and going to school is truly considered dependent. As far as most insurance policies are concerned, being a dependent has nothing to do with a student's income level, but whether or not she's under a certain age (usually 24) and whether she's a full-time student.

Using On-Campus Alternatives

One of the best-kept secrets in the war on student medical costs is medical and insurance alternatives offered through a college. This is especially true if a student is attending a college that has medical or nursing programs on-campus and uses the campus clinics as training grounds for their faculty. Although these might not be ideal places for brain surgery, they're great options for sore throats, sprained ankles, and hangovers from "study breaks."

There are really two distinct opportunities here for parents and students trying to squeeze through college financially. First and foremost, even if a student has insurance, visiting a free clinic for routine issues can save $20 to $50 per visit in deductibles or co-payments. Every student should pay a visit here first and then get a second opinion or outside treatment as needed.

Second, most colleges offer *group* or *blanket* health insurance plans for students that run from bare-bones coverage (accidents and major illnesses) to full coverage. Because these plans are offered on a group basis, students with preexisting conditions or a complicated medical history generally cannot be denied. These plans are a great alternative for students who do not already have coverage or those whose coverage costs will go up significantly under their parents' plan.

DEFINITION

Group or **blanket** insurance policies cover an entire group of people or provide blanket coverage for one type of accident or illness. If available, they can provide the ideal type of health coverage for college students because they are underwritten on a group basis and offer relatively cheap premiums in spite of medical history.

An Ounce of Prevention

As Ben Franklin once said, "An ounce of prevention is worth a pound of cure." In financial terms, "it's a lot cheaper to avoid sickness than it is to cure it."

The truth about college medical bills, which can push a family's budget to the breaking point, is that much of the money drama could have been avoided if everyone was more proactive about staying healthy. I'm not suggesting that you pump you or your student full of the latest vitamins, but I am suggesting that regular preventative care can go a long way toward cutting nuclear bomb–size expenses off at the pass.

Here are some of the easiest pieces of prevention to put into place:

- **Holiday check-ups**—One of the easiest ways to ensure your health is getting the attention it needs is to schedule a visit with your existing family doctor during the holidays and other visits home. That way, you're ensuring that you or your child gets the needed preventative care from someone you know and trust.

- **Connect your doctors**—Request a consent to release information from your hometown doctor, sign it, and keep it in a safe place. In an emergency, this can be handed to or faxed to a doctor at a campus's clinic, which will then allow him to share information with your trusted local physician. This helps to ensure prompt treatment and attention to problems, raising the quality of care and lowering the possibility of a large, unexpected medical bill.

- **Overfill your prescription**—As long as you're not sending your student off with highly dangerous or marketable drugs (such as Vicodin or Oxycontin), there should be no problem getting a three-month supply to send off to school. This will ensure that prescriptions needed to maintain health don't slip through the cracks of busyness or poor money management.

- **Get educated on remedies**—In the confined space of a college dorm and communal bathrooms, there's more than enough bugs to go around, and it's inevitable that a student is going to get sick. Unfortunately, bad advice on how to feel better is as prevalent as the germs and viruses leading to illness. Make sure your student understands the basics of over-the-counter medication (doses, effects, and so on), its interactions with his own medication, and its interactions with things like alcohol and caffeine. Unnecessary trips to the emergency room for reckless usage of medications start at about $300 per pop and go up from there.

- **Talk about depression**—Hands down, one of the most common ailments among students is depression. This is especially true among freshmen who are dealing with homesickness and social or academic pressure. Depression can start off as a mild case of the blues and snowball into a more severe case of clinical depression, quickly sinking a semester's worth of grades. Make sure your student knows the signs of both mild and more severe depression, encourage him to talk to you or someone else about it, and make sure he knows how to get in touch with the mental health clinic on campus.

CHEAT SHEET

An easy way to cut off homesickness at the pass, while also lowering your long-distance phone bills, is to invest in a cheap webcam. Thanks to free services like Skype and Apple iChat, students and their loved ones can now enjoy unlimited high-quality video chat for free. With webcams being as cheap as $50, it's a great investment on many levels.

Falling in Love

I realize that you might think me a little twisted and lacking in the romance department, but falling in love can definitely be a hidden cost of college. In fact, in my college planning workshops, I tell parents to go ahead and start saving for five years of college instead of four. When they ask why, I tell them that a marriage will likely cost them about the same as one year of tuition, and there is a darn good chance that their son or daughter will fall in love during or not long after college. Whether it is helping with the cost of a wedding, a honeymoon, or a ring, these are major costs that can come out of nowhere.

Now don't panic. I'm not telling you that you need to start saving up for a wedding or honeymoon if you haven't already started. But I am telling you that there is a good chance your student will find love in college, and that can result in some serious costs. What you do need to do is begin thinking about how you would handle the announcement of a cross-country relationship or—gasp!—an engagement.

Most importantly, begin setting reasonable expectations as soon as there's something on the radar. If your student comes home head over heels in love, be glad for her. Embrace it, investigate it, and encourage it if it looks healthy. And, when the time is right, talk about what you can and cannot do financially if a marriage or long-distance relationship is in the future.

Inflation Is Not Your Friend

The annual letter announcing the coming year's cost increases is one of the harshest "indirect expenses" of college that students and parents must come to terms with. When I started college nearly 20 years ago, the apologetic letter from my college's administrator announced a tuition increase that ranged between 4 and 6 percent. That amounted to roughly a $1,000 increase in tuition cost for each year of my undergraduate career. All that to say, you absolutely should expect your total cost of attending college to increase by 4 to 6 percent annually, whether you have a few years until college starts or this is your final year of paying tuition.

Unfortunately, like many of the other indirect costs in this chapter, there is not anything you can do to fight off *inflation*, but you can be aware of it and plan for it. In fact, it's so important that I've included it on your College Cash Strategy Worksheet in the "Adjust Your Annual Costs for Inflation" section as something that needs to be added back in after you've done all this hard work of cutting costs. Doing so will keep you from being surprised or thinking that you've substantially miscalculated both your direct and indirect costs.

DEFINITION

Inflation is the increase in the cost of a good or service over time. All goods and services are typically expected to increase in price over the years, but the cost of a college education has been increasing at 2 to 3 times the normal rate of inflation in North America.

Mathematically, adjusting for inflation is easy to do, so don't feel like you need a degree in economics. Simply add up your direct and indirect costs for one year of college (after you've worked your cost-cutting magic), and increase this amount 5 percent for each year that is going to elapse until you actually have to pay those expenses. (For the record, I chose a 5 percent rate of inflation for you because that's roughly the national average for all colleges.)

For example, if your first-year college costs will total $10,000 but you have one year until you will need to begin paying this, you should multiply $10,000 by 1.050. This yields $10,500, which equates to a 5 percent jump in costs. If you were also expecting to pay for a second year of college at the same initial cost, you would multiply it by 1.050 *twice* to account for two years of inflation. In this case, that would mean your second year of college would cost $11,025, or $10,000 × 1.050 × 1.050.

To make it easy for you, I've included a handy fill-in-the-blank table in Appendix B as part of the College Cash Strategy Worksheet. All you need to do is estimate your annual costs for one year of college right now, find the line with the correct number of years until you have to pay that expense, and multiply your cost by the number I've included there. There's your cost of that year's college education, including inflation. But before you burst into tears or start hyperventilating at the size of this number, I want you to look at that price tag and say out loud (yes, out loud), "I'm not scared of you! You're just a number!"

The Least You Need to Know

- The hidden costs of college can increase your costs 10 percent or more if you aren't deliberate about tackling them head on.
- Trendy technology is expensive; shop around for the basics and work hard to protect your purchases.
- Traveling at off-peak times and on alternative modes of transportation can save you thousands over four years.

- Use on-campus clinics and preventative care to keep medical expenses from putting your finances on life support.

- Set realistic financial expectations about the cost of long-distance love, weddings, and a honeymoon for students who find themselves head over heels prior to graduation.

- While you can't cut the indirect cost of inflation, you can estimate its effects on your cost-cutting efforts.

Tapping Your Assets Wisely

In This Chapter

- How far will your assets stretch?
- The best assets to tap first
- Why the type of account matters
- The nest eggs you shouldn't crack open
- Finding money in insurance policies

Kitchen sink financial planning—that's what I call it when people begin throwing every asset they have at a problem. They start liquidating all their investments, withdrawing money from retirement plans, tapping the equity in their homes, and selling their baseball card collections.

Unfortunately, liquidating every asset in sight, and doing it in no particular order, can wreak as much havoc on your finances as good. It's crucial to know which assets need to be the first to go toward paying tuition, which should be saved as long as possible, and which should not be touched at all. It's also crucial to think through your asset liquidation strategy now because there is a good chance you'll have to dig into some of your assets (if you have any) before some of the financial aid comes rolling in.

Calculating How Far Your Assets Will Go

You may think I'm crazy, but this is where the fun really begins. Maybe it's because I like solving puzzles, especially when I know they're not impossible. Or maybe it's just because I'm a numbers geek. Either way, the good news is that this is as big as this number will get. It will most likely only go down from here as you begin adding up what resources you have to meet this need, as well as developing a plan to make up for what you don't have.

So now, on your College Cash Strategy Worksheet in Appendix B or a piece of scratch paper, you're going to systematically begin listing the assets and financial resources that you have or can expect to have to offset the cost of college that remains after the first few chapters. Here are the things I want you to total up and begin subtracting to calculate your *Unmet Need* in Step #4 of the College Cash Strategy Worksheet:

1. Subtract any money you have specifically saved up to meet this person's college costs. Is there money in savings bonds, Section 529 accounts, custodial accounts, mutual funds, or insurance contracts that you have earmarked specifically to pay for college costs?

2. Subtract any financial help you can reasonably expect to receive from anyone else, besides outright scholarships. Did your parents, ex-significant other, neighbor, and so on, promise to help pay for college? If they did, sum up what they've promised to pay across all years of college and insert it on that next line.

3. Total and subtract any formal scholarships or other financial funds you already know you'll receive.

4. Subtract the total amount you've already added to your monthly budget to help pay for college. For example, some people know that they'll be able to pay $250 per month out of their wages and income toward college expenses. Again, you need to be sure to calculate this number for the entire length of college, so you'll need to multiply it by 12 months and then again by the number of years you'll be paying for college.

5. Subtract all these things from your original cost calculation for all years of college. This is your *Adjusted Need*. Hopefully it shrank some, or even a lot, from where you started. But if it didn't, don't panic. The remainder of this book is about finding the funds you need to cover whatever unfunded amount still remains.

What's left is the total amount of money you're going to have to figure out how to scrape together. I refer to it as your *Unmet College Cost*, and it's what much of the rest of the book helps you to systematically chip away at. But before we get to that, I want to make sure you're strategic in how you use up the assets that you have, so that you minimize the costs of liquidating your college accounts, while maximizing your chances for financial aid.

The First Assets to Go

There's a recipe, if you will, for which assets should ideally be tapped first to help pay for college. While your unique situation may not include some of these asset groups or may require you to slightly reorder their liquidation, the general principles remain the same. You want to get rid of the following assets first:

- **Aid-reducing assets**—Different assets, as well as who owns those assets, have varying effects on your financial aid package. In short, assets owned by your child lower your aid package the most and should be the first to go. Assets owned in the parents' names count against aid, but not as much as a child's assets, and should go next. Assets owned by extended family members (grandparents) and certain protected assets (such as retirement plans and insurance) won't likely lower your aid at all and should probably be held onto as long as possible.

- **Low tax assets**—Investments and assets that can be accessed without paying any tax should be considered for liquidation before those that will incur a large tax bill.

- **Low liquidation costs**—Some investments, especially if sold in a hurry, can experience a substantial decrease in their value. Assets that meet the other criteria, but are also low on liquidation costs, should be moved to the front of the line.

CHEAT SHEET

One of the best ways to minimize the tax costs associated with liquidating an investment is to make sure you time the sale to land in either this year or the next, depending when your overall tax bracket will be lower. Sometimes it even makes sense to sell part of an investment now and part of it in the coming year to minimize the taxes associated with it. Because the savings can easily equate to 5 to 10 percent of an asset's value, talk to a tax professional if you expect your taxable income to fluctuate significantly in the coming years.

In addition to these characteristics that make assets more preferential to tap early on in the college experience, other characteristics indicate an asset should not be tapped if possible. In particular:

- **Reserved for other goals**—If you have assets set aside for other goals, especially retirement, you should avoid tapping them as long as possible. Liquidating these assets to meet college costs simply creates a new problem while solving another.

- **Asset-based borrowing**—If you have an asset that is worth a significant amount of money, you should generally avoid using it as collateral to secure a loan. This is especially true if the asset is the roof over your head, the car you drive, or the business that puts bread on your table.

- **Superior rate of return**—Assets that have a proven potential for growth or income should not be used if you can borrow money (especially from Uncle Sam) at rates that are below what you're earning. By borrowing at a cheaper rate and earning at a higher rate, you get to keep the difference in income *and* the asset.

Bye-Bye, College Accounts

Just as little kids can get a little sentimental when it's time to give up their cherished (and raggedy) blanket or stuffed animal, it's not uncommon for parents to feel unsure about breaking open the college piggy bank. After all, there might be a substantial sum of money in there and it might feel wise to hold onto it in case unforeseen costs pop up.

But, for the sake of your wallet, it's time to bust open that account. That's because true college accounts (custodial accounts, Coverdell ESAs, Section 529 plans, and certain trusts, which I'll discuss in a moment) can hurt your financial aid options as much or more than other assets. Further, most of these accounts have rules that require you to do something else with the money or pay a penalty if it is not used for college.

The one college account you should liquidate last is the one that still has a grandma, a grandpa, an uncle, or an aunt as the owner (such as a Coverdell ESA and Section 529 plan). That's because accounts owned by extended family members are completely ignored for financial aid purposes under the current rules. With that in mind, you're far better off to empty your own account and increase your aid eligibility sooner rather than later and then to empty grandma's account and lower your aid package.

If you have any traditional college accounts, here is the order in which you want to drain them:

- **A child's savings bonds**—If you have Series EE or I savings bonds in your child's name, you'll definitely need to get rid of these to increase your financial aid eligibility. They count as a child's asset for financial aid purposes (35 percent *contribution rate*) and typically have a poor rate of return compared to other assets owned in a child's name.

DEFINITION

An asset's **contribution rate** is the percentage of its value an owner is expected to use in any given year toward paying for a college education. This rate effectively reduces the amount of financial aid that someone can expect to receive. Currently, when an asset is considered the property of a child, 35 percent of its value is expected to be used in a given year. When it is the property of a parent, 5.64 percent is expected to be used.

- **UTMA/UGMA custodial accounts**—These accounts, short for the Uniform Transfer to Minors' Act or the Uniform Gift to Minors' Act, respectively, count heavily against your financial aid eligibility. Further, they have to be turned over to your child between ages 18 and 25 (depending on your state), so you have no reason to keep these around. Getting rid of them will increase your chances of future aid and reduce the chances your child will come home with a Harley.

- **Crummey Trusts and 2503c Minor's Trust**—Although most people who are reading this book are unlikely to have set up one of these old-fashioned education trusts, it's very possible that grandma or a rich uncle might have. If your child has been named as the beneficiary (recipient) of one of these trusts, you'll need to begin making some phone calls to figure out how to gain access to it. Because these assets count as heavily against financial aid as a custodial account, there's nothing worse than receiving less aid and not knowing how to make withdrawals from a trust to compensate for it.

- **A parent's savings bonds**—If you have savings bonds in your name, you should get rid of them to take advantage of the tax-free withdrawals allowed to pay for college costs. The reason these are not liquidated at the same time as your child's savings bonds is that they count against financial aid at a lower rate. Again, they'd typically be liquidated before other assets that also count less against financial aid because savings bonds historically have a much lower average rate of return.

- **Coverdell ESAs**—Formerly known as the "Education IRA" or "ED-IRA," these accounts weigh against financial aid at a much lower rate than UGMA/UTMA custodial accounts. In fact, they weigh exactly the same as a Section 529 plan owned by a parent. But unlike a Section 529 plan, any unused funds in these accounts must be turned over to your child by the time he turns 30 or rolled over to another child.

- **Section 529 plan**—You almost hate to open the spigot on these accounts because they were so much fun to fill up. But, all the gains built up in this account can be withdrawn tax-free if they're used for college expenses, as opposed to being taxed and maybe hit with a 10 percent penalty if not used for college. Further, because they do count against financial aid at a rate of 5.64 percent (the same as Coverdell ESAs and other parent-owned assets), they're much better to get rid of than certain protected assets of the parents. (See Appendix F for a state-by-state list of Section 529 plans.)

Other Assets to Consider Tapping Early

There are a couple of other categories of assets to consider using early on in the college funding process. They involve a little more work and some outside-the-box thinking, but they can save you a good chunk of change.

> **WORLD WIDE WISDOM**
>
> A simple search of the Internet can turn up assets for a child that a parent has forgotten about or a deceased loved one failed to mention she had set aside. Most states offer free online searches for unclaimed assets and dormant bank accounts that companies were forced to turn over to the state after a certain amount of time. Visit your state treasurer's or secretary of state's website to learn more.

A conversation with a loved one might need to take place before using these assets, often because she has some real or emotional joint ownership over these assets. But, it is often worth it and the amount of financial pressure that it removes can be substantial.

Other Children's College Accounts

If you are planning on putting more than one child through college, there is a good chance that some money might be tucked away separately for each child. In fact, it is not uncommon for parents to have enough in multiple accounts for different children to pay for a couple of years of college outright for a single child.

So if you can do it without causing some major drama in your household, you might want to consider using the money you have set aside for multiple children to help fully fund your first child's education, then ideally replenishing those accounts later.

Even if you aren't able to rebuild your previous savings, you've delayed the need to take loans—and in turn, created a debt that collects interest—for a few more years.

Doing so can help you or your student avoid taking out costly student loans and increase your overall financial aid eligibility with future students. This becomes especially attractive if the potential earnings on your other children's accounts cannot exceed your expected cost of borrowing for your current student.

Of course, using money titled for one child for the benefit of another requires you to jump through some hoops. But don't worry, these tricks are completely legal and let you easily shift funds around:

- **For custodial accounts**—If you are the custodian (or can influence the custodian) of a UTMA or UGMA account that is for the benefit of a younger child, you can withdraw money to pay that younger child's living expenses. This would in turn allow you to redirect money that would have been spent in your monthly budget on that child toward the college expenses of your college student.

- **Section 529 plans and Coverdell ESAs**—These tax-advantaged college savings accounts allow you to roll over an account balance (Coverdell ESAs) or change beneficiaries (Section 529 plans), subject to certain limitations. If you own an account with a balance for a younger child, it might be in your benefit to roll it over and withdraw from it to benefit the older child.

Even if you're not comfortable using another child's college account to help with current expenses, it doesn't mean that there aren't other ways to benefit from the account. One technique that has become popular in rocky markets is to claim a loss on battered Section 529 plans. If you have a balance in a Section 529 plan for another child that has lost money, you can distribute and invest it elsewhere, claiming the loss on your tax return. This keeps the money working for that child but puts some tax dollars back in your pocket. See IRS Publication 970 for more details (available at www.irs.gov).

Assets Collecting Dust

Paying college tuition might provide the ultimate reason to de-clutter your life, especially of valuable nonfinancial assets that are taking up time, space, and energy. Whether it is the coin collection you inherited 10 years ago and haven't looked at since or that plot of land you own on the outskirts of town, you need to give serious consideration to whether collecting debt is more valuable than these things collecting dust. These things are hard to sell overnight without taking a major hit on the value, but they often can be sold within a semester or two of the start of college and can provide a major cash influx in time for the winter semester.

Tapping Your Retirement Funds

When it comes to paying for college, few things scare me more than the idea of people using their retirement nest eggs to pay for a college education. In fact, nothing derails more people's retirements than a failure to plan properly for a college education.

The peril isn't hard to see. Most people are between 40 and 60 years old when their first child heads off to college. At this point, they have somewhere between 5 and 25 years left to accumulate enough money to last them the rest of their retired lives. Because many of them are just reaching their peak earning years, this is the time when they should be playing catch-up, using their earning years to sock away money into retirement plans. Instead, paying for college forces them to do just the opposite. Not only do many people cease funding their company's 401k or an IRA for themselves, but they often dip into this money through a loan or withdrawal. All this leaves them staring down retirement with little hope of regaining their financial footing in time.

In short, using your retirement assets for a child's college education is the equivalent of a financial suicide mission. It'll probably do the trick, but you'll be the one to pay the price. Just remember, there are such things as student loans, but no such thing as a "retirement loan." You're much better off to have your student take out a loan and promise to help her repay it than give up your retirement funds and hope your student will take care of you.

Withdrawals Can Cost 45 Percent

Perhaps the most important thing to realize—and a fact that confuses many parents and students—is that a retirement plan withdrawal for college can cost you a ton in taxes. This confusion comes from the fact retirement plan withdrawals for college expenses are not subject to the 10 percent early withdrawal penalty. Many parents mistakenly think this means that these plans are also not subject to tax, which they usually are.

With the top federal income tax rate of 35 percent in 2010 and state income tax rates nearing 10 percent in some states, you could potentially lose up to 45 percent of a withdrawn amount to taxation. Even though that might still seem like something that moves you a step closer to solving the college money puzzle, it's one giant step backward for your financial future.

CHEAT SHEET

If you absolutely have to take a withdrawal from a qualified retirement plan to pay for college expenses, you might want to consider minimizing the taxes withheld by your employer or IRA custodian. Just because they want to withhold 20 to 30 percent for federal and state taxes, you might not actually owe that. If you typically pay little or no taxes every April 15, you will not likely owe much more with your withdrawal, especially considering the additional tax credits you will likely receive for paying education expenses.

Wisdom Against Taking a 401k Loan

Because 401k and other retirement plan loans are not subject to taxation on the loan amount, many parents and students see this as a viable way to access these balances. Generally, however, this is a very poor option in comparison to using a student loan, for a number of reasons:

- **Your assets freeze**—Most retirement plans remove (un-invest) assets equaling the loaned amount from your retirement portfolio. This means that the growth of these assets essentially freezes during the loan repayment period, except for the interest you pay into the account.

- **Your paycheck drops**—The payments for your retirement plan loan are typically made directly from your paycheck, which means the paycheck you were getting just got smaller. Many people living paycheck to paycheck who are also now struggling to pay tuition don't realize this and end up finding themselves financially overstretched after taking a 401k loan.

- **It still could be taxable**—If you quit, retire, or get fired from your employer before your retirement loan is repaid, it will be re-characterized as a taxable distribution. This means it is added to the income you have to report on your tax return, as well as possibly being subject to the 10 percent penalty.

Using Your Home Equity

For many people, their home is their single most valuable asset, often worth hundreds of thousands of dollars beyond what is actually owed on it. Sadly, as we've seen over the last decade, many homeowners have treated their homes like a giant ATM. Instead of properly planning for life's big expenses or taking the time to arrange alternative financing, they simply borrow money against their home equity as needed. Of course, many of these homeowners now owe more on their homes than they're worth, locking them into both a home and repayment requirements.

While tapping your home equity might be tempting, I strongly recommend using it as an absolute last resort. I even recommend a student choose a few years at a community college over unlocking a home's value. Of course, the banks and some talking financial heads will try to tell you differently. So you don't get railroaded, here are some of the primary arguments you'll hear for tapping your home's equity and the problems that exist with each:

- **The rates are low**—Although bankers will insist that their rates are low compared to other forms of borrowing and credit, they won't tell you that they can't compete with most federal student loan programs, especially those for students demonstrating substantial need.

- **Your interest will be deductible**—This statement is a half-truth that also ignores the deductibility of student loan interest (more on this in Chapter 11). In reality, a home equity line of credit interest is only deductible for a taxpayer on the first $100,000 in borrowed money. In fact, it can be even lower depending on certain tax formulas. Student loan interest is deductible up to $2,500 paid each year, which equates to roughly $30,000 to $50,000 in student loans, which is more than most people will end up taking out.

- **Easy access**—Proponents of using home equity lines of credit to fund college also tout easy access to your money on a moment's notice. As the last major economic downturn has proven, even the best borrowers can have their credit limits cut dramatically overnight as banks seek to cover their financial backsides. Counting on a line of credit can leave you between a rock and a hard place if your bank decides to batten down the hatches.

CHEAT SHEET

If you decide to borrow against your home, be sure to shop around and not just use your existing bank. Because banks and lenders know that their customers do not tend to compare rates, they often offer lowball rates. If you do find a better rate around town, be sure to take it back to your own bank or lender and see if they can beat the offer.

If you still feel tempted to tap the home equity in your home to pay for college, weigh the options carefully before signing up. Taking out a home equity loan is not a neutral event that has no negative effects on your ability to pay for college and your financial future.

First and foremost, you need to compare the rates offered on your home equity line of credit and the rates offered on the primary federal student loan programs (Stafford, Perkins, and PLUS loans). If your home equity line of credit has a higher rate or has the potential to rise above the rates offered on federal student loans, there is really no reason to use a home equity loan.

Second, you need to realize that home equity lines of credit *can* affect your ability to get financial aid down the road on a couple of levels. First, if you do either a cash-out refinance (where the bank gives you a large lump sum) or withdraw money that is not being used, these amounts can count as assets you're expected to use in place of receiving financial aid. Further, the fact that you have additional credit available and/or balances in your name can hurt your eligibility for federal PLUS loans, which do require a credit check unlike Stafford and Perkins loans.

Whole Life Insurance

Anyone who knows me knows that I'm not a fan of whole life (cash value) life insurance. This type of insurance costs substantially more than some other types of insurance, because it promises to also help you build a cash reserve known as a "cash value." I find that it is generally a colossal waste of money compared to term insurance (which only covers your risk of dying in a predetermined period, with no savings feature) and a horrible investment, despite what insurance salespeople might promise.

If you have a whole life policy, be it for your child or for you, you should consider tapping this asset to pay any bills left after your child's college accounts are used up. In the process, I strongly recommend first purchasing term insurance if you still feel coverage is needed.

FLUNK-PROOF FINANCES

One of the worst places to get an opinion on an existing whole life policy is from the agent who sold it to you. If you have a policy you think deserves the old heave-ho, contact a different agent who specializes in term life policies and get a second opinion.

I would not, as most agents will suggest, borrow against the policy. A policy loan, while cheap from a loan point of view, is very expensive overall because you must continue to pay a premium to keep the policy in force (unless paid-up). Not surprisingly, this results in an additional "renewal" commission for an insurance agent. All this increased annual cost, plus the cash value in your policy, represents money you could be putting toward your unmet expenses.

If cashing out a policy seems like the right move, make sure to get a cheaper term policy first, so you don't find yourself without coverage, even for a short period of time. Also, be sure to ask your agent whether any surrender charges are associated with making a partial or full surrender of your policy. Often (one more reason I hate these policies), money you've deposited in the last 5 to 10 years might have a surrender charge attached to it. If the surrender charges are generally less than what it would cost you to borrow money elsewhere for the coming year, go ahead and take the hit and leave your policy behind.

The Least You Need to Know

- Empty out college accounts held in your child's name first because these count the heaviest against financial aid.
- Avoid tapping assets destined for other financial goals and those with superior rates of return, until all other assets are used.
- Avoid tapping your retirement plans at all costs.
- Home equity loans should be used only as a last resort and when the rate is the same or better as other loan options.
- Consider trading your whole life insurance policy for a cheaper term policy and using any accumulated cash value to pay tuition bills.

Strategies for Borrowing

Part

2

In my previous books, I've warned time and again against the use of *almost* every kind of debt. One of the two exceptions to this piece of advice is the responsible borrowing of money to finance a college education.

The reason for this exception can be best summed up by one of America's top money gurus, Ben Franklin. Back in the day, Ben was quoted as saying "An investment in knowledge always pays the best interest." With a college degree resulting in nearly $1 million more in lifetime earnings than a high school diploma, I think Ben knew what he was talking about. *Borrowing to earn a degree can be the best investment you ever make.*

In this part, you learn how to borrow money at reasonable rates, even if you think your household makes too much money. Even better, you learn about repayment programs that don't strangle you as soon as you graduate and some nifty programs that might just wipe out everything you owe.

Student Loans Made Easy

In This Chapter

- Biggest student loan myths
- Popular federal loan programs
- Worst student loan mistakes
- Why drugs and loans don't mix

Borrowing is not bad, reckless, stupid, or an admission of some type of financial or parenting failure on your part. In fact, it might be one of the single wisest things you can do to ensure that you or your child gets the college education you or he needs.

Think about it—a family earning $150,000 per year earns more than 94 percent of all American households. They're easily considered high income and probably could be labeled rich by most people's standards. Yet, a year of college at many schools can easily cost $30,000, or one fifth of their annual income. If they live out of state, that same year of college could easily cost $50,000, or one third of their entire income.

Now imagine that they're the average American family, which means they've two kids in college at the same time or back-to-back, they earn half as much, and they haven't managed to save much for college. Their annual college costs can actually *exceed* their after-tax income for the year!

Regardless of how much money you make, how much you've saved for college, or how willing you are to apply for scholarship after scholarship, student loans might be a necessity for you. That's more than okay and should be embraced. Knowing that they're a reality, your job becomes using the right programs and using them wisely, as well as utilizing the best repayment options, which I talk more about in the next chapter.

The Truth About Student Loans

Student loans seem to be shrouded in more myths and misunderstandings than the first moon landing or the origins of Coca-Cola. Perhaps it's because many people's information comes not from official sources, but trickles down through the student-parent grapevine like a really bad game of telephone. By the time you finally hear the story of why the child of your neighbor's uncle wasn't able to get a student loan, the blame falls squarely on some grand conspiracy to stick it to the middle class.

First and foremost, it's important to realize that student loans can and should be used to help meet a student's reasonable living expenses (above and beyond tuition) while in school. The government fully expects this and encourages it. You can use these loans to help pay for room, board, books, and so on. You can even use them for things that are indirectly related (but still necessary) to a college education. While a new stereo or spring break trip would not be considered living expenses by the Department of Education, things like child care, transportation, overseas travel, and technology are all fair expenses for which to use student loan proceeds.

Who's Really Applying?

One of the biggest misconceptions about student loans is that it is the parents who are applying for them. In reality, even if Mom or Dad enters the information into the *FAFSA* form, it is the student who is truly applying for Stafford and Perkins loans. That means that it is the student who is on the hook for repaying the loans.

DEFINITION

The **Free Application for Federal Student Aid (FAFSA)** is the standard form used to apply for federal financial aid at all colleges. Its use has been adopted by most state and private financial aid organizations as well. The CSS Profile is an additional form used by some private colleges to apply for their own private aid programs.

It also answers another concern that many parents have about student loans, especially in a rocky economy: how will their credit score affect their ability to borrow. Thankfully, when it comes to Stafford and Perkins loans, the credit history of the parents doesn't have anything to do with a student's ability to qualify. In fact, a student's credit rating doesn't matter either because Stafford and Perkins loans are available without regard to a student's credit history, aside from previous student loan borrowing.

The one exception to both who applies for a student loan, as well as the lack of a credit check, is PLUS loans. These loans are most often taken out by parents who still need additional funds after all other financial aid has been received to meet their child's college expenses. PLUS loans do require a credit check to ensure that the borrower does not represent an above-average risk to government-backed lenders.

Upper-Middle Class Families *Can* Qualify

Over the years, I've heard all kinds of bogus rules of thumb about how much a family can earn or have in the bank and still qualify for federal student loans. Often, those using these benchmarks mix up someone's eligibility for scholarships, Pell Grants, and student loans. While Pell Grants, which are financial aid awards from Uncle Sam that do not need to be repaid, are based heavily on financial need, eligibility for student loans is far more lenient.

The reality is that virtually everyone who wants to borrow money from the government can, although the terms might be different for those who demonstrate financial need. In fact, even families with hundreds of thousands of dollars in income and liquid assets can still borrow large amounts of cash from Uncle Sam. The primary difference is that those demonstrating a financial need according to government formulas can qualify for more friendly loan programs and terms.

Subsidized Versus Unsubsidized Loans

One important distinction with student loans, especially federal student loans, is subsidization versus no subsidization. When a federal student loan is *subsidized*, the government actually pays the interest on the loan while they remain in school, as well as possibly providing a lower interest rate over the life of the loan.

By contrast, when a loan is *unsubsidized*, the interest on the loan is usually a higher percentage and is added to what is owed each year. This can easily amount to a few thousand dollars more in loans to be repaid after graduation for a student who did not demonstrate a need.

If an *independent student* or the family of a dependent student demonstrates substantial financial need, they might qualify for subsidized student loans. If a student or her family does not qualify for subsidized loans because of her income, assets, or other factors, she can still likely receive unsubsidized loans up to certain annual limits. Often, students receive a mix of both subsidized and unsubsidized loans, with a portion receiving a lower interest rate and that interest being paid while they're in school.

DEFINITION

An **independent student** meets one of the following criteria: is married, is a veteran, is a graduate student, is an orphan, has her own legal dependents, or is emancipated. If a student does not meet one of these criteria but wishes to file the FAFSA as an independent student, documentation of her financial independence must be provided to her school's financial aid administrator.

Federal Rates Are Great

Whether you qualify for a subsidized or unsubsidized loan, the rates are generally excellent compared to loans offered by private lenders who aren't partnered with the U.S. Department of Education. In fact, some rates will drop as low as 3.4 percent during the 2011–2012 school year, as shown in the following table. These rates are low enough that parents and students should not hesitate to borrow enough to meet their legitimate college costs.

Loan Program	Interest Rate
Subsidized Stafford loans	4.5% for 2010–2011 3.4% for 2011–2012 6.8% for 2012–2013+
Unsubsidized Stafford loans	6.8% for all years
Perkins loans	5.0% for all years
PLUS loans	7.9%–8.50% for all years

Likewise, state-sponsored loan programs often offer great loan rates to parents and students, especially those studying to become teachers or other types of public servants. To learn more about the availability of these and other state-based financial aid programs, visit the website for your state's financial aid commission, listed in Appendix D.

Applying Is Easy

One of the greatest things about federal financial aid, as well as much of what you can receive from your state and school, is that there is a single "button to push" to start the ball rolling. In other words, once you complete and submit the FAFSA form, you've officially applied for grants, Stafford loans, Perkins loans, and many of the unique programs offered through your state and school.

Of course, the FAFSA form has a reputation for making your tax return look like a child's coloring book, but this reputation is largely unfounded. Perhaps back before the FAFSA form was available online, it was more difficult. But now, thanks in large part to the Internet, it can be completed for the first time in 1 to 2 hours. In subsequent years, it should take no more than 30 to 60 minutes. Greatly speeding up this process starting for the 2010–2011 school year is a new feature offered through a partnership of the Department of Education and the IRS that allows the required information from your tax return to be automatically loaded into your FAFSA.

So if you are going to need financial aid in the coming school year and haven't filled out the FAFSA form, you need to put down this book and go to fafsa.ed.gov to get started. Time is of the essence, especially considering that state financial aid deadlines are often substantially earlier than the June deadline (historically, June 30) for federal aid.

Stafford Loans

Federal Stafford loans are the bread and butter of most students' financial aid package. In fact, they often represent the single largest source of aid received by many students. Unfortunately, they are also the most complex of the federal student loan programs, with a variety of rates and rules that can apply to each borrower. Still, they're not beyond the average parent or student's comprehension.

Stafford loans come in both subsidized and unsubsidized flavors. If they're subsidized, they potentially receive a lower interest rate (depending on the year) and all interest is paid (waived) while the student is still in college. All unsubsidized Stafford loans have an annual interest rate of 6.8 percent and interest *does* accumulate during the college years.

CHEAT SHEET

Under the Servicemember Civil Relief Act (SCRA), Stafford loans (as well as PLUS and consolidation loans) can have their interest rate limited to 6 percent if the loans were incurred before their active-duty started. Check with your potential lenders for more information if you plan on joining the military at some point.

Stafford Loan Eligibility

As previously mentioned, financial need is not a requirement to qualify for Stafford loans, although it is to qualify for subsidization on those loans. Aside from that, a student must meet the following requirements to receive a Stafford loan.

- Submit a FAFSA form
- Be a U.S. citizen or legal permanent resident
- Be at least half-time in his studies
- Attend a school eligible for federal financial aid
- Not be in default on a previous loan

Stafford Loan Upfront Costs

Stafford loans have historically been subject to two types of upfront costs, which are typically added to the overall balance of a student's loan. The first type of fee, an *origination fee*, has historically been as high as 3 percent but was eliminated in mid-2010.

The remaining fee, a *default fee*, is expected to remain at 1 percent on all disbursed loan amounts. This default fee is used to help the government offset losses from students who do not repay their loans.

Stafford Loan Borrowing Limits

Limits are placed on how much can be borrowed under the Stafford loan program, depending on what year of college (freshman, sophomore, junior, senior, or graduate) they're being borrowed for. These limits are broken down by both subsidized and total amounts. For example, a student can borrow up to $5,500 for her freshman year, with no more than $3,500 of her loan amount being subsidized. If she does not qualify for any subsidized loans, then she is permitted to borrow unsubsidized Stafford funds, up to that year's limit ($5,500).

The current Stafford loan limits, subject to change, are shown in the following table.

Stafford Limits for Dependent Students

School Year	Subsidized Limit	Overall Limit
Freshman	$3,500	$5,500
Sophomore	$4,500	$6,500
Junior	$5,500	$7,500
Senior	$5,500	$7,500
Graduate	$8,500	$20,500

Further, these limits are increased for students who are independent (no longer financial dependents of their parents) and for students whose parents applied for a PLUS loan and were denied.

Stafford Limits for Independent Students and Students Whose Parents Were Denied PLUS Loans

School Year	Subsidized Limit	Overall Limit
Freshman	$3,500	$9,500
Sophomore	$4,500	$10,500
Junior	$5,500	$12,500
Senior	$5,500	$12,500
Graduate	$8,500	$20,500

Stafford loans are also subject to lifetime limits on the total amount that can be borrowed. These limits depend on a student's status and the level of education she's pursuing.

Stafford Lifetime Borrowing Limits

Student Status	Lifetime Limit
Dependent undergraduates	$31,000
Independent undergraduates	$57,500
All graduate students	$138,500
Medical students	$224,000

Perkins Loans

With the exception of the 2010–2011 and 2011–2012 school years when Stafford loan rates temporarily dip, Perkins loans are considered the cheapest of the mainstream federal student loan programs. They are issued only in a subsidized format, with their 5 percent interest rate being paid by the government while the student remains in school.

Perkins loans are reserved for students demonstrating a high level of financial need, with many Perkins loan students also qualifying for the coveted Pell Grant. These loans are highly sought after by future teachers and certain other professionals, due to special loan forgiveness programs attached to Perkins loans.

CHEAT SHEET

The decision about which students receive Perkins loans and how much they receive is made by a school's financial aid administrators. With this in mind, it is important that a student actively communicate his need of and appreciation for such programs during the application process. Specifically, sending a letter to your financial aid department early on requesting the use of Perkins loans can help secure their use or a larger amount.

Perkins Loan Eligibility

The biggest nonnegotiable requirement for a Perkins loan is that the student demonstrate substantial financial need. There is no such thing as an unsubsidized Perkins loan for students who do not qualify based on financial need.

In addition, Perkins loans recipients must:

- Have U.S. citizenship or permanent residency
- Be enrolled on at least a half-time basis
- Make satisfactory academic progress (defined by the school)
- Register with the U.S. Selective Service as required
- Not be in default on any other federal loans

Perkins Loan Upfront Costs

Unlike Stafford and PLUS loans, Perkins loans are not subject to any upfront origination or default fees.

Perkins Loan Borrowing Limits

Perkins loans, although much more favorable on their loan terms than Stafford and PLUS loans, have a much lower lifetime limit on borrowing. Remember, though, that

Perkins loans can be used in conjunction with Stafford and PLUS loans, so the lower limit does not mean you will come up short on money if you are offered Perkins loans. It just means that any funds borrowed in excess of the Perkins loan limits will have to come from Stafford or PLUS loans.

For undergraduate students, the 2010 Perkins loan limits are $5,500 per year and $27,000 for a student's lifetime. For graduate students, the annual limit is increased to $8,000 and the lifetime limit is increased to $60,000.

PLUS Loans

The Parent Loan for Undergraduate Students (PLUS) loan is meant to be a loan that tops off a family's college funding tank. In other words, this loan is meant to make up the difference between what college actually costs and what other financial aid has already been awarded. *It has no preset limit on lifetime borrowing.*

FLUNK-PROOF FINANCES

Until recently, PLUS loans actually required the borrower (usually the parent) to begin repayment within 60 days of the first disbursement! Thankfully, this rule has been changed and parents can begin repaying these loans six months after a student graduates. However, this option needs to be requested at the time of application; otherwise, a bill will most definitely show up in your mailbox.

Unlike Stafford and Perkins loans, PLUS loans for undergraduate students are taken out by the parent of a dependent student; parents of independent students are not permitted to apply for PLUS loans. To make matters slightly more confusing, these loans that were designed for parents have also now been made available to graduate students who are not financially dependent on a parent.

As of the 2010–2011 school year, two possible interest rates are available on federal PLUS loans. Students that borrow them under the Direct program pay an annual rate of 7.9 percent, whereas students who borrow under the Federal Family Education Loan Program (FFELP) pay an annual rate of 8.5 percent. There is no such thing as a subsidized PLUS loan, with all borrowers paying one of these two rates, regardless of their financial need. PLUS loans are also subject to a 4 percent upfront fee (3 percent origination fee + 1 percent default fee), which is typically added to the balance of the loan.

As with Stafford and Perkins loans, PLUS loans are available only to U.S. citizens and residents attending school at least half-time. Unlike these other loans, though, PLUS loans are subject to a credit check and are regularly declined for borrowers with poor credit history.

State Loan Programs

Federal student loan programs aren't the only ones out there, although they're the easiest for most students to get their hands on. In addition to these student loans, many states offer student loans to their residents, with the amount loaned being coordinated with federal loans.

These loans often focus on low-income students and on certain professions such as nursing and teaching. Unfortunately, these programs are susceptible to state budget cuts, and students should be prepared to seek out financial aid elsewhere should these programs experience overnight cuts.

> **FLUNK-PROOF FINANCES**
>
> Many students going to an out-of-state school will not qualify for state-based loans during their freshman year. Unfortunately, many of these same students forget to go back and apply for state-based aid in later years after they've gained residency. Take the time to figure out when you might gain residency and make a note on your calendar to go back and apply for state-based aid at that point.

To find out more about loans available in your state, see Appendix D.

Student Loan Landmines

As quick as I am to recommend student loans as a safety net for most college educations, it's also important to mention a few holes that could put you at risk of hitting the ground at full speed. Time and again, students and parents not aware of the risks associated with student loan refunds, private loans, and casual drug usage find themselves in major trouble with no real options.

The Student Loan Refund

It's a simple question that can lead to complex consequences. When applying for financial aid, you'll be asked a simple "Yes or No" question about whether you want to apply for the maximum aid allowable. If you're only going to need a few thousand dollars in loans, saying "Yes!" might lead to an extremely large refund check that might be all too easy to spend—and a nightmare to repay.

When more money is received than a college can apply to future classes within a certain window of time, it is required to be refunded to the student. Part of the government's intention behind requiring the refund is that many students might need some or all of this money to pay their living expenses while in college.

Unfortunately, receiving a check for thousands of dollars in the mail is just too tempting for many students to handle responsibly. Money that should have been spent on tuition, room, and board often is spent on other items that suddenly become necessities, like a new wardrobe, paying off a credit card, or spring break.

To keep this money from burning a hole in anyone's pocket, consider the following tips:

- **Ask your school to hold the money**—Some schools will hold refund checks in the accounts of their students upon request. Where possible, it usually requires a written letter of instruction signed by the student and sent to the school's student accounts department. If this can be done, the money will simply sit in the student's account until the next tuition bill comes due.

- **Send the money back to the school**—There is nothing that keeps a student from turning around and re-depositing a refund check as soon as she receives it. This money will then sit safely with the school, which will apply it to tuition when it comes due.

- **Repay the money**—If you're pretty sure that the money is not going to be needed at all, there's no reason to hold onto it and have it accumulate interest. Because none of the major loan programs charge an early repayment penalty, consider sending it back to the lender and getting a leg up on the eventual repayment of your student loans.

- **Stick it in savings**—If you know you are going to need the money and you trust yourself not to spend it, stick it in a savings account and let it earn some interest. Better yet, stick it in a certificate of deposit (CD) that is timed to pay out when your next tuition bill is due.

Private, Nongovernment Loans

A few years ago, Gary Coleman of *Diff'rent Strokes* fame attempted to recapture some of his former glory by doing commercials for payday lenders. Unfortunately for Gary, payday lenders are the legalized version of a mob loan shark, and many networks weren't too excited about the bad press they were getting. *Thankfully* (please note my sarcasm and disdain), private student loan lenders stepped up to fill the cheesy and dishonest void in the advertising world.

Although many federal loans are made with the help of private lenders, *private student loans* are a different animal. These types of loans are made by corporations who choose not to be subject to federal regulations, in large part because they restrict the amount of profit they can wring out of students. As opposed to federal student loans, which charge between 3.4 and 8.5 percent, these private corporate lenders typically charge 10 to 15 percent. Even worse, lenders often jack up their rates at the first opportunity after a student has graduated, which leaves him little hope because these loans cannot be consolidated under a federal program.

Because there is really no reason to use these loans for most students, they should be avoided like the financial plague that they are. If someone other than your school's financial aid administrator offers to arrange a federal student loan for you, don't believe them.

> **WORLD WIDE WISDOM**
>
> Due in part to the incredible number of students borrowing money and the relative ease with which huge amounts are handed out, both student loan errors and fraud are skyrocketing. It's important that students review their account statements and credit history for unrecognized loans at least every six months while in college, as well as check their free credit history on a regular basis. To protect yourself, visit www.annualcreditreport.com to get free copies of your credit report.

Drugs and Student Loans

Without passing judgment on those who choose to indulge in chemically altered living, let me give you some fair warning. Selling or getting caught in possession of illegal drugs can and does lead to a loss of federal financial aid, including student loans.

If you didn't pass on the grass in your past and got busted for it, don't panic. The following drug-related "incidents" should not affect your financial aid eligibility:

- Arrests or convictions that did not occur while you were a student

- Arrests or convictions as a minor

- Convictions that were not in a federal or state court

- Convictions removed from your record

The Least You Need to Know

- Virtually everyone can qualify for federal student loans of some kind, regardless of how much money they earn.

- Filling out the FAFSA application is relatively simple and something every student should do regardless of whether he thinks he's eligible.

- Between Stafford, Perkins, PLUS, and state loans, students should be able to get all the low-cost loans they need.

- Students should avoid taking student loan refunds, opting instead to leave the money in their accounts or return it to their lenders.

- Avoid private student loans at all costs.

Loan Repayment Strategies

In This Chapter

- Your federal loan repayment options
- Choosing the best repayment plan
- Deferments and forbearances for hard times
- Simplifying life by consolidating loans

The funny thing about student loans is that even though your college is being paid, *you haven't technically paid for college*. In reality, a lender has paid for college on your behalf. With student loans, you start paying for college after you graduate and continue to do so for the next 10 to 30 years. So if you choose to use student loans, how you go about repaying them after college matters as much as anything you do with them during college.

Thankfully, the government is one of the most flexible creditors you'll have in your life. It gives you a buffet of repayment options, doesn't jack up its rates on you if you fall behind, and will even give you a temporary reprieve from repaying your loans should you fall on hard times. But, the great options it offers aren't automatic. If you do nothing, your student loan repayment plan will automatically be selected and missed payments will begin building toward a default.

In this chapter we take a look at everything you need to know to manage your loans wisely after you graduate and *really start paying for college*. You should make a point of reading it now, when you're still trying to figure out how to pay for college, so you have a handle on how student loans will affect your life and can decide if they are really worth it.

Federal Repayment Programs

The term *repayment program* refers to how the monthly payments are calculated for someone who is no longer in college. The term is often confused with *loan cancellation* and *loan forgiveness* programs, which I talk more about in the next chapter.

Federal repayment programs are not necessarily programs run directly by the government, but are formulas that government lenders are required to use to calculate how much you pay and when. If your funds were loaned to you indirectly through a corporate lender who was participating in a government student loan program, you'll be sending your money to that lender. If your funds were provided under a Direct loan—which represent the smaller portion of loans made—then you'll be sending your checks to the Department of Education. Either way, if your loan was a Stafford, Perkins, or PLUS loan, your options are set in stone.

To help illustrate the various repayment options, I'll be using the same imaginary graduate, Ima Graduate, with $40,000 in student debt at 6.8 percent, for each scenario. That way, you'll be able to see side-by-side how these programs stack up and what college will really cost when you get around to paying for it. All calculations are pulled directly from the Department of Education's student loan calculator, which can be found at www.ed.gov.

Standard Repayment

The Standard Repayment Plan requires the student to make equal monthly payments over 10 years, or 120 monthly payments. However, this plan also requires a minimum payment of $50 per month, which means loans below $4,500 (at 6.8 percent) will actually have to pay more than the calculated repayment amount, resulting in a payoff that is actually faster than 10 years.

CHEAT SHEET

Borrowers are automatically placed into the Standard Repayment Plan (10 years) unless they request otherwise prior to the end of the initial deferment period.

Of all the repayment plans, the 10-year Standard Repayment Plan costs the most each month but the least over time. In other words, because the graduate is putting a large amount toward her loan each month, it greatly reduces the opportunity for additional interest to grow on the amount that is owed.

For Ima, our hypothetical student with $40,000 in student loan debt at 6.8 percent, her monthly payment under the Standard Repayment Plan will be $460.32. Over 120 payments, this means she will pay a total of $55,238.40, or $15,238.40 more than she originally borrowed.

Extended Repayment Plan

For students with more than $30,000 in student loan debt, the government offers an extended repayment plan option. This option can be repaid over 25 years instead of the standard 10 years.

Under the basic Extended Repayment Plan, the monthly payment amount remains the same every month during that 25-year period. Naturally, breaking up a loan over 25 years is going to give you substantially lower monthly payments than breaking it up over 10 years. However, it is also going to give the loan much more time to accumulate interest, resulting in a much larger total cost over time.

For our student with $40,000 in loans at 6.8 percent, she can expect to pay $277.63 per month, compared to $460.32 under the Standard Repayment Plan. However, over the life of her loan, her total repayments will be $83,289, compared to $55,238.40 under the Standard Repayment Plan. That's roughly $28,000 more and twice what was originally borrowed!

CHEAT SHEET

As long as your student loan is in good standing and you meet a program's eligibility rules, you can switch from one payment plan to another without any cost to you. This is done using a simple form available from your lender.

Graduated Plans

In addition to the Standard and Extended Repayment Plans, the government allows students to add a "Graduated" option to these plans. Under the Graduated option, the monthly payment starts at a lower amount and then increases every two years. In fact, under both the Standard Graduated and the Extended Graduated, the initial monthly payment amount starts significantly lower and ends significantly higher than the level repayment options for those same plans.

Even though that might seem like it all balances out in the end, the Graduated options actually do end up costing a borrower slightly more in the end. In the case of a 10-year Graduated repayment, it increases the total cost of borrowing by approximately 5.5 percent. Under the 25-year Graduated plan, it increases the cost of borrowing by just under 8.5 percent.

In real numbers, that means that someone with $40,000 in loans at 6.8 percent will pay $58,222.23 (instead of $55,283.40) under the Standard Graduated Plan (10 years), broken down as shown in the following table.

Monthly Payment Under the Standard Graduated Plan (Based on $40,000 at 6.8%)

Years	Monthly Payment
1–2	$316.07
3–4	$384.26
5–6	$467.16
7–8	$567.95
9–10	$690.48

Under the Extended Graduated Plan, that same $40,000 in loans at 6.8 percent will cost $90,216.18, with payments starting at $226.67 in years 1 and 2, ending at $396.60 in year 25.

FLUNK-PROOF FINANCES

It's not uncommon to hear of students who dream up the "brilliant" plan to borrow as much as they need (or can get) during the college years, with the intention of declaring bankruptcy soon after college and erasing their debt. Unfortunately, as these financial whiz kids soon figure out, student loan debt is not erased by bankruptcy and the Department of Education isn't shy about garnishing your wages to get its money back.

Income-Based Plans

Over the years, the government has introduced a number of repayment plans designed to take into account what a borrower actually earns when calculating her monthly payment. These plans, which are only available to taxpayers earning typically below $50,000 to $75,000, use complicated formulas to determine the payment a household can afford without taking too much away from their quality of life. Borrowers participating in these plans either have their payments lowered or the payments remain the same as they would have under the Standard or Extended Repayment Plan they would have otherwise qualified for. Participating in these plans requires the ongoing submission of certain documentation, namely information from your tax return, to calculate the appropriate payment for a borrower's coming year.

Three income-based plans are currently available, all of which result in roughly the same monthly payment amounts. These plans, which are commonly referred to by their initials, are Income Based Repayment (IBR), Income Contingent Repayment (ICR), and Income Sensitive Repayment (ISR). The newest of these plans, IBR, is considered the most generous of the plans and is the one that students should consider. The largest single difference that makes this plan stand out from the older ICR and ISR plans is that there is the potential for loan forgiveness after as few as 10 years (more on this in Chapter 7).

WORLD WIDE WISDOM

Because the loan repayment programs that are tied to income have a lot more moving parts than the basic plans, you need to visit the Department of Education's income-based calculators (studentaid.ed.gov) to get a real handle on how much these plans might save you based on your unique situation.

The downside to all three of the income-based plans is similar to the Extended Repayment Plans. By paying a lower monthly amount and stretching these loans out as long as 25 years, many borrowers will pay much more over the long run than they would with a 10-year Standard Repayment Plan. This trade-off needs to be examined closely before someone settles into an income-based repayment plan because it is money that could have been used to reach other financial goals.

Because all repayment plans tied to income end up in the same monthly payment ballpark, I've included the calculations for the newer IBR program. Because this calculation also requires a borrower to provide her income level and family size, I've run it assuming our hypothetical student (with $40,000 in debt at 6.8 percent) is single and earning between $10,000 and $60,000, in $10,000 increments. Remember, under the original Standard Repayment Plan, the monthly repayment amount was $460.32 and the total cost at payoff was $55,238.40.

Comparison of IBR Plan at Different Income Levels for a Single Person with a $40,000 Loan at 6.8%

Income	Monthly Payment	Months to Pay Off	Total
$10,000	$0	300	$0
$20,000	$45	300	$13,500
$30,000	$170	300	$51,000
$40,000	$295	258	$76,059
$50,000	$420	137	$57,665
$60,000*			

* Does not qualify for IBR based on income and family size.

Did you notice anything interesting? If a borrower ends up earning very little money as a graduate, it's actually possible that she will have to pay back far less than she borrowed, even if the loan is not forgiven until its 25th year. On the flipside, if a person ends up earning more than $50,000, the monthly payment and total cost isn't much different from the Standard Repayment Plan because it is paid off in roughly the same amount of time. Most peculiar, though, is the person who earns somewhere between the extremes, whose total cost for the loan ends up being just over $76,000!

CHEAT SHEET

The conditions for loan forgiveness after 10 years under the new IBR program are broad enough that working a public service job should be a consideration for everyone borrowing substantial amounts of money. For example, for the student borrowing $40,000, complete loan forgiveness after 10 years of public service is the equivalent of nearly $4,000 in annual bonuses for a decade!

Before you get angry and think that this is some type of scam to bilk middle-income students out of what little money they have, you have to see the IBR for what it is. At its core, all it really does is move a borrower back and forth between three different programs based on her income level.

For those earning very little, it costs very little and eventually forgives most of the balance (making it a welfare program of sorts). For those people earning a moderate level of income, it essentially puts them on the Extended Repayment Plan, in fact costing them slightly less than that option. For those earning higher levels of income, it moves them toward a standardized, 10-year repayment plan. Best of all, it makes the changes for you as you go, simply by submitting your annual documentation.

Choosing the Best Repayment Plan

If you stop and think about it, the world of student loans is clearly detached from reality, which is something to be thankful for. Where else could an 18-year-old, with no job, credit history, collateral, or cosigners, borrow more than $100,000 simply on the promise that it'll be paid back? It's pretty wonderful, funny, and scary at the same time.

Well, my advice on choosing a student loan repayment plan takes advantage of yet another *Twilight Zone*–like feature of student loans. Namely, that a borrower's interest rate stays the same regardless of whether he's going to repay money over 10 years or take as long as 25 years. In the real world, the interest rate for two otherwise identical loans should be significantly higher for someone who wishes to borrow money for an extra 15 years. And yet, student loan interest rates stay the same.

The practical application of this loophole is that borrowers should opt for the lowest monthly payment and the longest repayment period possible *but repay the loan as fast as they can*. In other words, because your rate does not change, keep your commitment to your lender to a minimum but strive to pay off what you owe as quickly as possible. This will allow you the maximum flexibility to adjust your budget to other financial opportunities and surprises, while lowering the risk that you'll fall behind on your commitment to the lender.

For most people, this is likely going to mean one of three things. They'll need to use either the Income Based Repayment (IBR) program if they can qualify or the Extended and Graduated programs if they cannot. Again, the intent here is to make as much over these lower minimum payments as possible, assuming that they don't have other debts the borrowers need to pay down with higher interest rates. Ideally, these loans should be paid off in 10 to 15 years, but choosing one of these other repayment plans gives you maximum flexibility to adjust to post-college life.

Buying Yourself Some Time

Student loans come with a number of built-in deferral mechanisms that allow a graduate or someone taking a break from college to get her feet on the ground before she has to start repaying her debts. The initial deferments all students are entitled to last six months for Stafford and PLUS loans and nine months for Perkins loans. However, if you are or expect to be strapped for cash, additional *deferments* or *forbearances* can be applied for.

> **DEFINITION**
>
> Although the terms often seem to overlap, a **deferment** is a temporary suspension of loan payments being due, usually under an established program with standard criteria. A **forbearance** can include a temporary reduction in payments, a total waiver of payments, or a suspension of payments similar to a deferment. The big difference between the two is that a forbearance is typically granted according to the lender's internal standards and policies, as opposed to deferment standards set by the Department of Education.

Deferments and forbearances can be especially helpful if you are experiencing extenuating circumstances that are somewhat beyond your control and would benefit from delaying repayment past the standard 6 or 9 months.

Deferments

Deferments past what is initially granted for each type of loan might be requested for a number of reasons. If they are granted, loan interest will continue to be piled on top of your balance, with the exception of subsidized loans, which might have the interest accrual temporarily halted.

To qualify for a deferment, you must typically fall into one of the following deferment categories:

- **In-school deferment**—This type of deferment is available to students who re-enroll in school on at least a half-time basis. This type of deferment is valid for as long as a student remains in school.

- **Military deferment**—Students and graduates directly serving as active-duty personnel in a war, peace-keeping activity, or national emergency can defer their loans as long as they continue to serve, up to a 3-year maximum.

- **Economic hardship deferment**—If the household income for your family size is less than 150 percent of the national poverty guideline, you can request deferment every 12 months, for up to 3 years.

- **Parental leave deferment**—Students who become pregnant and need to take a leave from their studies can request a deferment of up to 6 months, as long as they are not working or attending school.

- **Working mother deferment**—If a borrower is not earning $1 per hour more than the federal minimum wage and has a child who is in kindergarten or younger, she can request a deferment of up to 12 months.

- **Public service deferment**—Students who are serving in the Armed Forces during peace time, in the Public Health Service, in the Peace Corps, in the National Oceanic and Atmospheric Administration, in the Action programs, or as a paid volunteer in certain tax-exempt organizations can request a deferment up to 3 years during their service.

- **Unemployment deferment**—Borrowers who are unemployed (subject to certain verification requirements) can defer for up to 36 months.

- **Disability deferment**—A borrower suffering from a temporary total disability (subject to a doctor's verification) can request deferment every 6 months for up to 3 years.

CHEAT SHEET

If you have any other debt you're struggling to pay, such as a car loan, a mortgage, or credit cards, consider taking a deferment on your student loans and redirecting that cash toward eliminating that higher interest debt. This is especially true of subsidized debt, where deferral also stops the accumulation of interest on your student loans.

Forbearances

Earning a forbearance is less predictable than a deferment. That's because deferments are granted according to strict government standards, while forbearances are granted according to a lender's own internal policies. What that means is that you should never count on a forbearance as a way to temporarily avoid making payments, because there's no guarantee you'll be granted one. If possible, you'll always want to use a deferment first. But, if you need a forbearance or you've exhausted your deferral options, you shouldn't hesitate to ask your lender for help.

Generally, a forbearance is granted when the lender thinks a temporary break in payments will actually raise the probability of paying off your loan later. So if you're going to ask for a temporary reprieve, you need to do it right. This means that you need to communicate hope in your situation changing, explaining that you should have no problem resuming payments once you get that new job, pay off another debt, or experience some other change in your circumstances.

Student Loan Consolidation

A lot of hoopla is made about student loan consolidations—too much hoopla in my opinion. Many people incorrectly think that consolidated student loans will lower the interest rates on their loans, when in fact they can actually raise them slightly—with one exception. This happens because a consolidated student loan actually just blends together the balances and rates on your existing loans, into one larger loan. In doing so, the new rate is simply the weighted average of the loans you had before, *rounded up* to the nearest one-eighth of a percent.

> **CHEAT SHEET**
>
> Your best bet for a reduction in your student loan rate is to make sure that you select a lender that offers incentives for paying your student loans on time. For example, many lenders decrease your student loan rate by .25 percent after you've successfully made 6 to 12 months of on-time payments or have signed up for an automatic withdrawal of your payment from your checking account.

For example, if a borrower has $10,000 in loans at 6.8 percent and $5,000 in loans at 5.4 percent, the new rate on the combined $15,000 consolidation loan would blend these two rates. How they are blended is based on the size of the individual loans prior to consolidation, known as a *weighted average*. In this case, the new rate would be comprised of two-thirds (the $10,000 divided by $15,000 in total loans) of 6.8 percent and one-third of 5.4 percent. This equals 6.33 percent, which then is actually *rounded up* to 6.375 percent, costing the student slightly more overall than before.

Why would someone bother with consolidation? There are four reasons you might want to consider a consolidation when you finally get around to paying for college:

- By consolidating your loans, a new longer loan period might be granted. Although this does not actually change your rate, it might lower your monthly payment by spreading the loan balance over a longer repayment period. Keep in mind, however, that spreading your loan over a longer period of time actually results in a greater out-of-pocket cost in the end.

- The idea of simplifying and having only one loan balance to keep track of is appealing to many borrowers. In truth, the actual slight increase that often accompanies a consolidation is a small price for some people to pay for the massive reduction in paperwork.

- Parents and students with PLUS loans might actually experience up to a .25 percent drop in rates with a student loan consolidation (the one exception I previously mentioned). Because the interest rate on a student loan consolidation is capped at a maximum of 8.25 percent, a parent or student consolidating a PLUS loan at the standard rate of 8.5 percent will save some dough. However, because the savings equates to only $25 per year for every $10,000 in unpaid balances, don't count on your payments dropping dramatically.

- A student loan consolidation allows a borrower in *default* to get a fresh start on his loans. By consolidating, a borrower can clean up his credit a tad and arrange new payment terms that weren't available under his defaulted loan.

DEFINITION

A federal student loan is considered in **default** after no payment has been received for 270 days. If a loan is in default, collection actions are imminent unless you contact the lender, make alternative payment arrangements, or attempt to "rehabilitate" your loan by making 9 on-time payments within a 10-month period.

The Least You Need to Know

- Federal student loans might be repaid under a variety of programs that range from 10 to 25 years and that include Level, Extended, Graduated, and income-based options.

- Students should opt for the longest repayment plan and lowest payment possible but commit themselves to paying it back more quickly than required.

- Deferments can be used to delay the repayment by up to 3 years for a variety of circumstances that include financial hardship, unemployment, and military service.

- Don't count on student loan consolidations to save you large amounts of money because they actually can cost you a little more!

Loan Forgiveness Programs

In This Chapter

- Loan forgiveness basics
- Do you qualify?
- The difference between loan forgiveness and forgivable loans
- Determining whether loan forgiveness is taxable
- The largest loan forgiveness programs

Over the years, I've done a lot of interviews about the ins and outs of paying for college. Without fail, each reporter invariably asks me what my number one "paying for college" tip is. Without an ounce of hesitation, my answer is always "loan forgiveness programs." I know that might seem far-fetched; the idea that you could borrow tens of thousands of dollars for college only to have some bureaucrat somewhere wave his hand and wipe it out. But, for once, something that is too good to be true actually *is* true.

It's not that the government randomly picks a few lucky graduates to let off the hook at the cost of taxpayers. Rather, federal and local governments use loan forgiveness programs to fill crucial holes in the employment landscape, such as teachers, nurses, and public servants. In doing so, they ensure the public continues to have access to quality services and professionals.

If loans are going to be a necessary part of paying for your or your student's college education, you'll need to pay close attention to this chapter and begin following these programs. Qualifying for them is in fact much easier than qualifying for many scholarship programs, and these can essentially pay for college with as little as 2 to 4 years of work in a certain profession or geographical area after graduation. Although there are no guaranteed silver bullets in paying for college, this is as close as it comes.

How Loan Forgiveness Works

Most loan forgiveness programs, regardless of their sponsors, generally work the same way. As mentioned, they're fairly easy to qualify for, but they do require the college graduate to be flexible in which jobs she takes in the first few years after graduation.

CHEAT SHEET

There are certain situations that no one should wish for, but that almost assuredly result in loan cancellation, which is virtually identical to loan forgiveness. If the borrower dies or becomes totally and permanently disabled, loans are typically forgiven. Additionally, if a student's school ceases to exist before she can complete her education, the school fraudulently certified the loans, or the student was subject to identity theft, any loan balances are likely forgivable. It's important to note, however, that filing bankruptcy *will not* usually result in loan forgiveness.

Before we break out the details and application process for loan forgiveness, let's clear up one misconception about loan forgiveness and payment. In most cases, loan forgiveness programs are offered by a government organization *in addition* to the paycheck your employer offers you—not *instead of* your paycheck. In fact, your employer has very little to do (if anything at all) with whether you are approved for loan forgiveness or how much loan forgiveness you receive. In short, loan forgiveness is like a bonus on top of what you're going to be paid to do your job. Great deal, huh?

Qualifying for Loan Forgiveness

Unlike many forms of financial aid, which are based on someone's lack of income or assets, most loan forgiveness programs don't even look in that direction. Whether you were born with a silver spoon in your mouth or grew up working at the local greasy spoon, you are welcome and encouraged to apply.

What really matters when it comes to applying for loan forgiveness is whether you meet the following criteria:

- **Qualifying job**—The vast majority of loan forgiveness programs are offered to people who are working in certain fields that benefit the public. In other words, if you are caring for the sick, providing legal services for the poor, or protecting your town's streets, there's a good chance you'll be eligible for loan forgiveness. In fact, most loan forgiveness programs won't even consider your application until after you've landed a job in such a field.

- **Qualifying degree**—Most loan forgiveness programs also require successful applicants to have received at least a four-year degree in certain subject areas. Many of the juiciest programs actually require you to have a graduate degree (Master's or Ph.D.) to earn loan forgiveness.

- **Geographical location**—Loan forgiveness is often based around graduates working in rural or urban areas that might otherwise have a tough time attracting certain professionals. So if you're willing to go to work in rural Arkansas or urban Harlem, you're more likely to qualify for loan forgiveness than if you want to work on the beach in Hawaii.

- **Time commitment**—Most loan forgiveness programs come with a requirement that the recipient continue to work in that field or geographical location for a minimum number of years. The average is approximately four years, but some loan forgiveness programs will wipe out a portion of your debt in as little as one year.

CHEAT SHEET

Because many loan forgiveness programs are dependent on a student having a state license or certification, and because the requirements for the same license vary from state to state, it's important to do your homework before you enroll at a school in a different state than the one in which you plan to work. To ensure that you don't spend extra time making up for missed requirements, request a list of certification requirements from both a school in your state and your out-of-state school.

Forgivable Loans Versus Loan Forgiveness

For every loan forgiveness program out there, there are probably two or three forgivable loan programs. Confused? Don't be.

Loan forgiveness is when a student takes out standard federal loans (Perkins, Stafford, and PLUS) that might be later forgiven if the student meets certain conditions after graduating. There is no guarantee that these loans will be forgiven, and the student does not need to make any promises to actually work in any specific field while he's going to school.

Forgivable loans, on the other hand, are typically state-based loans made to students under the assumption that they will work in a certain field immediately after graduation. If they do, then a portion of the loans will be forgiven each year. If not, they're on the hook for paying them off. Thus, these loans are almost "preapproved" in a sense for later forgiveness.

These are great loans to utilize if you're sure about your career path. If you're not, you might not want to use them because their interest rates might be higher than those of federal loans and they might lack many helpful repayment options, such as the federal Income Based Repayment (IBR) program (see Chapter 6). To find out more about these forgivable loans and their availability, visit the website for your state's student aid commission.

DEFINITION

Loan forgiveness refers to programs to which a graduate applies after he graduates and that erases his debt in exchange for service. **Forgivable loans** refers to loans that are made to existing students in exchange for a future commitment to work in certain professions. Students should utilize both types, if available.

Tax Consequences of Loan Forgiveness

One question that might have occurred to you by now is how does the IRS feel about someone getting thousands of dollars in loans wiped out. Isn't that the same as someone handing you that amount of money, and if so, wouldn't it be counted as income?

It's a valid question and one you should answer before you embark on a loan forgiveness program. Not because paying taxes on the forgiven amount is a rip-off, because it's not. It always makes sense to have a large amount of debt forgiven, even if you have to pay a relatively small amount of taxes to do it.

Rather, you need to understand the taxability of a forgiveness program because it can lead you to choose one job over another, or one loan forgiveness program over another. In comparing the benefits of one job or loan forgiveness program to another, you need to subtract the taxes you'll pay from the amount forgiven to determine your net benefit. For example, if you're offered a job paying $50,000 with no loan forgiveness and one paying $45,000 plus $7,000 loan forgiveness ($52,000 total), the taxability of that $7,000 in loan forgiveness will likely affect which job you should take.

To avoid having to include student loan amounts that have been forgiven on your tax return, the forgiven amounts have to meet certain criteria. If they don't meet these criteria, they're likely going to be fully taxable as income for both your federal and state income taxes.

The criteria for tax-free loan forgiveness are twofold:

1. **Required employment**—The loan forgiveness program must require you to work in a certain profession or position for a prespecified amount of time.

2. **Qualified organization**—The forgiveness must be provided by one of the following three types of organizations:

   • Federal, state, or local government

   • A tax-exempt public benefit organization running a hospital

   • A school that has a partner program with one of the previously mentioned organizations to help staff underemployed professions or geographical areas

> **WORLD WIDE WISDOM**
>
> Everything you need to know about the taxability of student loan forgiveness can be found in IRS Publication 4681, at www.IRS.gov/formspubs.

Even if forgiven loan amounts are considered tax-free, you'll still likely receive an IRS Form 1099-C for the amount that is forgiven each year; this needs to be included on your tax return. However, your tax preparation software or accountant will walk you through how to exclude this amount from the figure on which your taxes are actually calculated if you meet the previous requirements.

Loan Forgiveness for Teachers

One of the easiest ways to secure some substantial loan forgiveness is to spend a few years as a teacher. This might not be what you or your student wants to do with the rest of your/her life, but it can be a surprisingly lucrative detour with very little additional effort. In many states, obtaining a certification to teach requires only an additional 12 to 18 months of schooling on top of a student's primary degree.

Federal Forgiveness Programs

There are two primary federal loan forgiveness programs available for teachers. These programs offer much greater flexibility for teachers to work in any part of the country or any state that suits them, as opposed to state-funded programs, which lock teachers into that state. These two programs also tend to be the most stable from year to year and most likely to survive budget cuts because they're paid for out of the federal budget:

- **Perkins Loan Forgiveness for Teachers**—One of the juiciest loan forgiveness programs for teachers is the Perkins program, which forgives up to 100 percent of a teacher's Perkins loans. The amount forgiven depends on the number of years someone accumulates as a full-time teacher, with 15 percent of the person's loan balance forgiven for each of her first two years, 20 percent for years three and four, and 30 percent for every year after that.

- **The Stafford Loan Forgiveness Program for Teachers**—This program forgives between $5,000 and $17,500 in Stafford loans in return for five years of consecutive service in a designated low-income school. Loan forgiveness awards over $5,000 are reserved for certain high school math and science teachers, as well as special education teachers working with children with disabilities.

WORLD WIDE WISDOM

One of the most comprehensive and up-to-date directories of both federal and state loan forgiveness programs for teachers is maintained by the American Federation of Teachers (AFT). The directory can be viewed for free online at www.aft.org.

State Loan Forgiveness Programs

Many states offer loan forgiveness programs for teachers in their state. Although I've provided a full list of every state's teacher loan forgiveness programs in Appendix D, here are some of the largest programs. It's not unheard of for graduates to actually move to a state with a large need for teachers or a good loan forgiveness program, simply to erase their debts:

- **California APLE**—This program forgives up to $19,000 in student loans for teachers. To qualify, a teacher must commit to at least four years of teaching in an underserved subject area.

- **Teach for Texas**—This program forgives up to $5,000 per year in loans, or $20,000 total over a maximum of five years. To qualify, a teacher must be teaching in either a subject area or a geographical area experiencing a shortage.

- **Teach for New York**—For teachers willing to work in New York City, the state offers up to $4,000 in loan forgiveness per year ($24,000 maximum). Unlike many other programs, the Teach for New York program forgives several types of nonfederal loans, including private bank loans.

- **Illinois Teacher Loan Forgiveness**—This program matches federal Stafford Forgiveness amounts up to $5,000 after a teacher has five consecutive years of teaching in the state.

- **Florida's Critical Teacher Loan Forgiveness Program**—This program forgives up to $10,000 in either undergraduate or graduate loans for Florida teachers, with a minimum of $2,500 per year being forgiven. To qualify, a teacher must be teaching in a certified shortage area.

Loan Forgiveness for Medical Professionals

The good news is that loan forgiveness programs for medical professionals can forgive a ridiculous amount of money. We're talking well over $100,000 in student loans. The bad news is that these programs are heavily dependent on the type of certification or license that someone holds, with the bulk of forgiveness programs focusing on doctors and nurses. Additionally, many of these programs focus primarily on attracting medical professionals to urban and rural areas that are experiencing a shortage of professionals.

National Health Service Corps Loan Forgiveness for Medical Professionals

The granddaddy of medical loan forgiveness programs is the National Health Service Corps (NHSC) program. In 2010, the federal government allocated more than $200 million in funds to this program for loan forgiveness. It represents a huge opportunity for certain professionals to wipe out a large portion of their college costs.

Under the NHSC program, qualified medical professionals can receive up to $50,000 in loan forgiveness for a two-year commitment to serve in a designated shortage area. Professionals who can participate in this program are broadly defined and include:

- Physicians
- Primary care nurses
- Certified nurse-midwives

- Primary care physician assistants
- Dentists and dental hygienists
- Psychiatrists and psychologists
- Psychiatric nurses
- Licensed clinical social workers
- Marriage and family therapists
- Licensed professional counselors

WORLD WIDE WISDOM

The most comprehensive online database of medical loan forgiveness programs is run by the Association of American Medical Colleges. Its database allows you to search for both forgivable loans and loan forgiveness programs. Visit the site at www.aamc.org to learn more.

Nursing Education Loan Forgiveness Program

If the NHSC program is the granddaddy of all medical loan forgiveness programs, then you're about to meet grandma. The Nursing Education Loan Forgiveness Program can wipe out up to 85 percent of a registered nurse's student loans for just three years of full-time service at a nonprofit facility—although only a minimum of two years is required. As always, benefits offered under this program are in addition to the normal salary and benefits paid to the employee.

Other Medical Loan Forgiveness Programs

A large number of smaller federal loan forgiveness programs are out there that are geared more toward certain medical specialties and activities. Again, even though I've provided an extended listing in Appendix D, I want to give you a sampling of two of the more popular programs to give you hope and help you plan:

- **NIH research grants**—The National Institute of Health offers hefty loan forgiveness of $35,000 per year to medical doctors and Ph.D.s doing research in certain high-profile areas such as pediatrics and infertility.

- **State/federal partnerships**—Many states receive federal funds to help recruit medical professionals to serve in areas experiencing shortages. These funds are most often offered in the form of loan forgiveness, with annual amounts typically ranging from $10,000 to $30,000. Check with your state's medical board for more information about what might be available in your state.

Loan Forgiveness for Volunteers

Loan forgiveness for people volunteering their time isn't as substantial as for those working in professions experiencing shortages, but it can still be a pretty nice financial pat on the back for doing something you might already be inclined to do. Unfortunately, only volunteer service done through one of two primary organizations qualifies for federal loan forgiveness outside of the Income Based Repayment (IBR) program:

- **Peace Corps Loan Forgiveness**—Graduates with Perkins loans can have up to 15 percent of the loan balance forgiven for each 365 days of volunteer service during their first two years with the Peace Corps, as long as they serve in an overseas location. If they volunteer a third or fourth year, they can receive an additional 20 percent forgiveness for each of those years, for a maximum of 70 percent over four years of service.

- **AmeriCorps Segal Education Award**—If full-time overseas travel isn't your cup of tea, the AmeriCorps awards up to $5,350 (2010) per year for volunteering within the United States. This award can be earned a maximum of two times and can also be earned on a reduced basis by people not working as full-time volunteers. Even better, nearly 100 colleges around the United States will actually match any loan forgiveness amounts earned under the AmeriCorps program.

- The amount forgiven by the AmeriCorps Segal Education Award is tied to the amount awarded under the Pell Grant program. So if you have a few years until you're going to volunteer in the hopes of earning loan forgiveness, you can count on this amount increasing.

Other Loan Forgiveness Options

Although the loan forgiveness programs for teachers and medical professionals are the largest and most widespread, plenty of other programs are hiding out there for people willing to flip over a few stones. Many times, these programs are sponsored by local nonprofit organizations or smaller government programs that are having a tough time attracting teachers.

I cannot include an exhaustive list in this book, but I do encourage you to visit the websites provided, as well as CollegeSavings.About.com, which has a growing master list of all these programs. Also, be sure to check with the college of your choice, the professors in your (or your student's) major, and professional organizations in your area about loan forgiveness:

- **Lawyers**—Considering that even veteran public defenders make just a fraction of what a partner at a law firm makes, it's not surprising that many local governments have begun to offer loan forgiveness to try to attract quality attorneys. These programs do not exist in every area, but anyone considering a legal career should visit www.EqualJusticeWorks.org and www.abanet.org to find out about law schools and local nonprofits that help forgive the loans of attorneys in public service.

- **Child care providers**—Although the program has faced some funding shortfalls, the Federal Child Care Provider program still exists. Graduates working in low-income child care facilities can have up to 100 percent of their loans forgiven. Visit studentaid.ed.gov for more details.

The Least You Need to Know

- If you're willing to be flexible in your job choices, loan forgiveness can wipe out a huge chunk of your college costs.
- Forgivable loans, which are awarded while a student is still in school, should be used only if you're sure about your career path.
- Considering a career detour through teaching or volunteer work can shave thousands off your student loans.
- It's important to ask around about programs offered by your state and local government.

Increasing Your Aid Eligibility

In This Chapter

- The basic financial aid formula
- Three ways to lower your expected family contribution (EFC)
- Tips for increasing your aid award
- Mastering the CSS Profile for private schools
- Financial aid and non-nuclear families

We recently moved from the big city to a much more rural part of the country. In addition to all the other perks of smaller town living, I love the fact that people are just far more creative in their solutions to life's problems. They have home remedies for everything from a toothache to parenting problems. Of course, I've come to recognize that some of these solutions are absolutely useless wives' tales, like changing your diet to determine what gender your baby will be. I've also come to realize that others are actually downright harmful, like putting butter on a burn.

Over the years, I've come to recognize that eligibility for financial aid is not much different. There are a ton of myths and solutions floating around about how to increase your financial aid eligibility or how much financial aid you can actually qualify for. Further, many of these recommendations can actually harm someone's financial aid chances more than they help them.

To keep you from falling prey to useless or even destructive financial aid eligibility tricks, this chapter picks apart the financial aid eligibility formula and how it is really calculated. As a bonus, we'll walk through some of the broad techniques that really can make a difference in how the government and schools determine your financial need and what aid they'll provide.

Understanding the Aid Formula

Although every school and scholarship may use its own unique aid formula for the school-based scholarships it provides, they're all built heavily on the expected family contribution (EFC) model that is used for federal aid programs. EFC is a measure of how much a family is expected to contribute toward a student's education in any given year.

The EFC calculation itself does not have anything to do with the cost of the college you are attending; it is a separate calculation that is compared to the cost of college you are attending. In other words, someone's EFC for federal aid is the same whether he goes to Harvard or his local community college.

> **FLUNK-PROOF FINANCES**
>
> Many first-time parents and college students make the optimistic error of assuming that they will receive the difference between their EFC and their cost of attendance. In reality, this "unmet need" is just a starting point for financial aid, with many students not receiving nearly enough to cover it.

For example, let's say that a family had an EFC (more on the actual calculation in a minute) of $5,000. If their student plans on attending a school that costs $4,000 per year, they're unlikely to get any financial aid because their EFC actually exceeds their cost by $1,000. However, if their student was to go to a school with an annual cost of $20,000, this amount actually exceeds their EFC by $15,000. So the family will likely receive some financial aid.

In short, the closer your EFC calculation is to the cost of the attendance at the school of your choice, the less likely you are to get financial aid. This means, of course, that one of the primary goals in getting more aid is to legally lower your EFC number as soon as possible and for as many years of school as possible.

Ingredients in the Federal EFC Formula

Because the actual math of the EFC calculation is beyond what a parent or student needs to understand, we'll just take a look at the main ingredients that go into the EFC formula. The greater the dollar amounts of these individual ingredients that are added to your EFC formula, the greater the ending number and the lower your aid package.

At the core of the federal EFC formula, also known as the *Federal Methodology*, are the amount of income and the amount of assets a family has in the year leading up to when financial aid is being applied for. Naturally, the more income and assets that someone has, the more she'll be expected to contribute toward her or her child's education.

DEFINITION

Federal Methodology refers to the formula used to calculate the EFC for a student for federal financial aid purposes using information from the FAFSA form.

However, not all income and assets are created equal. The assets and income of a student are expected to be used at a greater rate than those of a parent. This is based on the theory that a student does not have many other financial responsibilities, while a parent clearly does. Of course, this is not always true, especially when the student is a parent herself. Further, some assets are completely excluded from the EFC calculation for both parents and students.

A household's EFC is also affected by the number of people in the household who are going to college at the same time. Although it might be a little too late to whip up an extra child, many creative parents are going back to college at the same time as their kids—thus lowering the EFC for each person and resulting in more overall financial aid for the household.

So, in a nutshell, here is how a family's EFC is calculated:

> A percentage of parent's unprotected income
>
> + A percentage of parent's unprotected assets
>
> + A higher percentage of a child's unprotected income
>
> <u>+ A higher percentage of a child's unprotected assets</u>
>
> = Expected Family Contribution

Dependent Versus Independent Students

Being viewed as an independent student in the eyes of the federal government and by colleges is a huge plus when it comes to the amount of aid a student or family receives. That's because, as you look at the previous formula, the income and expenses of the student's parents are removed, resulting in a much lower EFC. But getting classified as an independent student is a lot harder than just turning 18, declaring one's independence, and getting a place of your own. In fact, most students who move out, get a job, and are financially independent are still considered dependents for financial aid purposes.

To be considered independent, a student must meet one of the following criteria:

- Be at least 24 years old
- Have kids of his own
- Be married
- Be an active-duty military serviceperson or veteran
- Have been declared emancipated by a court
- Be pursuing a graduate degree
- Have other people who are his own dependents (siblings, disabled parents, and so on) living with him
- No longer have living parents
- Have been in foster care after age 13
- Be homeless

If someone does not meet one of these criteria and is truly financially responsible for himself, he can apply for a "professional judgment override." Under this provision, a school's financial aid administrator can rule the student as independent; however, this is rarely approved.

General Principles of Increasing Aid

The financial aid formula is far more complex than I can cover in this book. The federal guide to the EFC calculation is 35 pages by itself. So I want you to focus on a couple of general principles that will lower your EFC and increase your financial aid, instead of trying to master the ins and outs of the calculation:

- **Principle #1: Shift money to excluded asset categories**—In general, any net worth that a parent or child has that is tied up in a retirement account (such as IRAs or 401ks), a whole life insurance policy, or their primary personal residence is not counted as an asset for the federal EFC calculation. For example, you can have a $1 million home that is completely paid off, $1 million in a cash-value life insurance policy, and $10 million in your IRA and not be expected to use any of it toward college under the federal methodology. Of course, shifting money to these assets can result in an increased cost if you have to get it back out, so don't just stick everything into one of these after reading this.

- **Principle #2: Shift assets from children to parents**—Because the financial assets owned by a child (savings accounts, custodial accounts, and so on) count much more heavily against the EFC than those of the parents, it can make sense to shift this money to Mom and Dad if it can be done legally.

- **Principle #3: Minimize a child's wasted income**—Don't get me wrong; because the EFC expects you to contribute only *part* of what you or a child earns toward college, you're always better off to earn more money than to not. Don't ever turn down a promotion, a pay raise, or lottery winnings because you're afraid of hurting your financial aid eligibility. It just wouldn't make sense to earn $10,000 less to get $2,000 in financial aid. However, if your child has a job and is *wasting* all her earnings on her own leisure expenditures, your EFC will end up being higher with no extra cash to show for it. If your child is going to work during her senior year of high school or college years, make sure a substantial portion of her earnings goes toward lowering your overall cost of putting her through college because that income she's earning will decrease the amount of aid you're eligible for.

CHEAT SHEET

For an in-depth look at increasing your financial aid eligibility, check out *The Complete Idiot's Guide to Financial Aid for College, Second Edition* by David Rye (Alpha Books, 2008).

Simplified EFC Calculations

Many people would like to refer to these as rules of thumb, but there are actual provisions that allow a financial aid applicant to use a simplified EFC formula (which does not take into account assets) or even simply claim an EFC of zero. For the sake of figuring out how you're going to pay for college, you can be reasonably assured that you'll get substantial federal, state, and institutional financial aid if your EFC is zero or calculated under one of these simplified formulas.

To qualify for an automatic zero on the EFC calculation, a student's household must have had an income of less than $30,000; not have filed an IRS Form 1040 (only a 1040A or 1040EZ); and either have received federal poverty assistance (food stamps, Supplemental Social Security, and so forth) in the last year or had a dislocated worker as a family member. To qualify for a simplified EFC, which will result in a relatively small EFC, the income limit on these requirements is raised to $49,999 for 2010.

Keeping It Legal

As you evaluate the techniques for lowering your EFC in this chapter, as well as other suggestions that you'll inevitably hear from peers or find on the Internet, you need to make sure that you don't do anything illegal. The potential increase in aid you might receive will feel very small compared to a massive fine (as high as $20,000) and potential jail time (up to two years)!

The most common mistake many parents (often encouraged by their advisors) make is trying to somehow "hide" assets or income. They might do this by simply lying on their FAFSA forms about how much they have or make, or they might even go so far as to shift assets illegally or temporarily to unrelated parties in an effort to show a smaller net worth.

What most parents and students don't realize is that roughly 30 percent of all FAFSA forms randomly undergo verification, which is meant to catch both honest errors and dishonest cheaters. In fact, if you file a FAFSA form four years in a row, there's almost a 100 percent probability that your FAFSA information will undergo verification at least once.

Getting Your Assets in Gear

One of the most immediate things you can do to decrease your EFC and increase your aid package is to legally shift assets away from kids to parents, from parents to other family members, and from includable to excludable assets. Now, again, there are legal ways to do this and illegal ways to do this. The methods in this section constitute legal ways of shifting assets.

Shifting Assets from Kids to Parents

Financial assets that are considered the property of children are counted most heavily against the EFC calculation. In fact, assets that are technically the property of the child have a contribution rate of 20 percent toward the EFC, while those of the parents have a rate of only 5.64 percent.

Thankfully, very few types of assets are owned by the children that are counted in the EFC. The two most common are UTMA or UGMA custodial accounts, as well as true educational trusts. Any money in these, even though it might have received some favorable tax benefits during the years in which the balances grew, now becomes a hindrance for financial aid purposes because they're in the child's name. However, because these assets technically belong to the child, they cannot simply be transferred into the parent's name without you getting into some major hot water.

So savvy parents use these accounts as much as possible to legally pay a child's other living expenses (food, room, board, private school tuition, car purchases, and so forth) in the few years before college starts, instead of the parent paying for these things out of his own pockets. Using a custodial account or a minor's trust for the "general care" of a child is usually well within the scope of the law and can save you big bucks when you get your financial aid.

WORLD WIDE WISDOM

For more information on the laws pertaining to parents spending money out of UTMA and UGMA accounts, you'll need to do some research on your specific state's rules. Simply do a Web search for "UTMA laws" and your state's name, and you should find all the information you need.

For example, let's say a parent of a 15-year-old has $10,000 in his personal bank account and $10,000 in a UTMA custodial account for that child. If he uses the $10,000 in his own personal account to buy the child a car and the UTMA account remains intact until college, he'll be expected to use $2,000 of the $10,000 (20 percent) toward college costs. However, if he uses the child's custodial account to buy the car—which is completely legal if the parent is the named custodian over the account—his own $10,000 would remain intact until college. In this case, he'd be expected to contribute only $564 (instead of the $2,000) toward his child's college costs.

Shifting from Parents to Other Family

The only two parties whose assets and income count toward the EFC, and in turn against financial aid, are the parents and the student. Grandma and Grandpa, as well as other family members, are not reported on a student's FAFSA, regardless of how much money they have or how much they intend to help pay for. So if Grandma is the owner of a Section 529 plan, the assets in this plan do not reduce financial aid at all.

If you still have more than one year until college, you could consider naming another family member as the owner of a child's Section 529 account. As long as the amount of the account is under the annual IRS gift limit, you shouldn't have any tax problems in doing so. This would remove the assets from your net worth in plenty of time to honestly fill out the FAFSA form and exclude those assets. Of course, you have to trust that that person will not run off with the money and will use it exclusively for your child.

FLUNK-PROOF FINANCES

By all measures, Section 529 plans are relatively new. In fact, they're so new that the laws regarding financial aid and these accounts seem to keep changing. If you are going to use a strategy that involves shifting assets to a Section 529 account, or shifting your existing Section 529 assets to another family member, you'll need to double-check that financial aid rules haven't changed recently.

It is important to note that once this money is withdrawn and used to pay for college, it does count as income on the child's FAFSA form, which will hurt her aid eligibility in the following year. So many parents wait to tap Section 529 accounts owned by grandparents until the final year of college, when no more financial aid will need to be applied for.

Shifting from Includable to Excludable Assets

In addition to who "owns" an asset affecting how much that asset reduces potential financial aid, the type of asset itself can result in it being completely excluded from the EFC calculation. Naturally, it would make sense for parents to convert includable assets to excludable assets prior to filling out the FAFSA form, as long as there is not a high cost, major loss of value, or substandard investment return for doing so.

The easiest way to do this is to simply convert cash or investments into physical property that you are going to need to buy in the next couple of years anyway. For example, if a parent or student has a large amount of cash sitting in a bank account when she completes her FAFSA, this will count against her financial aid. However, if she uses this money to buy the computer, car, and clothes she'll need for college, these assets will all be excluded from the EFC.

More creative parents with more money than can be converted into necessary expenditures can consider using this money to pay off debts, pay down their mortgage, invest in their retirement plans, or purchase whole life insurance (although I generally advise against these expensive policies). Again, in all these situations, you need to consider the costs of getting at this money, such as interest to borrow against a home that has been paid down or penalties for removing money from an IRA, prior to trying to shelter available funds.

Intelligent Income Planning

Like assets, the income you and your child report can have a huge effect on the amount of financial aid you're eligible for. As I've mentioned, it would make no sense for someone to attempt to make less money to qualify for financial aid. However, controlling the timing and titling of that income can make a huge difference in how much aid you receive.

When it comes to *income timing*, accelerating or delaying income can make a huge difference. For example, if you accelerate or delay when you receive a bonus, a payout from a lawsuit, withdrawals from retirement accounts, or the sale of investment assets, it can help lower the EFC in the year you exclude it from. As a general rule, if you already expect to show $50,000 or more in income in any given year, you'll need to push as much income into that year as possible. Doing so won't really cost you much, if anything, in financial aid. Likewise, pushing income out of the years where your income is already going to be low—especially between $30,000 and $50,000 in total income—will greatly increase your chances of receiving substantial financial aid.

DEFINITION

Income timing refers to the deliberate choosing of one tax year over another to receive income in to lower one's potential EFC.

From the point of income titling, if there is any way that income can be legally reclassified as expense reimbursements (getting paid in mileage instead of wages) or that income can be paid to you instead of your child, you'll come out ahead. The most common instance of this is parents who own a small family business that employs their own children. By skipping the paycheck and having your kids help out for free around the shop, that money can either be paid as income to you (which is counted against your EFC at a lower rate) or be kept as part of the business's assets (which probably will not be counted at all).

The CSS Profile and Institutional Methodology

So far, everything we've talked about has revolved heavily around the FAFSA form and the Federal Methodology for calculating need. However, the FAFSA form and Federal Methodology are not required for financial aid programs using non-government money or for most institutions offering private scholarships to their students. In fact, many private schools use *both* the Federal Methodology that we've been tinkering with throughout this chapter as well as an *Institutional Methodology* that takes into account different factors in determining what your need is.

DEFINITION

Institutional Methodology is a formula used for private aid given by schools, using information found on the CSS Profile.

The numbers used for the Institutional Methodology are often drawn from a separate financial aid form known as the College Scholarship Profile, more commonly known as the CSS Profile. This form is used by hundreds of private schools around the country to award private financial aid and scholarships to students who attend their institution.

Ultimately, if you're required to complete the CSS Profile for financial aid at a private school, you need to be aware that some of the classic EFC reduction tricks that work for the FAFSA will not work for the aid provided by private schools. In addition to your income being counted in a different way, assets such as your home equity and retirement accounts might be factored in.

Although much more in-depth techniques can be found for maximizing financial aid when you are subject to both the Federal Methodology using the FAFSA form and the Institutional Methodology using the CSS Profile, I'm of the opinion that you don't need to bother. Some differences do exist between the EFC amounts that are calculated from these two different forms, but it's generally not huge for most parents or students with limited assets and income. Further, federal financial aid is usually the best bet for most cash-strapped students, so tweaking your assets and incomes to maximize this is usually the best choice for most students and families.

The Non-Nuclear Family and Financial Aid

Single parents, *blended families*, *shared custody*, and *unpaid child support* are phrases that apply to more families of college-bound students than ever before. These "non-nuclear" families, with a sticky web of intertwining obligations and complicated emotions, can create some major anxiety when it comes to filling out the FAFSA and other financial aid forms.

Many students have no clue how much one or both parents make, with at least one parent often reluctant to actually disclose his income or assets for fear of the other party taking advantage of him. Just as often, a student still dependent on one party doesn't even know how to get in contact with the other parent, who might have been out of the picture for years or even decades.

Even though the rules can be confusing at times, the single best option for making sense of them is to contact the financial aid administrator at the school you will be attending. He will be able to walk you through the unique facets of what is needed for your situation and what to do if you cannot get the information you need. But, as a general rule, here's who is responsible for filling out the FAFSA and helping to pay for the education of a child:

- **The custodial parent**—The parent with whom the child lives for the majority of the year and who provides the majority of the support is the one responsible for helping a student complete his FAFSA.

- **Noncustodial parents**—Depending on state law, a biological parent living separately from the custodial parent and child might or might not have a financial obligation to help the custodial parent pay for college. From a federal financial aid point of view, this parent's assets and income are not part of the student's EFC calculation. However, many private schools that rely on the CSS application *do include* the incomes and assets of both parents, even if they're no longer a couple, as part of their consideration for aid.

- **Step-parents**—If the custodial parent of a child remarries, the step-parent's assets are factored into the federal EFC calculation, even though the child is not the step-parent's biological child.

The Least You Need to Know

- If you want to increase your financial aid, you have to lower your expected family contribution (EFC).
- The assets and income of a student hurt financial aid eligibility significantly more than those of the parents.
- Students and parents should try to convert cash and other includable assets into protected assets, especially goods that will eventually need to be purchased anyway.
- If any existing income can be pushed forward or backward into a higher EFC year, it can result in more overall aid than if kept in the current year.
- If you're living in a non-nuclear family, you'll need to do your homework well in advance of financial aid deadlines to ensure that you have all the information you need.

Free Money for College

Thanks to the Federal Trade Commission, it's rare anymore that you'll see the word *free* without an asterisk next to it. Of course, that asterisk points to some fine print indicating that this *free** thing actually requires $19.99 in shipping and handling or an annual subscription. It turns out that *free* has become a dirty, untrustworthy word in our culture.

That's too bad, because there are a lot of legitimate opportunities to get free money to help pay for college, or even an outright free college education. Of course, because most people think that it is too good to be true, it remains so for them. Sadly, they miss out on piles of cash that are waiting for eager students.

In this part, you learn how to access free money from federal and state agencies, from the IRS, and even from colleges who like to educate people for free. Some of it is easy to get, some of it is a tad bit harder, but all of it is asterisk free.

Scholarships: Truly Free Money

Chapter 9

In This Chapter

- Scholarship myths
- Doing the research to find the right scholarships
- Developing your scholarship strategy
- Making an impact with your application

Every sport has its rare moments of peak performance. You've got the grand slam in baseball, the hat trick in hockey, and the slam dunk in basketball. Well, in the arena of college planning, landing a scholarship is truly that "superstar" moment for a parent or student. That's because scholarships, at their core, are free money that is awarded based on how well someone has performed, be it on the field, in the classroom, or on his scholarship essay.

Make no mistake about it, winning scholarships is a competitive sport. You're not just competing against yourself in terms of finding the right options, dressing up your application, and keeping track of key deadlines. You're also competing against every other person who is scrambling to pay for college, in large part because there are just not enough scholarships to go around.

But don't be discouraged. Winning scholarships is as much a test of someone's endurance and willingness to commit to a long-term process as it is about how qualified you actually are to win. To some degree, it's a numbers game, just like a hole in one in golf. You hit enough balls (or send enough applications), and you'll eventually get a hole in one.

Scholarships Myths

Unfortunately, there are more myths and misperceptions floating around about scholarships than there are truths. To make matters worse, a lot of so-called "professionals" promise to score you some big bucks if you're willing to dish out some cash. So before we go any further, I want to address some of the wrong information that is floating around out there, so you can find that happy middle ground between having false hope and having no hope at all.

> **FLUNK-PROOF FINANCES**
>
> I said it before and I'll say it again: don't waste valuable money paying someone to do research that you can do for free. Likewise, don't believe anyone who promises to get your scholarship application in front of the right people or on the top of the pile. I can guarantee that you'll come out ahead by keeping your $250 to $1,000, putting it toward tuition, and following the simple steps in this chapter.

Myth #1: Scholarships Are Impossible to Get

Chances are that if you told a stranger your child had received a scholarship, she'd ask you which sport your child plays. Likewise, if I were to ask you what chances you thought you had of receiving a scholarship, you'd guess little to none if you or your kid would rather crunch numbers than helmets.

In reality, though, there are hundreds of millions of dollars in scholarships out there that have nothing to do with athletics. They range from academic merit scholarships, to industry-specific scholarships, to geographical scholarships. In fact, there are so many scholarships out there that books trying to comprehensively list all scholarship programs usually range between 500 and 1,000 pages.

The point of all that is to say that doing your homework before you apply for scholarships, as well as applying for every scholarship that you have a legitimate shot at, will yield results. In fact, I would go so far as to say that if you apply for 10 scholarships for every $1,000 in unmet need you have, there is a good chance you'll get some letters in the mail that make you very happy.

Myth #2: Millions in Scholarships Go Unclaimed

Although scholarships are by no means impossible to get, especially for parents and students who send out a steady stream of quality applications, the idea that there are millions in scholarships that go unclaimed is completely bogus. In fact, anyone or any service that claims to be able to direct you toward slam-dunk scholarships is full of it.

In reality, even the smallest and least publicized scholarship funds get dozens of applications every year—if for no other reason than the people who are tied to the scholarship fund are constantly encouraging the kids of their friends and family to apply. But, as you'll see in a minute, these smaller scholarship funds are definitely programs you want to target because your chances are much higher with them than with programs that receive thousands of applications.

WORLD WIDE WISDOM

Although it's ridiculous to think that there are millions of dollars in scholarships that no one applies for, newly introduced scholarships often get substantially fewer applications because both students and scholarship services don't have them on their radars yet. The best way to get a heads-up on these new scholarships is to sign up for a free Google Alerts account and have it send you an e-mail any time the phrase "new scholarship" is in the news.

Myth #3: You Can't Qualify for a Scholarship

Just as with other forms of financial aid, many parents and students talk themselves out of applying because they believe they'll never qualify. Usually they think this because they make too much money or their grades are not at the top of their high school class. Thankfully, "qualifying" often has very little to do with who actually wins scholarships.

In large part, scholarship winners are decided on by a committee of people who take into consideration a number of factors, which vary widely from fund to fund. Some scholarships do hold very tightly to concrete standards, such as someone's financial need or academic record. More often, though, scholarship committees are given a lot of wiggle room to select candidates who really tug on their heart strings and seem to embody the reason that the scholarship fund was established in the first place.

Myth #4: It's Too Late to Apply

Perhaps the only time that it is too late to begin the scholarship hunt is a few months before you graduate; at that point you should probably be hunting for loan forgiveness programs (see Chapter 7). Any time prior to that, though, is as good a time as any to begin looking for some free money.

Granted, you'd ideally begin looking for scholarships at least 12 to 24 months before your freshman year of college starts. But, because most scholarships are initially awarded for only a one-year period, you have just as good of a chance of winning a scholarship in your sophomore or junior year as you do in your freshman year. In fact, you might have a better chance because you've already proven that there's a good chance you'll graduate. Scholarship funds hate giving away money to people who drop out of school after a year or two.

Additionally, many scholarship programs award amounts only to students entering certain years of college. It's not uncommon to find programs that are available only to junior, senior, or graduate students. Ironically, these might be some of the easiest scholarships to land because many families give up the scholarship hunt after freshman year. In short, you should view the scholarship application process as an ongoing cycle that you're committed to until six months prior to graduation.

If you find a scholarship that really seems to be your cup of tea but you have missed the deadline for it, you should still consider submitting an application. Many organizations, even though they have stated deadlines, will throw the late-comers in the pile as well. Regardless of the outcome, you should also add this scholarship deadline to your calendar for the coming year.

Myth #5: The Only Scholarship Worth Getting Is the "Full Ride"

Many students and parents don't take the scholarship process seriously because they think the chances of winning a scholarship that picks up the entire bill for college is pretty slim. Well, unfortunately, they're right about that. Unless you're a serious athlete or math-lete, you're probably not going to ever land the coveted "full ride."

Sadly, many parents don't realize that as the amount a scholarship offers drops, so do the number of applicants for that scholarship. In other words, you're going to get a lot more people applying for a scholarship that pays $25,000 per year for four years than one that pays $500 just once. But, if you're willing to hustle, you can probably scrape together a number of $500 and $1,000 scholarships that will go a long way toward meeting your unmet financial needs.

I'm not saying you shouldn't apply for a few huge scholarships. You never know—you might get lucky! But, you'll probably end up with more cash if you spend your time applying for smaller and better researched scholarships.

Finding the Right Scholarships

Although I wish I had the space to include a detailed listing of every scholarship out there, I don't. This book would have been three times as long and a lot less enjoyable to read. To really do the research you need, you're going to have to spend a little bit more money and purchase both a scholarship directory and sign up for a scholarship website.

All told, these two resources will probably cost you $20 to $30 per year, but they're absolutely necessary if you hope to find scholarships you'll have an above average chance of winning. In addition to the scholarship directory books I've included in Appendix C, you'll want to check out these free resources on the web:

- www.FastWeb.com, which is a free scholarship search engine

- www.SallieMae.com/scholarships, which is a scholarship directory and matching service

- www.CollegeBoard.com, which has a directory of unique state and local programs

Also check out Appendix E for a good starting point of the best scholarship programs out there.

> **WORLD WIDE WISDOM**
>
> Don't overlook your favorite Internet search engine in your hunt for scholarships, especially for smaller special-interest scholarships. Simply searching the Web for scholarships related to your unique special interests, such as "left-handed scholarships," will often yield results. (And, yes, there is actually a $1,000 scholarship for left-handed people.)

Drilling Down for Scholarships

When it comes to scholarships, there are really two kinds of scholarships in my opinion: primary scholarships and special-interest scholarships. *Primary* scholarships are those that are built around four main criteria and that offer the most scholarship opportunities across multiple organizations, as well as the largest amounts of money per award. *Special-interest* scholarships are those that are offered by smaller organizations and are focused on things that a large number of students might not be able to relate to or have any interest in.

The "big four" of primary scholarships are:

- **Academics**—Are your grades better than most?

- **Heritage**—Does your ethnic background provide opportunities?

> - **Career path**—Are you excited about a certain profession?
>
> - **Institutional**—Does your school of choice offer unique scholarships only open to its students?

If you solidly fit into one of these categories, you should spend the time "going deep" and finding every appropriate scholarship within that category that you might qualify for. For example, if you or your student has a 3.99 GPA, you should apply for as many academic scholarships as you can find. Likewise, if your ethnic heritage or your future career path qualify you for a certain pool of scholarships, spend a good portion of your time applying for these. In fact, if you qualify for one of these primary scholarship categories, every other application you write should go toward one of these primary scholarship sources.

CHEAT SHEET

Taking a hard look at your family tree can bear some serious financial fruit. Many scholarship organizations that award scholarships based on ethnic heritage require someone to be only one-eighth or one-sixteenth from that ethnic background.

Casting a Wide Net for Scholarships

Aside from those four primary categories of scholarships I just mentioned, there are thousands of other scholarships out there that cannot be neatly grouped into any one large category. In other words, you might find that you qualify for a few scholarships based on where you live, a few based on where you or your parents work, and one because you're an accomplished juggler. But no one of these special-interest scholarship categories will give you more than a few applications worth of work.

So with special-interest scholarships, you need to cast a wide net, leave no stone unturned, and get very creative in how and with whom you identify yourself. The best way to do this is to start by identifying potential special-interest areas around which you'll build your research.

Here are some of the special-interest scholarship categories you'll want to investigate:

> - **Employers**—You'll need to make a list of all of a student's, their parents', and even their grandparents' past and current employers. The scholarships from these sources are typically small ($250 to $1,000), but they tend to be some of

the easiest to get. In addition to researching on the Internet, you should make a call to each company's human resources department to see whether it offers any benefits.

- **Religious affiliation**—Whether you're Christian, Buddhist, Hindu, or atheist, I can guarantee you that there are at least a few scholarships out there for each group. In addition to the standard Internet search, be sure to check with your church's local and national offices or organizing body.

- **Geographical location**—Many communities, cities, and counties offer scholarships for current or former residents. Check with local community organizations, the chamber of commerce, and your local governing bodies.

- **Special skills or talents**—Although you probably won't find a scholarship for people who can tie cherry stems in a knot with their tongues, you'll definitely find them for things like juggling, poetry writing, musical skills, and bowling. Chances are, if you enjoy doing something that a lot of other people enjoy as well, there's a scholarship out there to go along with it.

- **Unique traits**—It won't surprise many people that there are plenty of scholarships geared toward women, but it might come as a shock that there are scholarships for twins, tall people, redheads, and just about every other unique trait under the sun.

FLUNK-PROOF FINANCES

There's a fine line between true *scholarships* and *scholarship contests*. The latter are where you simply enter your name, contact information, and a few basic details in the hopes of winning a few thousand dollars. Although these are legitimate opportunities for free money that you should always take 30 seconds to enter, don't confuse them with the real scholarships that you should regularly be applying for, which require more than the luck of the draw.

Athletic Scholarships: Smaller Schools, Better Odds

I haven't touched on athletic scholarships so far because the majority of people reading this book will not have enough athletic prowess to qualify. But, I know that some of the parents or students reading this book will have been decent athletes in their own right, even if they'd never be good enough to play for a PAC-10 or SEC school.

If you (or your child) were one of the better athletes on your high school team, you shouldn't give up hope of landing an athletic scholarship. The trick is to make sure that colleges who are less competitive athletically know that you'd be interested in playing for pay. In reality, many smaller schools do not have the recruiting staff of the larger sports powerhouses, leaving them to make do with what comes their way. Ironically, many of these second-tier athletic schools are first-tier when it comes to education.

Take my alma mater, Pepperdine University, as an example. Granted, they've had a few shining athletic moments over the years, but they are definitely not what most people would consider a top-tier contender in most college sports. However, they have deep pockets and are consistently ranked in the top 100 schools in the country by *U.S. News and World Reports*. During my time there, I knew a number of students who ended up playing a college sport as an afterthought, but who managed to earn a partial scholarship in the process.

The best thing to do if you were a competitive but not superstar athlete at the high school level is to contact your potential colleges' athletic departments and inquire about the possibility of athletic scholarships. In addition, you should do a search for respectable colleges who have second- or third-tier athletic teams in your sport and contact them to see whether there's any incentive for you playing for them.

Your Scholarship Battle Plan

When it comes to winning scholarships, it's a lot like getting in shape. There are no real magic bullets—just hard work and good technique. But instead of barbells and cardio, scholarships require you to apply often, paying close attention to what each organization is looking for. If you send out one great application and then quit, you're no more likely to win a scholarship than to get in shape after just one great workout. Likewise, if you send out a bunch of generic applications without paying attention to what they're looking for, you'll feel the pain, but not experience any of the gain.

CHEAT SHEET

The College Funding Plan that you began working on in the first chapter of this book has a Scholarship Battle Plan at the end of it that neatly summarizes these steps. After you read this section, you should pull out that original worksheet and map out your Scholarship Battle Plan, so that it doesn't slip through the cracks as you finish the rest of this book.

Step #1: Create a Routine

Just like a workout regimen works best when you get on a schedule, so does the scholarship application process when you get yourself into a routine. A routine is crucial for two reasons. First, if you try to do everything from researching to applying in one day, your brain will probably blow a fuse and you'll give up on the whole process. Second, landing scholarship dollars is a numbers game, meaning that you are going to need to apply for far more scholarships than you can accomplish in one day or weekend.

Here's how I recommend setting up a routine:

1. For every $1,000 in annual unmet financial need you have, you should apply for 10 scholarships, regardless of their dollar amounts. So if you are going to be $5,000 short, you should plan on applying for 50 scholarships over the coming year.

2. Because there is no way you are going to apply for 25, 50, or 100 scholarships in one weekend, spread out the work over the course of the year. Everyone needs a few weeks off for holidays, illness, and sanity, so divide the number of scholarships you should be applying for by 45 weeks. If you need to apply for 50 scholarships, that amounts to roughly one application a week. If you need to apply for 100 scholarships, that's two a week, while only 25 scholarships would be one every other week. To help you gauge your time, each application itself should take you roughly 2 to 3 hours the first time.

3. Go to your local office store and buy one of those big office wall calendars. After you've done your research and decided on which primary and special-interest scholarships you're going to apply for, mark their due dates on the calendar. This will be the roadmap you use to tell you what to be working on when.

4. As much as possible, pick a regular day to work on your scholarship applications. Sunday evenings seem to be a favorite for most people because the chaos of the week has not begun yet. If you are helping to fill out applications for someone other than yourself, this time slot can also present the least amount of conflicts. But, whatever day you pick, make sure it is one you can commit to and that won't get taken over with other priorities.

Step #2: Do the Research *Now*!

Doing some research throughout the year is a good habit, but it's important to do the bulk of your research on the front end of your scholarship hunt. That's because many of the scholarships have deadlines that you won't want to miss, leading you to prioritize which scholarships you apply for when.

Refer to the lists of primary and special-interest scholarships earlier in this chapter, and methodically go through each one of those areas, brainstorming on what you might think you qualify for. Just grab a pad of paper, write down the different categories (for instance, Academic, Religious, and so on), and put down any connections to that category that come to mind.

When that is done, begin looking for scholarships within each of those categories that fit you or your student. When you find one that might fit, even if it is a long shot, mark the page or print its web page and move on to the next. When you're done, sit down with a cup of coffee and take a deeper look at each scholarship, its requirements, and its deadlines. For those that fit, transfer the scholarship name, amount, and due dates to your oversized calendar.

☞ **WORLD WIDE WISDOM**

Parents who band together to figure out their college funding often get a lot more accomplished. Even if you do form a "scholarship support group" with some other parents or students, you should also seek out online forums where parents share tips and ideas.

Step #3: Start Applying

Now that you've done all the hard work of selecting scholarships that match your primary and special-interest categories, you have to get down to the business of actually filling out the applications. As a general rule, you'll need to have all applications in the mail no later than one week before the deadline, which means you should probably begin working on them no later than two weeks before the deadline.

Later in this chapter I discuss how to fill out applications and write essays in a way that sets you up for success. For now, here are some basic things you need to do for every application you send:

- **Type it**—While many scholarships allow you to fill out an online application, many others still require you to send in a paper application. If a paper application is required, go the extra mile and fill in the application form before printing it up or use an old-school typewriter for forms that cannot be edited online. The reality is that when a board is trying to decide between you and hundreds of other candidates, those who go the extra mile are going to stick out. Those who don't are going to be pushed to the side. Remember that scholarships are a competitive sport, and many of the people you are contending against will have typed their applications.

- **Proofread, proofread, proofread**—There's no quicker route to the bottom of the application pile than typos and grammatical errors. Scholarship committees will be praised or criticized on whether the students they give awards to build the reputation of the organization. If you have typos, they're likely going to take that as a sign that you're a less-qualified candidate.

  Consider recruiting someone who possesses both a love for you and a set of eagle eyes to be an additional proofreader for your applications. It takes only a few extra minutes to e-mail your English teacher cousin your application. Chances are, he'll be happy to help out and might even help you identify some areas where you should expand on certain things that make you unique. Don't forget to send him a gift card every once and a while as a thank you.

- **Don't guess on the postage**—Especially if you're going to be cutting applications close to their deadlines, you don't want your submission coming back to you due to insufficient postage. You did all that hard work, so walk the application into the post office or use your meter at work to ensure adequate postage gets on the envelope.

- **Keep a copy of your completed applications**—Many scholarships require a phone or personal interview before they're awarded. It's crucial that you make sure the information you give in your interview matches what is on your application. If you don't have a copy to review, you might come across a tad disorganized or, even worse, as a liar.

WORLD WIDE WISDOM

Many states provide a single online application that automatically enters you for dozens of state-based scholarships in one shot. For example, the state of Arkansas offers the YOUniversal application, which lets residents apply for 21 scholarships with a single application. Contact your state's Department of Higher Education (see Appendix D) to find out if it offers such an option.

You can and should reuse parts of your previous essays and short answers, especially if they've already won you some money. If you really like the way your bio or an essay's introduction looks on paper, there is no reason not to copy and paste from application to application. Just make sure you only borrow from yourself (not from other students' essays) and that you tailor each application to meet that organization's beliefs and goals.

Grabbing Their Attention

Although I'm a tad ashamed to admit it, I do watch *American Idol*. However, I usually only watch early in the season when the judges are still traveling from city to city and the contestants range from horrible to diamonds in the rough. One thing that I've noticed is that there are a lot of talented people who just miss making the cut. Usually one or two of the judges is mildly impressed, but one of the others feels indifferent. The contestant is usually ushered out of the room with a "maybe next year."

I want you to imagine scholarship committees like they're the *American Idol* judges. Just like being a pretty good singer is probably not going to get a contestant to Hollywood, being a pretty good applicant is not likely going to result in a student landing an award. In reality, you have to stand out. You have to wow the judges. You have to show them something unique, different, or promising. Although that might sound like a tall order, don't be intimidated. Wowing them is more about knowing what they want than what you have to offer. It's about packaging yourself in a truthful way that fits their organizational objectives.

Most people applying for scholarships spend all their time trying to highlight their laundry list of accomplishments—many of which have nothing to do with why the organization is offering the scholarship. The successful students are typically those who pay close attention to what the committee is looking for and design their application around that.

If you can weave the following things into your application, there is a good chance you'll make it into the pile of finalists:

- **The organization's purpose**—Most scholarship organizations believe strongly in something. Maybe it's diversity or maybe it's the place of beef on the American dinner table. Whatever it is, you need to sprinkle a shared belief in that cause throughout your application, essay, and interview.

- **The scholarship's purpose**—Many organizations that believe strongly in something offer multiple scholarships that work toward what the organization values. A typical organization might offer a scholarship to someone who has been impacted by their organization, as well as one to someone who can impact the world on behalf of their organization. Your application needs to show that you are the ideal candidate who meets the organization's goal of giving that specific scholarship in the first place.

- **Your belief in their organization**—Expressing your personal belief in the organizations from which you're seeking funds is crucial because organizations want their scholarship winners to be sources of publicity and public praise for the organization. If you can make it clear that you're going to spread the good news of whatever it is that they believe in, you'll be one of their top candidates.

Another great way to grab a scholarship committee's attention is to include timely comments about their organization in the news or the impact their organization is having on the current state of affairs in a community. This shows that you are truly interested in their organization and not just their money—something many people sending out mass applications fail to do.

CHEAT SHEET

If you have a good picture of yourself that you can shrink to wallet size, don't be afraid to include it. Doing so makes your application a lot more personable than the countless others without faces attached to them. If the organization specifically asks for one (which means everyone else will be submitting one), make sure you send a color picture. Simply clip it to the front; it's likely to boost your chances of making it through the first few selection rounds. In all cases, don't send a low-quality photocopy.

What Makes You Different?

Many people give the standard "Miss America" answers on their applications. They believe that children are the future, want to solve world hunger, believe in peace in the Middle East, and love Mom and apple pie. That means, of course, that if you build your scholarship around those things, you're probably going to sound just like everyone else. Now don't get me wrong, those are all great things. But what scholarship committees are looking for are individuals who stand out from the crowd, not people who think they deserve money for believing in the same unsolvable problems as every other applicant.

What you need to talk about is you. You need to tell them *your* story. You need to give them a moving look into who you are and how this money will help you become the person you've dreamed of being. Talk about that in real and honest terms, and again, you'll stand out from the masses of applicants who fail to differentiate themselves.

Taking a hard look at the previous winners of a scholarship can lead to some great clues about what to include on your application. Because many scholarship organizations put profiles of the winners on their websites, it should take you only a few minutes to find some great inside information about what type of applicants a scholarship committee tends to choose.

If the person applying for the scholarship has received any recent praise in the media, make a copy of the clipping or print the Web page and include it with your application (unless the organization requests only the application be submitted). This will build an organization's confidence that you can help expand their reputation and that you will represent them well.

Tips on Writing Your Essay

Some scholarships don't require an essay or answers to questions about why you deserve an award, but most will. For the student with average credentials, this is the place where you can easily snag scholarships out from underneath more qualified applicants.

In addition to ensuring that your essay or short-answers are typo free and reflect the core beliefs and purpose of the organization and the scholarship, you should try to do the following:

- **Use emotive language**—With thousands of applications in front of larger scholarship committees, I can promise you that they are dying for one thing: to be moved. That's why I told you to tell your own story instead of using the standard answers. To help beef this up, you need to use language that is more emotional than concrete. You should talk about hopes and dreams, using words like *joy, belief, change, impact, opportunity,* and so on.

- **Get to the point**—Especially with essays that require a shorter word count (250 to 750 words), don't beat around the bush with a long introduction or slow conclusion. Start with a bold statement about how the organization's goals overlap with who you are, talk briefly about how your achievements or involvement directly relates to the scholarship you're applying for, and close with a strong statement about the impact that this award would make on your own life.

- **Express your gratitude**—Wherever it fits naturally into your essay or answers, thank them for taking the time to review your application and recognize all the hard work they do. If it doesn't fit in naturally to your essay, handwrite it in the margin of the front page of the application. Something as simple as "Many thanks for taking the time to review my application!" will set you apart from the multitude of people who are simply sending out hundreds of applications in a nonstrategic manner.

Strategic Follow-Up on Your Applications

A few years back, there was a job I wanted more than probably any other job in my life. At the time, it seemed like the dream job, running a gorgeous retreat center in the mountains for an organization I had climbed the ranks in. Sure as shooting, I was one of two finalists in the running for this juicy dream job.

They flew my wife and I across the country for an in-person interview in front of the search committee. I decided, because I wanted the job so badly, that I needed to play it cool in the interview and not let my hopes show too much. I tried to be a team player and talk about how I would happily continue in my old role if they didn't want to give me this job, yadda yadda yadda. In the end, when I didn't get the job and asked why, I was told simply that the other guy had appeared to want it a lot more.

CHEAT SHEET

Many scholarships require a brief phone interview with the finalists. You can ace these phone interviews by simply revisiting your research on the organization the day of the call; reviewing the application you sent; and doing the interview in a calm, quiet location. Don't forget to keep a glass of water handy in case you get a tickle in your throat!

I share that story because I think the logic holds true for scholarships. Committees would much rather give money to someone who is hungry for it and does back-flips when they get it than those that seem to be indifferent about a scholarship from that organization. So if there is a decent amount of time between when you submit an application and when the award decision is made, you should continue to show them you are hungry for the scholarship.

Let me be clear: the wrong way to do this is by calling and asking whether they've made a decision yet. That makes you look pushy and childish. Rather, you should consider doing one of two things. First, if you accomplish something major (or a number of minor things), send the organization an updated list of your accomplishments, asking them to add it to your file. This shows them that you are serious about receiving a scholarship from their organization. Second, if you don't get the scholarship, be sure to reapply in the following year, indicating that you are "excited to again be considered for an award from your organization!" Further, do some homework on who actually won the scholarship in the previous years and do some comparison to see what they had that you did not.

Because many scholarships are renewable from year to year, any scholarships you win need to be nurtured and cared for. Be sure to contact the organization that awarded you with the scholarship and ask them what criteria they'll be looking at for renewing your scholarship in future years. Then, make sure you meet every one of the requirements, notifying them as you do!

The Least You Need to Know

- No student should consider scholarships out of reach for herself, regardless of her lack of academic and athletic credentials or her year in school.
- Smart parents and students thoroughly research primary and special-interest scholarships to ensure that their efforts are targeted toward awards they can actually win.
- You should plan to apply for 10 scholarships for every $1,000 you need each year.
- The key to successfully applying for a large number of scholarships is to develop a weekly goal for how many applications you'll send out.
- Make sure that each application is targeted toward the heartstrings of the organization and their goal for establishing the scholarship.

Grant Programs

In This Chapter

- Overview of grant awards
- The federal Pell Grant
- Supplementary federal programs
- Grants for state residents

Grant programs are the single most attractive form of financial aid out there because they're essentially a scholarship from the government. Financial aid does not get any better than these awards—grants do not have to be repaid, do not generally require the student to be an extraordinary student, and are often available to students attending school on a part-time basis. Even if you don't think you'll qualify, every parent or student should make sure that he's in the running for every grant program possible.

That's not to say that grants don't require you to show some financial aid IQ and don't come with some potential drawbacks. Just the opposite. By understanding how much you're likely to receive under certain grant programs, the stability of those grant programs, and the not-so-rare situation where certain former students end up owing Uncle Sam some money, you'll be able to know exactly how much of your college costs grants will cover and how much more you'll need to scrape together.

The Basics of Grants

As the name implies, *grants* are essentially a right or a gift that is bestowed upon someone by someone else. For example, if you lived in fifteenth-century Europe, a member of the royal family might grant you the right to rule over a portion of their kingdom. When it comes to education in the twenty-first century, the government awards you money for college instead of a castle and a few hundred miles of country-side. Further, these modern educational grants, which typically range from $1,000 to $6,000, are not made to the wealthy, talented, or favorites of the ruling class. They're designed for the rest of us peasants.

DEFINITION

A **grant** is a financial aid award given to a student with no expectation of repayment after graduation. However, students failing to complete the courses paid for by the grant are often obligated to repay the grant amounts in a much shorter period of time than a student loan.

Because grants are awarded strictly based on a student's demonstrated financial need—typically using the expected family contribution (EFC) as a measure (see Chapter 8)—there is no need to impress anyone, write a great essay, or ensure that your grades are at the top of your class. But, it is critical that anyone wanting grants not miss their federal or state financial aid deadlines. Due to the sheer number of people applying for these, the government just does not care about your sob stories of why your application is late.

Although grant programs have come to be a staple of many lower- and middle-income Americans' college funding plans, they should not be taken as a given or accepted without some thought. First, these programs, much more so than student loans, are subject to funding cuts that occur regularly at the state level and could definitely occur at the federal level. Just because someone received a grant his freshman year of college, does not mean that the programs themselves will even exist the following year.

Second, due to the large scale of these programs with hundreds of thousands of grants being handed out annually, as well as the "free money" nature of grants, there's very strong antifraud rules surrounding grants and students who drop out of school. And although I'm sure none of the readers of this book are considering committing fraud, students who start a program funded by grants but do not finish it are often expected to repay some or all of the money within a matter of months.

The Pell Grant

When I was a kid, everyone would run outside on Christmas morning after the unwrapping had ended and compare notes on who had gotten what. Whatever the hot toy was that year, there were always a lot of kids who struck out and a few lucky souls who got whatever it was that everyone else wanted. Like Tickle Me Elmo, a Cabbage Patch Kid, or the Storm Trooper Helmet that I drove all over the state to find a couple of years back, the Pell Grant is the must-have item for college students. If you get one, you're likely going to be the envy of a lot of other students.

The Pell Grant program was initially introduced as the Basic Grant Opportunity Program in 1972. It was renamed in 1982 after Senator Pell, who helped create it. It has been expanded every few years to include different definitions of students, as well as to up the amount of the award. It continues to be one of the single largest sources of financial aid in the United States, handing out well over $10 billion annually to students.

WORLD WIDE WISDOM

To learn more about qualifying for the Pell Grant, potential award amounts, and restrictions on who can receive the Pell Grant, visit the official Pell Grant homepage at ed.gov/programs/fpg.

Eligibility for the Pell Grant

Everyone would love Pell Grants, but the hard truth is that Pell Grants don't show their love to everyone. In addition to the income and cost of attendance limits covered in the next section, Pell Grant recipients must meet the following requirements:

- Demonstrate a substantial financial need
- Be a U.S. citizen or eligible resident
- Be under age 24
- Be in their first four years of earning an undergraduate degree
- Not have any felony drug convictions

One notable exception to these eligibility requirements is that Pell Grants might be used in limited cases by graduate students who are earning their teaching credentials. However, not all post-graduate teaching credential programs qualify for Pell Grants, so check with your graduate school's financial aid administrator before making a decision about where to attend based on the hope of Pell Grants.

The Pell Grant Formula

The amount someone receives under a Pell Grant varies widely, up to the annual Pell Grant limit ($5,550 for the 2010–2011 academic year). The actual amount is dependent on a combination of the following factors:

- Enrollment status (full-time, three-quarter-time, and so on)

- The student's unique EFC

- The student's cost of attendance (COA)

In fact, if you can determine these unique variables for yourself, you can make an accurate guess about what you'll receive under the Pell Grant, based on a series of easy-to-use tables provided by the Department of Education. Although these amounts aren't guaranteed, you'll be able to get close enough to actually include them in your College Cash Strategy Worksheet (see Appendix B).

CHEAT SHEET

Students right on the cusp between one student status and another should strongly consider taking an additional class and raising their status to max out the amount of their Pell Grant because these grants can be used only in the first four years of college, regardless of how much is actually awarded.

Of course, the easiest way to estimate how much you'll receive in Pell Grants is to visit www.fafsa4caster.com, a website provided by the Department of Education to help parents and students estimate their future financial aid. But, for those of you who want to see how the numbers really work, you can visit studentaid.ed.gov and search for the Pell Grant Award Charts. When you find them, here are the steps to follow.

Step #1: Determine Your Status

The number of credits you're taking in a semester determine which chart you use to calculate your Pell Grant award amount. Full-time students taking 12 or more units (or the equivalent if a different system is used) are the only ones who can receive the maximum Pell Grant award. Students taking fewer than this fall into one of three other categories:

- **Three-quarter-time**—At least nine units or 75 percent of equivalent units

- **Half-time**—At least six units or 50 percent of equivalent units

- **Less than half-time**—Fewer than six units or 50 percent of equivalent units

Step #2: Find Your EFC

After you've figured out your student status and located the appropriate table online, you need to calculate your EFC. Again, the easiest way to do this is visit www.fafsa4caster.com or another online EFC calculator. After you've done that, you can find the appropriate column across the top of the Pell Grant table.

Step #3: Determine Your Cost of Attendance

You need to find the annual COA for the school you will be attending, on the left side of the Pell Grant Award Chart. These amounts are broken down into $100 increments, up to the maximum COA covered.

FLUNK-PROOF FINANCES

For Pell Grant award purposes, the COA estimate is supplied by the school, not calculated by a parent or student. In attempting to estimate the total COA, a call should be made to your school's financial aid administrator.

Step #4: Find Where EFC and COA Meet

After you've found the right Pell Grant Award Chart for someone at your student status level, all you need to do to estimate your award is find where your EFC and COA intersect. For example, on the full-time Pell Grant Award Chart for 2010–2011, an EFC of $1,000 and a COA of $4,500 intersect at a box with an award amount of $4,290. Hence, that is the student's estimated Pell Grant award amount for that school year. Likewise, after you calculate your expected Pell Grant award amount, add it to your College Cash Strategy Worksheet under the "Calculate Your Unmet Need" section.

Other Major Federal Grants

Although the Pell Grant is the 800-pound gorilla of federal grants, it's by no means the only game in town. In fact, a number of other substantial grants might be available on top or in place of the Pell Grant. Most of these programs are designed primarily for undergraduate students earning their first college degrees, although some are designed for or can be used by graduate students.

The Academic Competitiveness Grant

The Academic Competitiveness Grant (ACG) is awarded only to students who are also eligible for a Pell Grant. It's essentially a bonus grant for Pell Grant recipients who have demonstrated they can handle academic rigor by passing a certain amount of core classes in high school or by maintaining at least a 3.0 in their freshman years of college.

> **CHEAT SHEET**
>
> If you have one or more students who still have a couple of years left of high school, you can greatly increase your chances of qualifying for the Academic Competitiveness Grant by taking certain classes. The current requirements include four years of English; three each of math, science, and social studies; and one year of a foreign language.

The maximum ACG grant for someone's freshman year of college is $750, with a maximum of $1,300 being awarded in a student's sophomore year. No awards are made for junior year or later. Eligible students who file a Free Application for Federal Student Aid (FAFSA) form will automatically be notified if they're eligible to receive the ACG grant. If eligible, a student must provide additional information and documentation to her college of choice to complete the award process.

The Federal Supplementary Educational Opportunity Grant

The Federal Supplementary Educational Opportunity Grant (FSEOG) is awarded to students demonstrating an extreme financial need. In other words, you're probably not going to get this unless your EFC is zero. But, if you do qualify, it can be worth up to $4,000 (for 2010) on top of the Pell Grant.

The FSEOG is a bit of a hybrid grant, mixing both a college's budget for financial aid and federal financial aid. Specifically, the federal government will match 3 to 1 whatever a school is willing to award under FSEOG. So if someone gets a $4,000 FSEOG award, that means that the school kicked in $1,000 and the federal government kicked in $3,000.

The determination of who gets an FSEOG is actually left up to a school's financial aid advisors, within certain restrictions, to award the money to low-income students. So there is no preset formula that allows you to estimate whether you'll win this award or how much you'll receive. No separate financial aid application is required; your school will do the rest after you file for your FAFSA.

The FSEOG is not available at every school. If you believe you're going to be able to demonstrate extraordinary financial need with an EFC of zero, you'll need to double-check that you're attending a school that participates in this program. Failure to do so could cost you up to $4,000 in lost aid, should you select a non-FSEOG school.

The National SMART Grant

The National Science and Mathematics Access to Retain Talent (SMART) Grant can award up to an additional $4,000 to students who are eligible for the Pell Grant. They can receive this in their third and fourth years of their college program. If they are part of a legitimate five-year program, the award might also be made for that fifth year.

To be eligible, a student must be enrolled in an eligible degree program in one of the following subject areas:

- Science
- Math
- Engineering
- Computer science
- Foreign languages
- Technology

Additionally, students must maintain a 3.0 GPA. Unlike other programs, however, there are no requirements about which field a student must work in after graduation. Students eligible for a SMART Grant are automatically notified by their college's financial aid administrator after completing their FAFSA forms. If you are not notified early in your academic year, you should make a trip to the financial aid office and ask why you haven't been notified.

The TEACH Grant

The Teacher Education Assistance for College and Higher Education (TEACH) Grant awards up to $4,000 per year for students studying to become K–12 teachers in either public or private schools. Each TEACH Grant received, though, does require the student to serve four years as a teacher; otherwise, the grant turns into an unsubsidized Stafford loan that must be repaid. Applications for the TEACH Grant can be requested from a student's financial aid office.

To be eligible for a TEACH Grant, a student can be either an undergraduate or graduate student. He must also meet the following requirements:

- Complete a FAFSA form
- Be a U.S. citizen or eligible noncitizen
- Be enrolled in a program leading to certification as a teacher
- Meet the current academic requirements for a TEACH Grant (a 3.25 GPA and top 75 percentile of scores on high school standardized tests)

State Grant Programs

Many states, especially the most populated states, offer their own internal grant programs. These programs are meant to be a complement to the Pell and other federal grants. For the most part, you must be considered a resident of these states to participate in these programs—something that might take a student a year or more to gain if moving from out of state.

The majority of states have a separate application deadline for state-based financial aid, so it is important to ensure that you know exactly when your application's deadline is. Further, some states require a student to submit an additional form besides the federal FAFSA form, so be sure to read the application requirements carefully.

The Least You Need to Know

- Grants are essentially free money and should always be applied for even if you don't think you can qualify.
- A completed FAFSA form is absolutely necessary to be considered for all federal and most state grants.
- Parents and students should attempt to estimate their Pell Grant eligibility to help shape their remaining financial aid efforts.
- If you qualify for the Pell Grant, you might also qualify for thousands of dollars in additional grants, based both on financial need and academic merit.
- State grants can offer substantial funds for low-income students but require a separate application, often with a different deadline than federal aid.

Free Money on Your Tax Return

In This Chapter

- Federal credits and deductions for education
- Tax benefits for Section 529 plan contributions
- Financial aid and taxes
- Avoiding taxes on your education savings

There's a famous proverb that states "the enemy of my enemy, is my friend." In other words, even though I might otherwise dislike you, the fact that we have an enemy in common makes us temporary allies. Nowhere is this more true than with the IRS, who is happy to lower your tax burden if you're in the midst of trying to fund a college education.

That's because the IRS, as instructed by Congress, is willing to hand you back some rather large piles of money simply for paying college tuition. These sums are so substantial, in fact, that they can virtually wipe out any unfunded college expenses for students attending lower-priced colleges. Unfortunately, they can only be utilized when you file your income tax return, so you might have to wait up to a year and a half from when you initially pay your expenses to receive a benefit.

Of course, all the tax opportunities presented in this chapter take some knowledge of tax laws and proper income tax preparation to take full advantage of, so if you are not comfortable using a program like TurboTax, you might want to seek professional tax help. Naturally, if you're already paying someone to prepare your taxes, you'll need to point out the fact that you're paying college expenses when you go to your annual appointment.

Federal Income Tax Credits

Before we go any further, it is important to have a short discussion about the difference between a tax deduction and a tax credit because both will come up in this chapter. It's an important discussion because a tax credit can be worth three to seven times more than a tax deduction, depending on your income tax bracket.

> **WORLD WIDE WISDOM**
>
> Everything you need to know about education expenses and your federal income taxes can be found in IRS Publication 970. You can find it on the Web at www.irs.gov/formspubs.

To understand the difference, you need to understand how the taxes you end up paying each year are calculated. Although your personal situation might be complex, the actual formula is pretty straightforward. Here's the ultra-simplified version:

1. The total income, or *gross income*, is added up for everyone in your household who is reported on your tax return.

2. You are allowed to subtract from your total annual income *deductions* that are permitted by the IRS. These can include things such as donations to charity, your mortgage interest, and certain education expenses.

3. After these deductions have been removed from your reported income, you are left with what is called *taxable income*. It's called this because it is what your tax is actually calculated on, using a series of increasing, or *progressive*, tax brackets. For example, the first $16,750 in 2010 is taxed at 10 percent. Then the next chunk of your taxable (not gross) income is taxed at a higher rate, and so on.

4. After the total taxes are calculated, you are then permitted to directly offset, or lower, what you owe by any *tax credits* you're permitted to take.

5. You (or your tax preparer) compare what you still owe after all tax credits are applied against what was deducted from your paychecks. If more was deducted than what you owe, you get money back. If less was collected, then you owe the IRS money.

CHEAT SHEET

The expenses eligible for educational tax credits or deductions are reported annually to you by the school on IRS Form 1098-T. However, some expenses such as books and certain qualifying expenses for supplies might not be represented on this form and must be added to your total prior to putting it on your return.

So in summary, tax credits *directly offset what you owe*, while tax deductions *only lower the amount of income your taxes are calculated on*. This means that a tax credit is typically worth its full computed amount. By contrast, a tax deduction is only worth a fraction of its initial amount because it only reduces the amount of income that you would be taxed on.

The American Opportunity Tax Credit

For whatever you think of President Obama, when it comes to paying for college, you owe him a thank you. The American Opportunity Tax Credit (AOTC) he pushed through, even though watered down from his campaign promise, puts up to $2,500 back in the pockets of students and parents. It's a big deal and something that you need to take advantage of if you're eligible.

The AOTC, with its higher dollar limit and broader eligibility, was originally enacted only for the 2009 and 2010 tax years and replaced the existing Hope Scholarship tax credit. It's likely that the AOTC will be renewed, but if it is not, the old Hope Scholarship will once again become available.

Here's how the AOTC works:

1. The first $2,000 in qualified expenses (tuition, fees, textbooks, and course materials) for 2009 or later receives a dollar-for-dollar tax credit. In other words, if you spend $2,000 on qualified expenses in 2010, you will owe $2,000 less in federal income taxes.

2. The next $2,000 you spend on qualified expenses receives a 25 percent credit. In other words, if you spend an additional $2,000, you will receive a $500 tax credit ($2,000 × 25 percent).

3. If you owe absolutely no taxes, meaning that even everything taken out of your paycheck for federal taxes was refunded to you, then the AOTC might also be refundable at a rate of 40 percent. For example, if you earned the entire $2,500 credit and had no taxes to use the credit against, the IRS would send you 40 percent of the credit, or $1,000 ($2,500 × 40 percent).

Is that a great deal, or what? For most American families, that means that spending $4,000 really costs them only $1,500. There are few limits on who can use this, so I want you to only add this to your College Cash Strategy Worksheet in Appendix B, under the "Spending and Savings Strategies" section, for each year you qualify.

To qualify, a student must meet all of the following criteria:

- Be in any of his or her first four years of undergraduate education.

- Be enrolled more than *half-time* at an eligible institution (a school eligible for federal financial aid).

- Have an adjusted gross income of less than $80,000 for single households or $160,000 for joint filing households (for 2010; this might increase in subsequent years). Above these amounts, the credit is phased out. A *phase-out* refers to tax benefits that are slowly decreased for a taxpayer after his income exceeds a certain amount. All the educational tax credits are subject to phase-outs, although the threshold for these has been substantially increased in recent years.

- Not be claiming the Tuition and Fees Deduction or the Lifetime Learning Credit for the same student in the same year.

DEFINITION

Many of the government tax benefits for education are based on **half-time** enrollment. However, the IRS remains nebulous on what this means, saying that half-time is determined by each school, based on the full course load for a student at that school. However, the IRS does use the Department of Education's definition of half-time as a minimum in determining this. According to the Department of Education, half-time is generally defined as at least 12 semester hours per year.

The Lifetime Learning Credit

If you are ineligible for the AOTC, you can probably claim the Lifetime Learning Credit. It can still knock off a significant chunk (up to $2,000) from what you owe Uncle Sam on your taxes, but you have to spend a lot more to get it.

The Lifetime Learning Credit is calculated by multiplying your qualified college expenses (tuition, fees, books, and other materials) by 20 percent. The maximum amount of expenses on which this can be calculated in any one year is $10,000 per student, resulting in a maximum credit of $2,000. Unfortunately, this credit is not refundable like the AOTC for taxpayers who owe no taxes is.

However, the Lifetime Learning Credit has two key advantages over the AOTC. First, it can be used for any year of college, even graduate school or continuing education at your local community college. Second, students do not have to be enrolled at least half-time to claim the credit. Thus, even if you take one cooking class per year at your local community college, you can claim this credit.

CHEAT SHEET

Occasionally, the tax credits for education might be increased to help students living in disaster areas get their feet back on the ground. In recent memory, this has included students living in areas affected by Hurricanes Katrina and Rita, as well as devastating tornadoes and storms in the Midwest. If you live in an affected area, you need to keep checking with the IRS and your tax preparer for updates.

Claiming Your Credits

As previously mentioned, you have to file a tax return to be able to claim these credits. If you haven't needed to or don't expect to file a tax return, you should talk to an accountant to see whether it is worth it to claim either of these credits. If you are paying for a student to attend college and he is considered your dependent for tax purposes, you can claim these credits on your return.

To claim these credits, you have to use a special IRS form (Form 8863 in 2009) that must be filled out and returned along with your regular tax return. This form is the supporting documentation for the credit that you are actually claiming on your main IRS Form 1040.

It is important to note that the IRS hates "double-dippers" and will come after you with a vengeance if you do it. No, I'm not talking about sticking a half-eaten chip back in the dip (though I wouldn't do that in front of an IRS agent either). I'm talking about trying to claim more than one credit for the same person, in the same year. In other words, you cannot claim both the AOTC and the Lifetime Learning Credit in the same year for the same person. Further, you cannot claim the Tuition and Fees Deduction, which I discuss a little later in this chapter, at the same time you claim either credit for a specific student. *That's double-dipping.* However, you are free to claim the same or different credits for different members of your family, as long as they each have valid educational expenses.

CHEAT SHEET

You can still claim an educational tax credit or deduct your tuition even if you paid for college with borrowed funds.

Federal Tax Deductions for Education

These deductions for educational expenses aren't as juicy as the tax credits we've just discussed, but they're still better than a sharp stick in the eye. Of course, what they'll actually save you depends on your marginal tax bracket, so you need to know how to find that.

U.S. taxpayers are taxed in progressive brackets. That means that as someone makes more and more money, some of his income will fall into the higher brackets, resulting in it (but not all of his income) being taxed at a higher rate. So unlike the value of a tax credit, which directly offsets taxes owed, a tax deduction only reduces the amount of income that is taxed at a certain bracket.

For example, if a married couple reports $74,000 in taxable income, everything above $68,000 is taxed at 25 percent for federal income tax purposes. So if someone claims the maximum $4,000 Tuition and Fees Deduction (not a credit), it reduces the amount of income that will be taxed at 25 percent by $4,000. This in turn saves this specific taxpayer $1,000.

The Tuition and Fees Deduction

Although not as hefty as the AOTC or the Lifetime Learning Credit, the Tuition and Fees Deduction is still considered meatier than many other deductions. That is in part due to its above-the-line status, which means you don't need to itemize your other deductions to claim this. Normally, with things like medical expenses and charitable deductions, you are able to claim them only if all your deductions exceed a certain combined amount. Again, the Tuition and Fees Deduction, which is technically known as an adjustment to income, does not require a taxpayer to itemize her deductions on a Schedule A to reap the benefits.

The Tuition and Fees Deduction for 2010 is $4,000, meaning that if you have $4,000 in qualified education expenses for a student, you can deduct them from the income you report on your tax return. Again, you cannot use both this deduction and one of the education tax credits previously covered. Because there is no way that this deduction can hold a candle to the AOTC, this deduction is primarily used by students and parents whose income is too high to be able to claim the Lifetime Learning Credit.

The Student Loan Interest Deduction

If you're currently making student loan payments or will in the future (and there is a good chance you will if you're reading this book), it's important to realize that you can deduct the interest you pay in any given year. Notice that I said interest you *pay*, not interest that is *charged*. That's because you can only deduct the interest portions of payments you actually made. If $1,000 in interest was added to your loan this year, but you did not actually make a payment, you cannot deduct anything.

Don't get too hung up on the computation here, though. Thankfully, your student loan lender will send you a form at the end of the year—called a Form 1098-E—identifying exactly how much student loan interest you paid. All you need to do is plug that number into your tax preparation software or hand it to your tax preparer, and you're all set.

Like the Tuition and Fees Deduction, the Student Loan Interest Deduction is also an above-the-line deduction, meaning you don't need to itemize your other deductions to be able to utilize it. But, the deduction itself is limited to $2,500 for 2010.

> **CHEAT SHEET**
>
> There's no rule that says you can't begin repaying student loans while you're still in school. In fact, many students make a point of paying the interest that accrues on their student loans each month to keep the loan from growing and to capture an extra deduction. If you have some spare cash lying around after you pay your college expenses, this would be a great use for that money.

State Tax Deductions and Credits

The federal government isn't the only one hooking you up with tax benefits for paying college costs. A number of states are getting in on the action. Unfortunately, because state income tax rates are generally much lower, the dollar amount of your savings will not be gigantic. But heck, money is money. Even saving $100 might help offset the cost of a textbook.

Here are some states offering deductions or credits for tuition and fees paid to a school (amounts are for 2009):

- **Alaska**—50 percent tax credit, on up to $100,000 in tuition expenses per year
- **Arkansas**—Up to a $3,029 deduction per year, per student, depending on the type of institution
- **Louisiana**—50 percent of the amount of tuition expenses, up to $5,000
- **Maryland**—100 percent tax credit for graduate students pursuing a teaching degree, up to $1,500 per student
- **Michigan**—8 percent tax credit, up to $375, per student

- **New York**—4 percent tax credit, up to $400 per student, or a tax deduction of up to $10,000

- **South Carolina**—25 percent credit of tuition spent, up to $850 per year ($350 for two-year colleges)

- **Wisconsin**—$6,000 deduction per student for tuition and mandatory fees paid to schools in both Wisconsin and Minnesota

In addition to these few states offering deductions for paying tuition and fees for college, a large number of states offer deductions or credits for contributing to Section 529 college savings plans. Even though that might not sound like an opportunity for someone who is about to start school, it most definitely can be. That's because most states have no rules about how long you have to wait after you deposit money into a Section 529 plan before you take it out and spend it.

This means a parent or student who is about to pay $1,000 in tuition could hypothetically deposit it in a Section 529 plan on a Monday, claim the tax deduction for funding a Section 529 plan, and then take a distribution and pay tuition with the money on Tuesday.

States might slowly close these loopholes, so you need to be sure to check with an accountant familiar with your home state's laws. You also need to be sure you understand the withdrawal rules and fees for any Section 529 plan before you use it, although the benefits of a substantial deduction will likely outweigh the costs of withdrawing money from a Section 529 plan. (See Appendix F for more on Section 529 plans by state.)

States Offering Tax Deductions for 529 Contributions (for 2009)

State	Amount
AL	$5,000 per contributor
AR	$5,000 per contributor
AZ	$750 per contributor
CO	All
CT	$5,000 per contributor
DC	$4,000 per contributor
GA	$2,000 per child
ID	$4,000 per contributor
IL	$10,000 per contributor
IA	$2,685 per child

State	Amount
IN	20 percent tax credit up to $1,000
KS	$3,000 per contributor
LA	$2,400 per contributor
ME	$250 per child
MD	$2,500 per child
MI	$5,000 per contributor
MS	$10,000 per contributor
MO	$8,000 per contributor
MT	$3,000 per contributor
NE	$5,000 per return
NM	All
NC	$2,500 per contributor
NY	$5,000 per taxpayer
OH	$2,000 per child
OK	$10,000 per contributor
OR	$2,000 per contributor
PA	$13,000 per contributor
RI	$500 per contributor
SC	All
UT	5 percent tax credit, up to $87
VT	10 percent credit, up to $250
VA	$4,000 per account
WV	All
WI	$3,000 per child

Tax Tricks for Your Assets

There are a few other tax tricks out there that can indirectly lower your costs of a college education. Unlike the tax deductions and credits that directly reduce what you owe, these tax tricks for assets keep you from paying additional taxes when you tap certain assets to pay for college. Again, the tax rules on these can be a little complex at times, so my hope is that you'll identify opportunities as you read through this section and seek out professional tax help if you're not completely comfortable preparing your own taxes.

Section 529 and Coverdell ESA Withdrawals

If you were fortunate enough to be able to squirrel away some money in a Section 529 plan or Coverdell Education Savings Account (ESA), now is definitely the time to consider tapping those. As a general rule, these should be the first assets to go, especially before you tap into your retirement accounts, your own personal investments, or your home equity.

What makes tapping into these so attractive is that the IRS, as well as your state's tax department, will allow you to withdraw the money without paying *any tax* on your accumulated gains, as long as the money is spent on college costs. That means that someone who originally deposited $1,000 that has now grown to $2,000 can permanently avoid paying tax on the gains if he withdraws the money and uses it to pay educational expenses.

One catch is that exclusion from tax on withdrawn gains can only be as large as your actual out-of-pocket expenditures for that year. This means you must subtract any scholarships, grants, or employer tuition assistance from your eligible costs to determine how much you can withdraw tax-free.

To be eligible for tax-free withdrawal, the money must be spent at an institution that is eligible to receive federal financial aid funds and the expenses must fall into one of the following categories:

- Tuition
- Fees
- Books
- Computers
- Equipment and supplies if required for enrollment
- Room and board, subject to certain limits (student must be more than half-time)

Waiving the Withdrawal Penalty on Retirement Accounts

If you decide you have to tap your retirement assets to help pay for college—something I generally advise against—you should know that you can do it *penalty-free*. Notice, I did not say *tax-free* necessarily, but penalty-free.

When it comes to pulling money out of retirement plans (as opposed to simply taking a loan against your balance), the 10 percent early withdrawal penalty for people under age 59½ is waived if the money is spent on qualified higher education expenses for themselves, their spouse, or their children. However, income taxes will still be due on all Traditional IRA withdrawals, as well as any gains withdrawn from Roth IRA accounts.

When withdrawing the money, be sure to indicate on the withdrawal form (there's usually a box to check) that the withdrawal is for education purposes. This will ensure that you avoid the 10 percent penalty, although income tax might still be withheld. At the end of the year, you'll receive a tax form from your IRA custodian that shows the withdrawal amount, which needs to be included on your tax return.

Income Exemption on U.S. Savings Bonds

Series EE and Series I savings bonds cashed in during any year when someone pays for college expenses for herself, a spouse, or children might be free from income taxes on her accumulated gain.

To be eligible, the person cashing in the bond must be at least 24 years old by the issue date listed on the face of the bond and the money must be spent at an institution eligible for federal financial aid. The funds can only be spent on tuition and fees, not on room and board.

Keeping Your Eye on Taxable Aid

Many people rightfully wonder how financial aid is treated for tax purposes. After all, having a school or an organization hand you tens or even hundreds of thousands of dollars can seem like too much money for the government to not try to grab a slice of. Thankfully, most financial awards are tax-free, but you need to keep your eyes on some notable exceptions.

CHEAT SHEET

Money received as part of a tuition assistance program provided by your employer is considered tax-free, up to an annual dollar limit ($5,250 in 2009). Because any amount above this is considered taxable income, smart students often delay taking additional classes that would result in assistance above that limit until a new calendar year starts. In doing so, they avoid paying taxes on the excess amount.

The single biggest factor that affects the taxability of a financial aid award is whether the student is working toward a recognized degree. Financial aid for programs that only lead to certificates or are from schools other than recognized colleges or vocational schools will likely be considered taxable aid, regardless of how the money is used.

If the student is working toward a legitimate degree or to acquire job skills and the school is an accredited institution, financial aid and award money used for the following expenses are most likely tax-free:

- Tuition
- Fees
- Books
- Supplies

However, if upon receiving the money, the student uses it for something else, it would be considered taxable income. Financial aid and award money used for the following expenses is subject to income taxation:

- Room
- Board
- Travel
- Research activities

The Least You Need to Know

- The American Opportunity Tax Credit (AOTC) can put up to $2,500 back into most undergraduate students' pockets.
- The Lifetime Learning Credit is a great back-up credit for those who don't qualify for the AOTC.
- The IRS does not allow double-dipping on tax credits and benefits, so don't try to claim more than one for the same student.
- Don't overlook opportunities to deduct the cost of college on your state income tax return.
- Take advantage of tax-free and tax-favored withdrawals from Section 529 plans, Coverdell ESAs, and U.S. savings bonds.

Tuition-Free Colleges

In This Chapter

- Tuition-free colleges are real
- Well-known tuition-free colleges
- Expenses you can still expect
- Tips for getting admitted

On one recent trip to the mall, my adorably clueless five-year-old fell in love with a litter of brand-new puppies at the pet store. After we left, with him nearly in tears, he asked (begged) if we could get a puppy. Being the stereotypical dad, I searched frantically for some way to avoid being the bad guy, and unfairly dished it off on my wife. I told him that "it wouldn't be fair to Mommy to bring a puppy home without talking to her first." His reply was that we could get Mommy a puppy as well. Trying not to laugh, I retreated to the old stand-by of, "We just don't have the money to spend on a puppy right now." To this he replied, "Duh, Dad, just go to the ATM!"

My son's very simple view on problem-solving left me rolling my eyes, much in the same manner as when parents tell me about the financial impossibility of sending their child to college and I recommend that they simply send their child to a "free college." I usually get some combination of dirty looks and an "Okay … free college …. Gee, why didn't I think of that?!"

But as absurd as it sounds, there is really such a thing as "free college." Or, at least it's free in the sense of not having to paying large amounts of cash out of pocket. No, I'm not talking about cheap community colleges, free online classes, or classes offered in the back of your local bowling alley. There really are legitimate, accredited colleges that for one reason or another let the majority of their students attend without paying a dime in tuition.

Is Free College for Real?

Although *tuition-free colleges* exist for a number of reasons, their existence is a reality all the same. The biggest source of funding for free colleges is ridiculously wealthy dead people who decided that their legacy would be ensuring that their wealth would help to educate people who might otherwise not get an education or to help a cherished school or subject matter advance its place in national education. These selfless individuals, sometimes individually and sometimes in conjunction with thousands of other donors, donate enough money that a college can literally operate off the interest that it earns on its endowment. In fact, many people don't realize that many of the top private colleges in the United States actually would be much more expensive if it weren't for these sizable endowments helping to lower the costs, even if students still have to pay a sizable amount.

> **DEFINITION**
>
> A **tuition-free college** is different from a full college scholarship in that everyone attending the tuition-free college is going there for free. After she's accepted to a tuition-free college, a student can rest assured that the majority of her education expenses will be paid for as long as she meets the school's academic standards.

Wealthy donors are no doubt the largest source of funding for private colleges, but many others enjoy partnerships with government organizations or professional organizations that use the college as a training ground for sorely needed professionals in a variety of fields.

The Top Tuition-Free Colleges

Tuition-free colleges fall into four primary categories: undergraduate, graduate, military, and international. Of these, undergraduate are typically the hardest to get into because of the sheer number of people seeking undergraduate degrees without having to join the military or leave the country.

Undergraduate College

Some of the most well-known and free undergraduate programs in the United States include the following schools:

- **College of the Ozarks**—This Christian college in Missouri provides a four-year degree to students who demonstrate substantial need. All students are required to work throughout their time at the college, often in agricultural jobs tied to the school's programs.

- **Cooper Union**—This historic college in the center of New York City offers degrees in engineering, architecture, and fine arts, as well as graduate degrees in engineering and fine arts. Admissions are based on a student's academic performance during her high school years.

- **Deep Springs**—Located in the Nevada desert, this all-men's college offers a general studies education in a unique and small self-governing community.

- **F. W. Olin College of Engineering**—This Massachusetts college offers four-year engineering degrees valued at over $80,000 to all students accepted. Admissions are very competitive and based on academic merit.

- **Curtis Institute**—Located in historic Philadelphia, this highly selective music academy accepts students based on the needs of its orchestra and music programs.

- **Alice Lloyd College**—A co-ed educational institution in the Appalachia region of Kentucky, it offers a variety of degrees and requires a minimum of 10 to 20 hours of work-study each week.

- **Berea College**—Also located in Kentucky, Berea College offers a number of degrees to lower-income students who rank in the top 20 percent of their high school classes.

- **CUNY William Macaulay Honors College**—A program within the large, multi-campus City University of New York (CUNY), it awards free tuition and special advising to top high school students.

- **CUNY Teacher's Academy**—Another program offered by the City University of New York (CUNY), it educates future teachers at no cost.

- **Webb Institute**—Located in a gigantic mansion on the Long Island Sound in New York, this exclusive school offers free tuition to all its students who earn degrees in marine engineering.

- **Barclay College**—This private Christian college in Kansas offers more than a dozen degrees and minors.

In addition to these colleges offering free tuition to all students, a number of colleges around the United States offer *tuition waivers* to students who meet certain criteria, even though not all students at those colleges will receive free tuition. The schools offering these programs usually require students to be *National Merit Scholarship Finalists*, their class valedictorian, or be in a predetermined top percentage of their class, or have household incomes of less than a certain dollar amount.

> **DEFINITION**
>
> A **tuition waiver** is when a college waives tuition for a certain class of students, such as National Merit Scholarship Finalists or people with incomes below a certain dollar amount. A **National Merit Scholarship Finalist** is one of approximately 15,000 students who demonstrates exceptional academic ability on the PSAT exam taken by high school students. With this title comes many offers for free or discounted educations around the country.

Before you get too excited, don't think this means that you get a free pass into Harvard, Stanford, or Dartmouth just because you meet their criteria for a tuition waiver. Tuition waivers have nothing to do with getting into these schools; they only have to do with helping you pay for them once you're there. Whether you're a low-income family, your child is valedictorian of his or her class, or your child is a National Merit Scholarship Finalist, you still have to beat out everyone else who is competing for admission. Further, virtually every school reserves the right to retract its tuition waiver program for the upcoming year if they get overwhelmed with applicants.

Some of the most popular schools offering tuition waivers are …

- **Harvard**—The best-known college in the United States is free for students whose families earn under $60,000 per year.

- **Stanford University**—Yes, the same Stanford. Tuition is free for accepted students whose families make under $100,000 per year.

- **Dartmouth**—Families making less than $75,000 per year receive free tuition.

- **Massachusetts Institute of Technology (MIT)**—Famed MIT allows students from families making under $75,000 to attend for free.

- **University of Pennsylvania**—Tuition is waived for all families earning under $90,000. Free room and board is also awarded for families earning under $40,000 per year.

- **SOKA University**—This Southern California school with Buddhist roots offers free tuition to all students whose families earn less than $60,000 per year.

- **Texas A&M**—This school offers free tuition for families earning under $60,000 per year.

- **Texas Tech**—This school offers free tuition for families earning under $40,000 per year.

Of the more than 100 colleges offering free tuition for National Merit Scholarship Finalists, some of the top-name colleges include:

- Arizona State
- Auburn
- Ball State
- Baylor
- Florida A&M
- Mississippi State
- Memphis State
- Nebraska State
- Oklahoma State
- Purdue
- University of Wisconsin—Eau Claire

Military Colleges

Although most Americans are familiar with the concept of someone "graduating from West Point," many do not know exactly where it is or what exactly happens there. It is, in fact, one of a number of service academies (military colleges) that offers a free education to all those who attend, as part of preparing them to serve in the U.S. military.

West Point, located in New York, admits more than 1,000 students per year, offering them a free college education on the road to becoming an officer in the Army. As with all the U.S. service academies, the cost of attendance is free but service in the U.S. military is required after graduation.

In addition to West Point, four other service academies offer a tuition-free, four-year college degree to future military personnel:

- The U.S. Naval Academy (Annapolis, MD)
- The U.S. Air Force Academy (Colorado Springs, CO)
- The U.S. Coast Guard Academy (New London, CT)
- U.S. Merchant Marine Academy (Kings Point, NY)

CHEAT SHEET

If you're interested in a free education without leaving the comfort of your home, you'll need to check out the University of the People, headquartered in Pasadena, California. Their degrees in business and computer science aren't accredited *yet*, but thousands of students have chosen the "UoPeople" as an alternative way to educate themselves. To learn more, visit uopeople.org.

Graduate Schools

Most graduate schools charge tuition to many of their students, but almost all graduate schools offer a free education to a certain portion of students. Many times, virtually all the students in a school's Ph.D. program receive free tuition, room, board, and even a spending allowance, in exchange for performing research duties and teaching classes to undergraduates.

Although there is no definitive list of the thousands of colleges that offer a free graduate education to a select portion of their student body, an Internet search of schools offering the degree you're interested in will turn up plenty of results. As a general rule, the more exclusive the school and recognized the program, the more likely that a student will receive a free graduate education.

International Colleges

Many countries outside the United States offer free or low-cost college educations to their citizens. But before you ask, no, American citizens can't just move there overnight and get a free education. But, if they have dual citizenship or have lived in a country long enough to apply for citizenship or to become a certified resident, a tuition-free education might be attainable. Although this might seem a little far-fetched, this can be a very good option for footloose and fancy-free students who are willing to take a few years off prior to starting their schooling. It might take a long time in some countries to qualify for citizenship and a free education.

Countries that offer free (or very low-cost) college educations to their citizens and residents include:

- Denmark
- Finland
- France
- Germany
- Ireland
- Italy
- Portugal
- Spain
- Sweden

Not Everything Is Free

Just because you or your student gets into a free college or a college that offers a tuition waiver that doesn't mean you won't have to come up with *some* money out of your pocket. Some colleges, especially smaller and more exclusive free colleges, might cover all basic expenses, but there might still be some sizable expenses you'll need to cover.

FLUNK-PROOF FINANCES

Most tuition-free colleges not only come with strong expectations about their students' academic efforts after enrollment, but also often come with strong work-study expectations. In fact, many of the basic operations of these colleges are staffed by the same people who are there for an education.

Parents and students considering this route should still take a serious look at what direct and indirect costs they could potentially incur. In addition to many of these programs not covering books (which can run $1,000 or more per year), most tuition waiver programs still do not cover room and board. Additionally, none of these programs cover the indirect costs associated with college, such as travel, clothing, or the income that is lost when a student stops bringing home a paycheck. If these costs are still going to be an issue, a student should look into financial aid options, especially federal student loans (see Chapter 5).

Getting the Invite

Guess who wants to go to college for free? *Everyone!* So don't expect to just waltz into a tuition-free college without having to take a number. Similar to applying for a scholarship, you have to be strategic in how you present yourself to a tuition-free school.

In baseball, the sweet spot is the mythical spot on a baseball where hitting it just right gives it some extra oomph to take it over that outfield fence. Well, you want to be a sweet spot candidate when it comes to applying to a tuition-free college. You want to be that homerun pitch the school is looking for, out of thousands that are coming across its plate. That means you need to ensure that you do a number of things:

- **Visit the school**—Every tuition-free school is going to get thousands of applications for a small number of spots. They realize that most of these people are hoping for a miracle and that this application is just one of many they've blindly sent out. Although they're sympathetic to that, there's no doubt that they favor people who have actually seen the campus and still love it, its mission, and its culture. The last thing they need is to be giving away four years of college to students who transfer out after their freshman year.

- **Understand their mission**—Every tuition-free college has a mission behind it. Maybe it is excellence in a certain subject matter, or maybe it is developing Christian leaders. Whatever it is, you need to be sure you understand their mission, are on board with it, and can talk the talk.

- **Get mission-related references**—Because these schools are heavily focused on their missions, you'll need letters of reference from as many persuasive people within that field as possible.

- **Demonstrate community**—Most of these colleges are very small, close-knit communities. It's crucial to them that the students they recruit don't upset the harmony they work hard to achieve. Make sure your application reflects extracurricular activities that highlight your sense of community.

- **Apply early, follow up often**—Again, these schools will look only at students who are truly serious about going to their specific school, which means they typically ignore students who ignore them. Apply as early as possible and then follow up your application with updates about your achievements, grades, extracurricular activities, and so forth.

WORLD WIDE WISDOM

Want to get the inside information on what it takes to get into a tuition-free college? Your best bet is to talk to another student who did it. Because most of these colleges have groups on the major social networking sites (such as Facebook and MySpace), you can easily pop into their discussion forum and ask for advice on getting into the school.

The Least You Need to Know

- Tuition-free colleges really do exist and offer great educations for little or no money out of pocket.
- Students wanting to gain entrance to a tuition-free college need to work hard to show that they're on board with the school's mission and culture.
- The five U.S. service academies (military colleges) offer top-notch educations in exchange for four or five years of service.
- Students with dual citizenship from another country should look into low-cost or free university degrees offered within that country.
- National Merit Scholarship Finalists, valedictorians, and low-income students may receive free tuition at over 150 colleges, should they beat out everyone else for that coveted acceptance letter.

Best-Kept Funding Secrets

Tom Robbins, 1970s hippie author of *Even Cowgirls Get the Blues*, was once quoted as saying, "Stay committed to your decisions but flexible in your approach." For those hungering for a college education, wiser words may have never been spoken.

In all my years of hiring people for different jobs, it never really mattered where they went to college or how they paid for it, simply whether they went to college or not. Their degree was their ticket in the door and created an opportunity for them to prove themselves.

In this part, we look at some of the ways flexible people can take a sledgehammer to their college tuition bills. Sure, it might involve moving, marching, or moonlighting, but these programs are a dream come true for those who can go with the flow.

Tuition Reward Programs

In This Chapter

- How tuition reward programs work
- UPromise, BabyMint, and the SAGE Scholars Program
- Maximizing your program earnings
- Using tuition reward credit cards

There was a time when savvy consumers earned ticket after ticket on their favorite airline by exploiting the ins and outs of mileage programs. Heck, I remember one guy who earned a handful of free tickets on American Airlines simply by buying Kellogg's cereal every time it went on sale.

Well, many of those globe-trotting mileage hunters have gotten the travel bug out of their systems, have settled down and had kids, and are now facing a new challenge. Instead of worrying about first-class upgrades, they're scrambling to pay tuition. Thankfully, old habits die hard and these resourceful folks are proving that you can earn just as much free tuition as you could frequent flyer miles.

In this chapter, we look at the new programs that have developed to reward the shopping habits of parents and students with tuition dollars. Further, I point out some of the top tips and tricks to get the most out of these programs. By harnessing the power of these programs, you can easily begin racking up $500 to $1,000 per year toward your tuition bill or to help pay off existing student loans.

The Basics of Tuition Reward Programs

At their core, it's important to understand that *tuition reward programs* are marketing gimmicks. They're used by for-profit corporations to try to get parents to choose certain products or services over others. This means that using them will not make you more than you spend; it will only redirect some of what you're already spending toward a child's college education. In other words, don't go spending thousands more than you already do on groceries because it'll only put a few hundred extra dollars back in your pocket.

> **DEFINITION**
>
> **Tuition reward programs** are programs that set aside money into a separate account for future students every time a participating parent uses a credit or debit card or shops at participating retailers.

But with this in mind, a parent or student who chooses to be strategic in how and where he spends can easily save thousands. The trick is to know these programs inside and out, to have a good handle on what your existing and future living expenses will be, and to get as many relatives participating as possible.

Most of these programs work by having you register your existing credit and debit cards online with the program sponsor. Then, every time you shop at a participating retailer, they automatically send a percentage of what you spend to your tuition rewards account. This amount does not increase the cost of the goods or services you buy, but it is more like a discount that each partner company gives to attract and reward customers. The organization running the program then takes a cut of the money you earn as its compensation, without charging you anything additional.

Some of the more substantial amounts you can earn on things like mortgages or cell phone service require additional steps, such as notifying a salesperson ahead of time that you are participating in one of these programs. Failure to do so can result in you missing out on hundreds or even thousands of dollars in tuition rewards. Again, that's why it is important to know the fine print of these programs.

It's Never Too Late to Start

Although you might not pile up tens of thousands of dollars in one of these programs, if your tuition bills are due in just a few months, you can still offset some of what you will inevitably owe. In fact, some programs such as UPromise, which I discuss a little later in the chapter, even let you continue to participate after you graduate, directing your earnings toward repaying any student loans you might have.

Because most of the programs are quick and free to join, you shouldn't move on to the next chapter without signing yourself up. I can guarantee that you'll be pleasantly surprised by how much you can earn and thankful that you did it, even if your earnings help pay for only one over-priced textbook.

Rope in Friends and Family

One of the single best things you can do to supercharge any tuition reward program you're using is to sign up your friends and family, if allowed. Getting grandparents, godparents, and extended family without children of their own to register can increase your earnings by 200 to 300 percent!

Although most of these programs have an automated feature that allows you to send e-mails to the people you know would be happy to contribute, I strongly recommend making an additional announcement on your own because many people and their Internet providers can think your invite is spam. Just make an announcement at the next family gathering or send an e-mail from your own e-mail account because you know it'll be read.

Be sure to emphasize the following to the friends and family you invite to participate:

* These programs are free to participate in.

* After they sign up, they don't need to do anything besides shop as they normally do.

* Their shopping history and transactions are confidential and not shown to you.

* The websites where they submit their information are secure and safe.

* They can stop at any time.

* The program might allow them to split their contributions among multiple children, so they don't have to play favorites.

FLUNK-PROOF FINANCES

One plan that often backfires on well-meaning parents and students is paying their tuition with a credit card. It might seem like an easy way to rack up to thousands of points or miles, but it can quickly backfire with only a month or two of interest charges.

Don't Be Penny-Wise and Pound-Foolish

Because I don't want this to be a solution that ends up costing you more than it is worth, I want to reemphasize that you should not buy something simply to earn tuition. Although a dinner at a participating restaurant can earn you $5 toward college, spending $50 to get the reward makes sense only if you were already planning to eat out.

Likewise, if you choose to buy your groceries, gas, or airline tickets somewhere that offers a reward, the prices you pay should still be competitive with other retailers who do not participate. It wouldn't make any sense to buy gas at $3 per gallon to earn one penny per gallon when the gas station right across the street is selling gas for $2.90 per gallon, with no tuition reward.

UPromise Could Be Worth $500 per Year!

As I was writing this book, I received an e-mail advertisement from UPromise stating that the average household using UPromise was earning $443.25 per year in tuition rewards. Frankly, I think this number is a tad low, with the average being thrown off by families who have signed up but aren't using the program. In reality, a family who heavily uses the UPromise account can very easily rack up $500 to $1,000 annually.

Such a high amount is possible because, to a large degree, UPromise was the first major player in the tuition rewards game. Further, after a good run on its own, it was snapped up by student loan giant Sallie Mae, leaving most major retailers clamoring to participate. To this day, it remains a free program, with Sallie Mae making its money by taking a slice of the tuition rewards that companies send your way.

CHEAT SHEET

One of the best-kept secrets about the UPromise program is that you don't even need to be a current or future student to use the program. In reality, anyone can sign up for the program, even naming herself as the beneficiary of the account.

At the heart of the UPromise program are its vast partnerships, with more than 22,000 grocery stores, 8,000 restaurants, 700 of the Web's largest shopping sites, and a wide variety of specialty retailers and service professionals. When money is spent with any of UPromise's partners using a registered credit or debit card (from any bank), a contribution ranging from 1 to 25 percent is made to your child's UPromise account.

Here's a small sampling of some UPromise partners that will reward you with tuition when you shop:

- **Grocery and drug stores**—Kroger, Ralphs, Vons, Pavilions, Food4Less, Albertsons, CVS, A&P, Wegman's, Kings, Brookshires, and ShopRite

- **Online shopping**—Apple, Old Navy, Gap, Target, Macy's, PETCO, Victoria's Secret, Office Max, Office Depot, and L.L. Bean

- **Travel**—Orbitz.com, Travelocity.com, Southwest Airlines, Marriot, Avis rental cars, and Budget rental cars

- **Other services**—Century21 Real Estate, ExxonMobil Gas stations, Sprint, XM satellite radio, and TurboTax

Obviously, none of the following tips and tricks will do you any good if you don't visit UPromise.com and sign up, so make that your first task after you finish this chapter. Aside from that, here are some of the tips and tricks the smartest parents and students have used to max out their rewards:

- **Register every card you have**—One of the mistakes many parents make is not registering every card they have, especially if spouses or partners have different card numbers. You also need to be sure to register new cards that replace your expired cards, so your earnings don't grind to a halt.

- **Plan seasonal shopping**—Some of the biggest opportunities to earn tuition through UPromise come around the holidays and when it is time to update wardrobes. By planning ahead and deliberately shopping online, instead of casually at the mall, you can put an extra few hundred dollars per year into your UPromise account.

- **Use the restaurant.com partnership**—Because you're already looking to trim some expenditures from your budget, UPromise offers you a great opportunity to do it while also padding your rewards account. Restaurant.com lets you buy gift certificates for local restaurants at a substantial discount (that is, a $25 gift certificate for just $10) while also earning tuition on your purchase.

- **Hang around the UPromise forums**—If you think I'm smart, you should check out the UPromise junkies hanging around the UPromise user forums. They'll keep you on top of every new savings opportunity and need-to-know piece of fine print.

BabyMint

BabyMint (www.BabyMint.com) functions almost identically to UPromise, with parents and students registering their credit or debit cards and receiving contributions from participating retailers. However, the number of participating retailers in the BabyMint program is substantially smaller than UPromise.

That's not to say you shouldn't sign up for BabyMint; you most definitely should. Some great national restaurants and retailers have chosen to participate in the BabyMint program but not the UPromise program. By signing up for both programs, you'll be sure you don't miss a chance to earn some additional tuition.

But, the biggest difference between the two programs is BabyMint's partnership with the SAGE Scholars Program (discussed in the next section). Under this program, earnings from BabyMint are matched, with the matched amount directly reducing a student's cost of attending more than 240 colleges around the United States.

CHEAT SHEET

Although UPromise, BabyMint, and the SAGE Scholars Program are some of the oldest and most popular programs, others like Future Trust are popping up all over the place. Because most of the older programs use the same shopping partners as these newcomers do, you don't really need to sign up unless they offer a unique partner or retailer you know you're going to use often.

SAGE Scholars Program

The Savings and Growth for Education (SAGE) Scholars Program is a unique college savings program that rewards parents and students with discounts on tuition at participating colleges. These discounts are earned by either investing money with one of the SAGE Scholars partner organizations, which range from large employers to boutique investment firms, or earning rewards on your BabyMint account.

For example, if a parent has earned 2,500 SAGE Scholars rewards points, this could be converted into a $2,500 tuition discount at a school such as the University of San Diego. The maximum that can be earned is one year's worth of tuition at any participating school, with unused amounts being rolled over to a student's siblings. Unfortunately, if a student decides to go somewhere else besides one of the partner schools, the benefits are not transferable.

As with UPromise and BabyMint, there is no reason not to enroll in SAGE Scholars Program because it is free. If nothing else, money you earn through your BabyMint participation is matched in the form of tuition discounts at participating schools. If your child doesn't go to one of those schools, you're not really losing anything.

You should, however, do some serious comparison shopping before deciding to do business with one of SAGE Scholars' limited menu of financial partners. There's a good chance that you could find a better deal on your mortgage, investment services, or insurance products by shopping around. To learn more about the SAGE Scholars Program, visit them on the Web at www.sagescholars.com.

Tuition Reward Credit Cards

In addition to UPromise and BabyMint both offering their own branded credit cards, a number of other options are out there that aren't tied to one of these reward programs. For a family that is a heavy user of credit cards, earning 1 percent or more on your purchases can easily rack up $1,000 or more a year in tuition. Of course, this can be easily offset by carrying a balance and paying 20 to 30 percent in annual interest, so I do not recommend starting to use a new card if you are not already showing good discipline in using the one you have.

Additionally, credit cards that reward their users with tuition need to be compared against other credit cards with other nontuition reward programs. You can do this by simply calculating the net benefit you receive for the amount of money you spend on the card annually. For example, if you receive $500 in cash back from a card that also costs you $100 per year, your net benefit is $400. If you had to spend $20,000 to earn that $400 after fees, your reward ratio is 2 percent ($400 divided by $20,000). If this is what your existing card earns you, and a college tuition card offers only 1 percent, obviously you shouldn't switch.

WORLD WIDE WISDOM

Before you run out and sign up for a new credit card, spend some time surfing the Web for the fine print and third-party ratings on the various cards. One of the best websites for finding the right credit card is CardRatings.com.

With all of that in mind, here are some of the most popular college tuition credit cards. Keep in mind that the fine print of these cards might have changed since the book was published:

- **Fidelity 529 credit card**—This card rewards you by depositing 2 percent of your purchases into any Fidelity 529 account. Even better, if friends and family sign up for the card, they can earn tuition for your child as well.

- **Bank of America UPromise credit card**—This card, which is linked to your UPromise account, pays 1 percent on most purchases, 2 percent on gas from certain companies, and up to 10 percent on certain items at the grocery or drug store.

- **BabyMint Platinum Visa**—Similar to the UPromise card, the BabyMint Visa is linked to your BabyMint account, depositing your rewards as you earn them. For families not heavily using the BabyMint savings program, this card may not be as attractive as the Fidelity or UPromise card because it pays only a flat 1 percent on purchases, with no bonus opportunities.

- **FutureTrust Mastercard**—The FutureTrust MasterCard does exactly what the BabyMint credit card does, awarding you 1 percent on your purchases. Because this is a much smaller program than UPromise and BabyMint, this card is most likely to be a best choice only for those that primarily use the other features of the FutureTrust savings program.

- **Nontuition credit cards**—Consider looking at what other nontuition-based credit cards have to offer, especially from the Discover Card family. Often, the rewards on these cards are heftier, with additional perks like waived interest for paying on time (for example, the Discover Motiva card). These cards might save you more than you'd earn by using one of the other cards that promises to help you pile up tuition dollars.

The Least You Need to Know

- Everyone should be using tuition reward programs, regardless of where they are in the process of paying for college.
- Getting family and friends to participate can turbo-charge the rate at which you accumulate rewards.
- Maximize programs such as UPromise and BabyMint by planning your seasonal shopping and largest purchases in advance.
- Review the current list of schools participating in the SAGE Scholars Program to see whether you should sign up.
- If you're a frequent credit card user, consider signing up for a card that earns you tuition instead of points or miles.

Challenge and Employer Programs

In This Chapter

- How challenge programs work
- State and local challenge programs
- Getting your boss to pay the bill
- Major employers that offer tuition reimbursement

Years ago, my wife and I worked with at-risk high school kids. Many of these teens didn't get enough attention at home or got the wrong kind of attention. One day after a football game, we took a bunch of kids out to eat, including a kid whose mom refused to let him eat anything with even a trace of sugar in it. While we were all looking at the menus, I caught a glimpse of him out of the corner of my eye, frantically ripping open sugar packets and dumping them into his mouth. I remember thinking that the old saying held very true, that "desperate times call for desperate measures."

If you're staring down some massive tuition bills and starving for some cash, the techniques in this chapter might be right up your alley. Like sugar straight from the packet, they can provide a huge dose of the cash you need. But they might require you to make some strategic and desperate moves, literally.

Employer tuition reimbursement programs, as well as state and local challenge programs, do something that was unheard of in college planning until a few years ago. They give you money, sometimes a lot of it, simply for working for the right employer or living in the right ZIP Code. In fact, many employer plans pay for tuition tax-free up to the IRS limit ($5,250 in 2010), and some state challenge programs pay nearly the entire cost of college.

Is that worth packing up your desk or your house and making a switch? It probably depends on how employable you are and how movable your family is. But it is something you should consider, especially if you have a few years until college starts or will be putting multiple people through college. When you do the math, making a move can be the equivalent of receiving a $5,000 to $20,000 raise in pay.

The Basics of Challenge Programs

You have to give credit where credit is due. A few years back, some incredibly gracious companies like Murphy Oil decided to give back to their communities in a very major way, through what were initially called "promise" programs. In doing so, they inspired a wave of programs that have collectively put as many kids through college as any single private scholarship program out there.

These "challenge" programs, as they came to be known, are meant to inspire high school students to stay focused and pursue a college education. To accomplish that lofty goal, these companies promised to pay for some or all of the college tuition of students living in the towns in which their businesses were based.

FLUNK-PROOF FINANCES

Most challenge programs require a student to be a resident of the area covered by the program for a minimum number of years, with the benefit amount increasing for every additional year the student has lived in the area. In other words, you can't typically move into an area covered by a challenge program six months before college starts and hope to get the free money.

Most of these programs require students to maintain only a C or B average, stay out of legal trouble, and attend a reasonably priced state college, in addition to living within the geographical area named under the plan. Most plans have minimum residency requirements as well, meaning that you could not move into town a week before college starts and hope to get full funding. But many programs do reward students who live in a covered geographical area for as few as four years and attend a local high school during that time.

Major Challenge Programs

Challenge programs are really broken down into two categories, although both of them revolve around where a student lives prior to attending college. *State* challenge programs are offered by a state government, usually covering all residents of that state. *Local* challenge programs are funded by companies and local donors, usually in the town where they themselves are located.

State Challenge Programs

More and more states are beginning to implement challenge programs for every student in their states. Like local challenge programs, these state-run programs only pay tuition and fees, leaving students and parents to fend for themselves when it comes to room and board.

In addition, many of these programs place limits on where the students can go to school, usually gearing their benefits toward students who attend in-state colleges. For those programs that do allow students to attend college out-of-state, the amount that the sponsoring state is willing to pay is usually limited to the cost of the average in-state school.

The following states offer some version of a challenge program:

- Alabama
- Arkansas
- Idaho
- Michigan
- Mississippi
- Missouri
- Oklahoma
- Tennessee
- Washington
- West Virginia

Corporate and Local Promise Programs

Since the first local promise program was started a few years ago by Murphy Oil, a new local program has developed every year or two. It's likely that as other communities witness the success and impact of these programs, more programs will be created, grandfathering in existing high school students in their coverage areas.

Although none of these programs pays for 100 percent of tuition at all colleges, some will truly pay a student's way through a state college education. Even those that don't offer full rides still offer a substantial amount of money that, when combined with grants and loans, can easily eliminate any remaining need a student has.

Should you move to get the free money? Here's where you'd have to plant new roots:

- **El Dorado Promise**—This program is for students of the El Dorado, Arkansas, area and is sponsored by the Murphy Oil Company. The program pays a maximum of $6,500, depending on how long a student has lived in the El Dorado area.

- **Pittsburgh Promise**—Awards up to $20,000 over four years for students who have attended a Pittsburgh area high school from grades 9–12. The initial funding for the program was provided by the University of Pittsburgh Medical Center.

- **Kalamazoo Promise**—Funded by anonymous donors, this program pays up to 100 percent of the tuition to attend a Michigan state university or community college. Students must attend grades 9–12 in the Kalamazoo Public School District.

- **Detroit Promise**—Although not as hefty as some of the other programs, the Detroit Promise plan still provides up to $2,000 for college to Detroit public school students.

- **Pinal County Promise**—Provides up to four semesters of free tuition at any school in the Central Arizona College system. To be eligible, the student's parents must sign a contract committing to the program by the end of their child's 8th grade year.

> **CHEAT SHEET**
>
> Money received from challenge programs is considered tax-free and is generally paid directly by the sponsoring state or program to the student's college.

Employer Tuition Programs

I have to admit that I didn't think very many employer tuition programs existed until a few years ago when I started teaching at the University of Phoenix. But I consistently run into employee after employee who is getting money from his company to pursue his Bachelor's or Master's degree. Even better, these students weren't just getting a few hundred bucks; most of them were getting their tuitions reimbursed up to the IRS limit for tax-free tuition reimbursement—or $5,250 in 2010. Considering that many of my students were making only $25,000 per year at their jobs, using their employers' tuition reimbursement programs was equivalent to a 20 percent tax-free raise!

Most often, tuition reimbursement comes in one of two forms:

- **Direct bill**—Under this arrangement, the college an employee attends simply submits a bill to the employer, who then pays it. However, employees might still be responsible for paying registration and other fees, as well as for their books.

- **Voucher**—Although not as common, some employers provide their employees with a voucher or coupon that they can use at any accredited school. The school in turn submits this voucher to the employer for reimbursement.

The Fine Print of Employer Reimbursement

There are literally thousands of employers that reimburse tuition, but these programs are not without some fine print. It's important to understand how these programs work before you take a few classes and then find yourself stuck with a hefty bill.

Here are some of the key components you need to consider before you begin:

- **Length of service**—Many employer tuition reimbursement plans do not kick in until an employee has been there for at least 6 or 12 months. The exception is usually free tuition for employees of an actual college, which often begins immediately or within 30 days.

- **Upfront payment**—Some plans require an employee to pay the tuition upfront, only being reimbursed after she successfully completes a class. Many nontraditional schools do offer more flexible payments terms for students using employer reimbursement to help minimize their out-of-pocket expenses.

- **Minimum grades**—Most tuition reimbursement programs will not reimburse students for Ds or Fs. In fact, some programs reimburse employees 100 percent only if they receive an A, with Bs and Cs being reimbursed at a lower percentage.

- **The IRS limit**—The IRS places a limit on the amount of tuition reimbursement an employee can receive before taxes kick in. For 2010, an employee can receive $5,250 in tuition reimbursement tax-free. Anything above this amount is taxable, with money owed to the IRS usually being withheld from the employee's paycheck.

Finding a Job with Tuition Reimbursement

Before you decide to move across the country to try to land a job at a company that offers tuition reimbursement, you'll need to check what's available in your own backyard. As a general rule, the larger and more profitable a company is, the more likely it is to offer tuition reimbursement for its employees.

> **CHEAT SHEET**
>
> You might not have to switch jobs to get tuition reimbursement. Consider asking your boss to institute a tuition-reimbursement plan as an employee benefit or to give you part of your next raise in the form of tuition reimbursement. In doing so, both you and the employer avoid paying payroll taxes on that money (roughly 8 percent each), as well as you having to pay income taxes on it under the annual IRS limit.

So start by doing an Internet search for the largest employers in your county and state. When you find local companies that look like they could be a good fit for you, simply pick up the phone and call that company. Ask to speak to someone in their human resources department and then tell them that you're considering applying for a job with them and were wondering if they offer tuition reimbursement to their employees. If they say "yes," see whether you can get any additional details, such as how long you have to wait before you're eligible and how much it covers.

If no major companies are headquartered or have operations in your area, grab a copy of *Forbes* magazine's annual list of the 100 Best Companies to Work For. Not only do the majority of these companies offer some level of tuition reimbursement, but their other benefits also make picking up your life and moving elsewhere all that much more worthwhile. The annual list of Fortune 500 companies (America's biggest corporations) is also a great place to begin doing research and making phone calls because these companies have deep enough pockets to offer employee tuition reimbursement.

Lastly, even though it is a bit of a long shot, you can try calling your local college and asking to speak to someone in the student billing department. Because these individuals are the ones involved in the billing and reimbursement process with local businesses, a sympathetic soul might be willing to rattle off a few company names if you tell him you're trying to find a future employer who takes care of its employees.

Tuition for Employees' Children

Many of employer tuition reimbursement programs have been expanded in recent years to include putting one's spouse or children through college. Although this is still relatively rare, students with children of their own should consider jobs at these companies to be worth their weight in gold. The easiest places to find jobs that offer tuition to spouses and children are the colleges themselves, so check to see whether any schools in your area are hiring.

It is important to note that some of these companies that do offer benefits for family members allow only *one* family member to use the tuition benefit at a time. So if you're the parent of twins or triplets, you might be out of luck.

Large Employers with Substantial Programs

This list only scratches the surface of major employers offering tuition reimbursement programs, but I hope it encourages you that tuition reimbursement is a very attainable reality. For an expanded list of schools, visit the Employer Tuition Reimbursement Directory at CollegeSavings.About.com:

- Alcoa
- Allstate Insurance
- AMD Microchips
- AT&T
- Blue Cross
- Boeing
- Campbell Soup
- Caterpillar
- Chase Bank
- Clorox
- Colgate-Palmolive
- Department of Homeland Security
- IBM
- Internal Revenue Service (IRS)
- John Hancock Insurance
- Kroger
- Lexmark
- Lucent Technologies
- Merck Pharmaceuticals
- NASA
- Oneida
- Pacific Gas & Electric
- Philip Morris
- Starbucks
- QWEST Communications
- Raytheon

- Saturn Automobiles
- Verizon
- Virginia Department of Transportation

- Von's Grocery Stores
- Wal-Mart
- Xerox

The Least You Need to Know

- Challenge programs pay for the college educations of students with average grades, simply for living in the right city or state.
- Challenge programs are subject to funding cuts, so even students who have already begun college might suddenly find themselves without funding.
- Employer tuition plans typically provide up to $5,250 in tax-free tuition reimbursement each year.
- If you're considering a job change to gain employer tuition reimbursement, start by researching the largest companies in your area.
- Many employer reimbursement plans only pay for classes if the student earns a certain grade and remains employed throughout the entire class.

College for Military Service

Chapter 15

In This Chapter

- Overview of military education benefits
- The Montgomery and Post-9/11 GI bills
- Military loan forgiveness programs
- Financial assistance for reservists
- Transferring benefits to family members
- The option to "opt out"

Nuclear option is a military phrase whose use has spread to many other arenas, from sports to politics. In the classic military sense of the word, it refers to a country pulling out all the stops in a war and dropping the big one. It's an option that takes no prisoners and absolutely decimates the competition.

When it comes to paying for a college education, joining the military is the financial equivalent of the nuclear option. If all other funding plans fail, a student can "nuke" his college costs with a relatively short commitment to a very short haircut and some less-than-fashionable footwear. In fact, this can be one of the single most attractive options for people who find themselves between a rock and a financial hard place.

How good are military education benefits? Well, if you're willing to go the distance, not only can you get an undergraduate education completely paid for, but you can also get your graduate degree in certain areas. Add it all up, and this can amount to over $300,000 in college funding, with very few hoops to jump through on the front end.

Your Uncle Sam Is Rich!

One of the best things about the education benefits offered by the military is that there is no limit to who can participate in the most basic programs. Unlike scholarships, which go only to a few candidates whose qualifications outshine the rest, military education benefits are made available to all who meet the service requirements.

In 2010 alone, the U.S. government will pay out nearly $3 billion in education benefits. Most of this goes to first-time college students with average high school grades and test scores who are pursuing undergraduate degrees. That means that if you're willing to serve, you're going to get the majority of your college expenses paid for.

Here's a basic overview of some of the benefits you can obtain through military service:

- Under the older Montgomery GI Bill, military personnel could receive nearly $50,000 for college.

- Under the alternative Post-9/11 GI Bill, military personnel can have 100 percent of their tuition and fees paid (up to certain state maximums).

- The Yellow Ribbon program is a partnership between the Veterans Administration and certain schools. Under the Yellow Ribbon program, expenses not covered under the Post-9/11 GI Bill might be waived by participating schools, and the VA will match any tuition discount given to a veteran by the school. A full list of participating schools can be found at www.gibill.va.gov.

- Graduate students (medical, dental, psychological, nursing, and veterinary), who apply prior to attending grad school, may be selected to have all of their educational costs at any U.S. college paid for in return for military service after graduation. Additionally, they can receive more than $1,000 per month in spending money throughout graduate school.

- Law and seminary students who commit to military service can have their degrees paid for.

- Military personnel can qualify to have classes waived at civilian colleges, based on their military experience.

- *Reservists* and certain family members might be eligible for benefits as well.

> **DEFINITION**
>
> **Reservists** refer to military personnel who sign up to serve on a limited basis each year but who can be called up to active service in times of crisis.

Tuition Assistance for Full-Time Military Service

The granddaddy of military education benefits are the GI bills, whose actual name has varied slightly as different programs have been introduced or phased out over the years. Although there are a lot of wrinkles to the various GI bills, the basics remain the same.

The actual amount that is paid under the GI Bill program, what is required to earn benefits, as well as how long someone has to claim her benefits, varies slightly depending on which version of the GI Bill program the service member is participating in. The two current versions of the program are commonly referred to as the Montgomery GI Bill and the Post-9/11 GI Bill programs; each has slightly different rules, provisions, and benefit amounts.

The Pre-9/11 Montgomery GI Bill

Although GI bills supporting education and other benefits have been around since the end of World War II, the Montgomery GI Bill will be one of the best known to most readers of this book. The Montgomery GI Bill was introduced in 1984 and was advertised heavily on TV throughout many of our childhoods.

Under the Montgomery GI Bill, active-duty personnel can earn the right to reimbursement for college costs, up to a certain annual and lifetime dollar limit. These benefits increase each year, to keep up with the rising cost of college. Further, the Montgomery GI Bill has very broad definitions of where money from the program could be used.

Key components of the Montgomery GI Bill program for 2010 include:

- **Basic benefit amount**—For the 2009–2010 academic year, the maximum GI Bill monthly tuition reimbursement amount is $1,368. This can be paid out for a maximum of 36 months or a lifetime maximum of $49,248.

- **Additional benefit amounts**—The pre-9/11 Montgomery GI Bill might offer "kickers" or increased benefit amounts of up to $950 per month for enlistees with certain valuable skills. Additionally, recruits might choose to "invest" up to $600 additional, which is matched on an 8-1 basis by the military. Thus, a $600 buy-up on the part of the soldier results in an additional $4,800 in benefits.

- **Housing allowance**—Someone receiving a monthly reimbursement check under the pre-9/11 Montgomery GI Bill can choose how to divide the amount between tuition and living costs.

- **Length of service required**—The amount reimbursed depends on someone's length of active-duty service (even if not deployed in a war zone). It ranges from 40 percent for service lasting between 90 days and 6 months to 100 percent for 36 months of service.

- **Time limit to use benefits**—Benefits must be used within 10 years of someone's discharge from the military.

- **Cost**—$100 per month for the first 12 months of service will be deducted from the service member's paycheck. There are no additional contributions after this point.

The Post-9/11 GI Bill

The "new" GI Bill, properly known as the Post-9/11 GI Bill, funds a service member's college costs using a substantially different formula than the older Montgomery GI Bill. Although the benefits under the new GI Bill can amount to substantially more, in certain cases someone eligible for both might want to opt for the older program.

The decision on which one to use really comes down to the price of the school the service member is attending. The more expensive the school, the more likely that someone who qualifies for both bills would want to choose the newer, Post-9/11 GI Bill. The reason for this is that the new Post-9/11 GI Bill might pay up to 100 percent of tuition and fees. The new GI Bill also includes a substantial housing allowance and book stipend.

Again, for a student attending four years of an inexpensive local college, he can actually put some money in his pocket by opting for the old Montgomery GI Bill. But for someone attending an expensive school, the fact that the new GI Bill might cover 100 percent of the costs can mean substantially more dollars for a service member.

CHEAT SHEET

In addition to the official military education benefits listed in this chapter, many enlistees can receive signing bonuses. With some of these bonuses exceeding $10,000 to $20,000, this can provide a large shot in the arm to any student saving up for college or trying to pay off loans.

Key components of the Post-9/11 GI Bill program for 2010 include:

- **Basic benefit amount**—For the 2009–2010 academic year, the maximum benefit amount is 100 percent of the cost of tuition, up to a maximum set for the state in which someone is attending college. This benefit ranges from as little as $805 per term for the state of Arkansas to $62,000 per term for Florida students! On top of the tuition reimbursement received, the new GI Bill also provides an annual book stipend (allowance) of $1,000.

- **Additional benefit amounts**—Like the older Montgomery GI Bill, the Post-9/11 GI Bill might offer "kickers," or increased benefit amounts, of up to $950 per month for enlistees with certain valuable skills. There are no buy-up provisions, however, that allow a service member to contribute additional funds in return for a higher payout later.

- **Housing allowance**—All veterans (as opposed to active-duty personnel) also receive a monthly housing allowance of roughly $1,000, with the actual amount varying by ZIP Code. Active-duty personnel, because they are already provided some form of housing or stipend, are not eligible for an additional amount under the Post-9/11 GI Bill.

- **Length of service required**—The amount reimbursed depends on someone's length of active-duty service, after September 11, 2001 (even if not deployed in a war zone). It ranges from 40 percent reimbursement for service lasting between 90 days and 6 months to 100 percent for 36 months of service.

- **Time limit to use benefits**—Benefits must be used within 15 years of someone's discharge from the military, as opposed to the 10 years under the old Montgomery GI Bill.

- **Cost**—There is no cost to newly enrolled service members. Those enrolled under the old plan who want to switch to the new GI Bill might be required to pay a prorated amount of the $1,200 they would have previously been charged.

Health Professionals Scholarship Program

Similar to the loan repayment programs discussed later in this chapter, the Health Professionals Scholarship Program (HPSP) will fork over a substantial amount of cash for someone to become a certified health professional. In fact, for many professionals, this program will pay 100 percent of the graduate school tuition up-front (prior to serving in the military), in exchange for one year of service for every year of school paid for. That means that the HPSP program could potentially pay for more than $250,000 in graduate schooling!

To be eligible, a student must have graduated from an accredited undergraduate program, be a U.S. citizen, and be otherwise qualified to serve in the military. The health professions covered include the following:

- Dentist
- Medical doctor
- Nurse
- Optometrist
- Psychologist
- Veterinarian

Other Programs

From time to time, other programs are introduced and phased out among the various *branches* of service. In fact, the branches themselves are not required to offer the same programs and can even introduce their own specialized programs to attract and retain personnel. Parents or students considering the military as their "nuclear" funding option for college will need to be sure that they continue to check with recruiters from other branches before making a commitment. If a new program has been introduced prior to you or your student actually signing your enlistment papers, you might want to make a switch.

> **DEFINITION**
>
> **Branches** refer to the various sections of the U.S. Armed Services someone can serve with, namely the Army, Navy, Marines, Air Force, and Coast Guard.

Other programs you might want to consider include:

- **Bachelor's Degree Completion Program (BDCP)**—Similar to the HPSP program, which pays for a student to attend graduate school prior to serving, the selective BDCP program pays for future Navy personnel to complete their Bachelor's degrees prior to actually serving.

- **JAG scholarships**—For existing military personnel interested in becoming a military lawyer, a limited number of scholarships are available.

- **Seminary scholarships**—Civilians interested in becoming a military chaplain might be eligible to receive a scholarship to attend a civilian seminary (of any faith background) in return for future service.

- **Reserve Officers Training Corps (ROTC)**—Students who participate in ROTC at their high schools or colleges might be eligible for a limited number of scholarships in return for later service. In addition to paying up to 100 percent of a student's tuition, fees, and books, these scholarships can include a monthly living allowance while in school.

> **WORLD WIDE WISDOM**
>
> There are a lot of scholarships out there for children and relatives of someone who has served in the military. Because these scholarships are not actually administered by the military, a simple Web search for "military scholarships" will turn up a wide variety of options.

Loan Repayment for Active-Duty Personnel

The military has some of the juiciest loan forgiveness programs around, especially for health-care professionals with graduate school loans. As always, someone pursuing this type of financial assistance should be sure he sees everything in writing and fully understands the fine print of the program before enlisting or committing to serve.

The two main programs available for active-duty personnel are the Military College Loan Repayment Program (CLRP) and the Health Professionals Loan Repayment Program (HPLRP). Both of these programs forgive a substantial amount of student debt, but they have different rules and requirements you need to understand.

One important fact to keep in mind with military loan repayment programs is that the forgiven amounts are considered taxable income. This means that income tax withholding occurs on these programs, reducing the actual dollar amount of forgiveness by roughly 25 percent initially, although this can rise or fall when someone actually files each year's tax return.

Here are the basics:

- **Military College Loan Repayment Program (CLRP)**—Depending on the branch, this program might exist under a different name or with slightly different rules, but the premise is the same. Up to $65,000 in student loans is forgiven for three to four years of military service. But to receive this benefit, a service member has to give up his rights to any additional tuition assistance under the GI Bill.

- **Health Professionals Loan Repayment Program (HPLRP)**—This program primarily forgives the student loans of health professionals with graduate-level degrees, along with registered nurses. Although the amount itself varies with the person's health profession, loan forgiveness amounts can easily exceed $100,000. The typical commitment is for four years of military service.

> **FLUNK-PROOF FINANCES**
>
> One of the biggest worries of many people considering the military to help fund their education expenses is the chance that they'll be injured or killed in service. For those wanting to minimize their chances of becoming a casualty, they should consider the Coast Guard, the Air Force, and the Navy, in that order.

Military Benefits for Reservists

So far, all the military benefits described have been for students who commit to serving in the military full time. However, the U.S. Armed Forces does offer a number of financial incentives for people who enlist as reservists and are not considered full-time active duty. It's worth noting that if someone is a reservist and gets called up to active duty, she might be eligible for a much higher level of benefits, similar to regular, active-duty personnel.

The two primary classes of financial assistance for reservists are tuition assistance and loan repayment. The tuition assistance programs work almost identically to what active-duty personnel receive under the GI bills, except that reservists qualify for a lower amount. Loan repayment programs for reservists work very much like the loan forgiveness programs discussed in Chapter 7, with the military providing funds to pay off existing loans after a certain amount of service.

For 2009–2010, the current benefit amounts are as follows:

- **Tuition assistance**—Although the details can vary by military branch and the current promotions being offered, a reservist with six years of continuous reserve duty can receive $250 per month for up to 36 months of college. Again, certain reservists that meet other standards or that see active duty might be able to claim a much higher level of reimbursement.

- **Loan repayment**—Under loan payment programs for reservists, up to $65,000 in student loans might be forgiven depending on someone's background and the skills she brings to the reserves. Be sure to request information in writing, however, before you sign on in hopes of earning loan forgiveness. A simple misunderstanding could lead to a number of wasted years.

> **WORLD WIDE WISDOM**
>
> For students entering the military with existing student loans, a deferment is available that puts all payments on hold for up to three years. For more information and the necessary forms, go online to studentaid.ed.gov and search for "Deferments."

Transferability of Benefits

One of the great things about some of the most substantial education benefits for military personnel is that they can be transferred to the service member's spouse or children. That means that if your parent (living or who died during active duty), spouse, or ex-spouse is entitled to education benefits, they might be transferable to you or your child in certain circumstances. The only benefits eligible for transfer, however, are those offered under the Montgomery and Post-9/11 GI bills.

The rules can be quite complex and should be thoroughly discussed with someone's benefits contact within the military, but here are the basics:

- **Benefit amount**—The amount transferred is the unused portion of the original service member's amount. So if he has used half, his spouse or child could use only the remaining half.

- **Housing allowance**—No housing allowance is offered by the military under transferred benefits.

- **Length of service required**—The service member must have served at least six years active duty, National Guard, or Select Reserves, *plus* have enlisted for four more years.

- **Time limit to use benefits**—Spouses have 15 years from the service member's retirement or date of active-duty death to use his benefits. Children have until their 26th birthdays to use benefits.

- **Control over benefits**—It is at the service member's discretion whether a spouse, an ex-spouse, or a child can use the benefits. Further, the service member can revoke someone's right to use it at anytime, even after that person's education has started.

"Opting Out" of Classes

In addition to the military helping to pay for a college education, many schools are willing to count military training toward a future diploma. In other words, certain military training and experiences allow a student to opt out of specific classes, in turn lowering the overall college costs. It's not unheard of for former military personnel to test or "qualify" out of up to one-third of a four-year degree before they ever set foot on a campus.

The Defense Activity for Non-Traditional Education Support (DANTES) program is the broad program under which a variety of college equivalency tests are offered for little or no cost. In addition to the CLEP test, personnel can take what are known as DSST and ECE exams. Each of these exam formats offers tests in a wide variety of subject areas. You can prepare for many of these exams through free classes offered at military installations around the world. To learn more about the DANTES program, visit the official website, dantes.doded.mil.

In addition to the opportunity to test out of required college classes, the American Council on Education (ACE) partners with the military to award college credit for specific trainings provided and documented by the various military branches. Because there are literally hundreds of standard military trainings that can count toward a college degree, anyone with military experience should visit the searchable directory of equivalent courses at militaryguides.acenet.edu.

The Least You Need to Know

- Serving in the military for as little as 36 months can pay for a student's entire college education.
- The HPSP will pay for a health professional's entire cost of medical or graduate school, in return for a commitment to serve 2 to 4 years.
- Reservists are also eligible for education benefits, though at a lower rate.
- The military offers numerous loan forgiveness programs for existing college graduates willing to enlist.
- Education benefits received under the GI Bill might be transferred to a spouse or child if certain conditions are met.
- Many schools are willing to count military training toward a future diploma, allowing a student to "opt out" of certain classes.

The Peer Lending Alternative

In This Chapter

- Peer-to-peer lending 101
- When to use peer-to-peer lending
- Peer-to-peer lending pitfalls
- Finding the best deals

One of my contentions in Chapter 6 is that, if all else fails, federal student loans can save the day for most college students. Throw in the use of forgivable loans and loan forgiveness (see Chapter 7), and borrowing money for college ends up being some people's single best plan for funding the high cost of higher education.

But, there will be times when federal and state student loans just can't come through in a pinch like you hoped they would. Sometimes it's because a parent or student let the federal or state application deadline slip through his fingers. Other times, a person is maxed out on how much he can borrow or his credit isn't good enough for certain programs, such as PLUS loans. Still other people qualify for the loan and will receive the money in the near future, but they need the cash now to enroll.

In all these cases, peer-to-peer lending, when used wisely, can be a lifesaver. Of course, peer-to-peer lending, when done poorly or without the proper research, can leave borrowers with higher-than-expected interest rates, damaged relationships, or broken kneecaps. As a side note, always avoid borrowing money from people who have a utensil as part of their name, such as Johnny the Knife or Mike the Fork.

The Basics of Peer-to-Peer Lending

Peer-to-peer lending, or P2P, is just a fancy term for borrowing money from another individual. It can range from a very informal and unwritten lending agreement between family members to a formal agreement between strangers, complete with fine print.

> **DEFINITION**
>
> **Peer-to-peer lending** involves loans that are made between private parties, as opposed to those made between a business or the government and a borrower.

The loans made under these agreements—especially more formal agreements—are typically shorter term and range from 3 to 10 years. The interest rates on these loans can vary from 0 percent when borrowing from generous family members to well above 10 percent when borrowing from strangers. Further, these loans might have no set-up or origination fees when done informally; however, you can face origination fees (typically 1 to 3 percent) and servicing charges (usually a flat dollar amount paid monthly or annually).

When to Use P2P Lending

Like all the tools in your college funding toolbox, there are right and wrong times to use peer-to-peer lending. In general, though, these loans should not be considered as an equal substitute for federal student loans. Likewise, they should not be considered as heinous as many of the private student loans available through corporate loan sharks that don't participate in the normal public lending channels.

Ultimately, using them comes down to two things: financial cost and borrower flexibility. Typically, both of these are more favorable under government loans—but not always. If any of the following situations exist, you should consider doing some deeper analysis:

- **Rates are significantly lower**—Although you wouldn't want to opt for the more restrictive nature of P2P loans over government loans for a savings of just .25 percent, a difference of more than 1 percent begins to beg the discussion. As P2P loan rates drop further from this point, they become a very real consideration that every student or parent should consider.

CHEAT SHEET

If P2P lending is going to be part of your future, you'll need to do more research than just reading this chapter. Check out *The Complete Idiot's Guide to Person-to-Person Lending* by Curtis E. Arnold and Beverly Blair Harzog (Alpha Books, 2009).

- **You're maxed out**—If you cannot get any additional student loans (remember, Stafford and Perkins loans are subject to lifetime limits), these might provide an attractive fallback.

- **You're a parent with bad credit**—Because PLUS loans taken out by parents do require a credit check, P2P loans might be a good fallback for those who can't qualify. However, because Stafford and Perkins loans do not require a credit check on the student borrowing the money, they should not replace these loans unless the rates are substantially better.

- **You need a swing loan**—If tuition is due now but your next financial aid disbursement is months away, you might want to use a P2P loan to fill the gap and then use your future financial aid disbursement to pay off the P2P loan. Before you do this, though, check to see what your school's policy is on late payments. If it'll give you a grace period or charge a rate of interest lower than your potential P2P loan, you should avoid borrowing.

- **For surprise expenses**—Whether it is replacing a crashed laptop or a crashed car, a P2P loan can cost a lot less over time than charging those amounts to a credit card with an annual interest rate of 29.99 percent.

- **Your only other option is raiding your retirement**—Because you might lose anywhere from 10 to 50 percent of your retirement account's value when raiding it for college-related expenses, taking out a P2P loan might give you time to figure out other options without forking over a substantial slice of your retirement to the IRS.

- **You'd rather pay interest to family**—Although a student or parent should always think of her own finances first and foremost, the idea of paying 8.5 percent annually to Grandma might be a lot more attractive than handing it to some of the financial giants that spent part of the last decade ruining our economy. I talk more about intrafamily borrowing a little later in the chapter.

Potential Problems with P2P Lending

Borrowing money from private parties, be they complete strangers or blood relatives, has its advantages; however, it also has a number of potential problems that every parent and student should consider. The biggest drawback of course is that these are not federal student loans. Those loans come with a built-in bevy of features designed to keep costs low, help cash-strapped graduates, and forgive unpaid amounts after certain periods of time. Specifically, P2P borrowers need to take into account the following drawbacks to using a P2P student loan:

- **Noncompetitive interest rates**—In general, formal P2P loans between unrelated parties have substantially higher interest rates than government loans, although their rates are often lower than those of loans issued by private corporations. This is especially true of subsidized Stafford and Perkins loans, with rates dipping below 5 percent in the next few years.

- **No deferments and forbearance**—Although P2P loans from family members or friends can be more flexible, anonymous P2P lenders want their money and they want it when it is due. They don't care that you're unemployed, returning to school, or suffering from an illness. Failure to pay will land you in collections.

- **Lower credit score**—Even if you don't end up getting approved or taking the offer, applying for a P2P loan might lower your credit score. Because credit scores are affected by the number of inquiries against someone's credit report, you should move forward with an application only if you're reasonably sure you're going to use the loan if it's granted.

- **No interest subsidization**—One of the great things about government loans for students demonstrating substantial financial need is that the interest is subsidized while they remain in school. That means that the government actually pays the interest on the loans, instead of that interest being added to the loans and increasing what has to be paid back. Formal P2P loans do not offer this feature, and family members making a loan would usually feel taken advantage of if they didn't earn any interest for the first four years.

- **No loan forgiveness**—Federal and state loan forgiveness programs only forgive government loans. Money borrowed from a private individual, even through a formal loan agreement, will not be eligible for most loan forgiveness programs.

- **Damaged relationships**—If the peers you're borrowing from are also relatives, even one late payment can make the next family reunion a lot more awkward.

- **Quicker collections**—The collections process on private P2P loans is typically a lot faster than on government loans, which can often take up to a year past the first late payment to begin collection actions.

- **Collateral requirements**—Federal student loans do not come with any collateral requirements, where the borrower is required to pledge an asset (his house, car, or bank account) as collateral for the loan. P2P loans, depending on the lender's unique requirements, might very well require you to sign over some of your property as collateral that they can seize if the loan does not get repaid.

- **Possible lack of tax deduction**—Normally, student loan interest is deductible in the year it is paid. When loans are made between related parties such as a P2P loan among family members, this interest is not deductible.

CHEAT SHEET

Although the collections process is generally much quicker for P2P loans, these loans can also be more easily erased under a bankruptcy filed by the student. By contrast, student loans made through federal programs are almost never discharged under bankruptcy proceedings.

Finding a P2P Lender

Like so many other industries, the arrival of the Internet has changed everything when it comes to P2P loans. But even though many people who have recently discovered P2P lending think it was created in the Internet age, it has actually been around forever. If you dig up a classifieds section from a large local newspaper from the

1970s or 1980s, you'll find plenty of people looking to borrow or lend money. Heck, just this morning I saw a classified in my local paper for someone looking to borrow $30,000 for five years.

If you think P2P lending is something that will be wise or necessary for you to use, you can find the best loan and rate by shopping around. You'll find a much wider variety of rates and options in the P2P loan market than in the highly regulated federal and state student loan market.

Follow these steps to find the best loan for you:

1. **Hit the Net**—Visit all the major P2P websites to see if you meet each site's standards and to request potential rates from interested borrowers. Although a quick search will bring up a whole host of services that match P2P borrowers and lenders, you should also check out Prosper.com, LendingClub.com, Fynanz.com, and GreenNote.com.

2. **Run an ad**—Most newspapers' classified sections will let you run a regular ad for little or no cost. So there's no harm in running an ad saying you want to borrow money and at what rate. To avoid scam artists, be sure to use a site such as VirginMoneyUS.com to arrange the transaction.

3. **E-mail family and friends**—While you shouldn't spam everyone you know, if there are people in your life who might be open to loaning you money and earning some interest in the process, send a generic e-mail to all of them. Make it clear that you're not putting any pressure on them and that they don't even need to reply if they're not interested.

If you do end up borrowing money from friends or family, consider putting the deal in writing, even if they're promising you great terms like no interest or a deferment on when you have to begin paying it back. It protects you and them. (Use the following sample loan agreement as a guide.) You can calculate the payments based on various interest rates at sites such as Finance.Yahoo.com, using a simple Excel spreadsheet, or with the help of a friendly accountant or financial planner.

Loan Agreement

This document serves as official student loan agreement between
_____ (borrower) and _____ (lender).

The amount to be borrowed is $_____ and will be used only for the purposes of paying college tuition and/or living expenses directly related to college. It will not be used to purchase unrelated personal or leisure items, to pay off any other debts, or make an investment of any kind.

The interest rate on this loan is _____ percent, compounded annually on the loan's anniversary date, with interest being added to the base loan amount and with subsequent periods' interest calculated on this new total amount.

Repayment of this loan will begin six months after the student's official graduation date, or by _____, whichever date comes first.

The loan will be repaid in equal monthly installments of $_____ by the first of each month, lasting for _____ years. Any payments not received within _____ days of each month's due date will be subject to a $_____ penalty.

In the event that payments are received late for three consecutive months, the lender has the right to demand repayment of the entire loan amount in one lump sum, use a third party to collect the outstanding balance, or to take ownership of the following collateral:

_____

Both parties agree to these terms, which may not be altered without both parties' signed written consent.

_____   _____
Borrower   Date

_____   _____
Lender   Date

The Least You Need to Know

- Peer-to-peer lending (P2P) should be used as your primary student loan only after you've exhausted other loan options or when interest rates are substantially lower.

- P2P lending can offer a cheap alternative to credit cards and other short-term loans when cash is needed for only a short period of time.

- P2P lending does not come with all the great features of federal loans, like interest subsidization, deferment, and loan forgiveness.

- Loans among family members can be a great deal for both parties, but steps need to be taken to ensure that relationships don't get damaged.

- When looking for a P2P student loan, be sure to visit the major lending sites, run an ad in your local paper, and e-mail friends and family members who might be interested in lending you money.

Thinking Outside the Box

Part 5

There are few movies lines more parodied than "Luke, I am your father" from *Star Wars*. Poor Luke, in one heck of an awkward moment, his whole way of seeing things shifted dramatically. From that point forward, Father's Day took on a whole new meaning.

This is that moment for you, except that I'm pretty sure I'm not your father. No, I'm here to tell you once and for all that the majority of Americans no longer ship themselves or their kids off to a four-year college, join a frat or sorority, or travel Europe on their summer breaks. In reality, the majority of Americans have realized this is either unproductive or unattainable and are pursuing much more effective alternative approaches.

In this final part, we take a step back and examine some of the new paradigms in earning and paying for a college degree. We talk about the wisdom behind community college, online degrees, and vocational programs. We also examine some of the biggest college money mistakes made by well-meaning students, as well as what to do if you have some time left to save.

Nontraditional College

In This Chapter

- The explosion of nontraditional educations
- Saving money with nontraditional educations
- Nontraditional education modalities
- The vocational school option
- Financial aid for nontraditional students

If there has been a buzzword in education during the last decade or two, it is *nontraditional*. There are nontraditional colleges, nontraditional students, and nontraditional methods, all of which I talk about in this chapter. Of course, the reason I talk about them is that nontraditional educations offer some interesting options when it comes to the costs and financial rewards associated with earning a degree.

Now, it wouldn't be fair if I didn't state my bias on the front end. *I love the nontraditional approach to education!* In fact, I love it so much that I've spent a lot of time working in that environment over the last couple of years, having worked as an instructor at Webster University and an instructor/administrator at the University of Phoenix. Given the choice of teaching in one of these environments versus a traditional college environment, I think I'd almost always choose the nontraditional college setting (unless Harvard calls).

It's in large part because I truly believe that many (but not all) nontraditional students get more out of their educations than those in the traditional two- or four-year college environment. Nontraditional schools seem to place a much higher emphasis on how the quality of the curriculum and educational setting prepare people for their future careers. Further, I've found that nontraditional educations seem to provide a much healthier work and life balance, something especially important for the droves of older students returning to start (or finish) their degrees.

The Shift Toward Nontraditional Educations

Although there have always been correspondence schools and vocational schools, the nontraditional college movement encompasses so much more than this. So before you figure out how this might apply to the burning issue of paying for college, it might be helpful to define some terms:

- **Nontraditional education**—Refers to an education received in some manner other than attending face-to-face classes on a full-time basis. It allows the student to get an education in some other format than attending school full time, taking multiple classes during the week at a physical campus. Nontraditional educations can include online, accelerated, or 100 percent evening or weekend classes.

- **Nontraditional college**—A school that focuses primarily on educating students through an alternative format (such as online or distance classes) or a different type of schedule (part time, intensive, or alternative hours).

- **Nontraditional student**—A term used to both describe someone who attends a nontraditional school or receives a nontraditional education, as well as those that don't fit the classic profile of a college student. This might include people returning to school after a number of years in the workforce and older first-time students.

To a large degree, the growth of nontraditional college educations has been all about lowering one's college costs and increasing earning potential. As you read this book and wrestle with how you're going to pay for a traditional education, you need to weigh the merits of shifting to a nontraditional education.

Truly Nontraditional Schools

Although it seems that virtually every school is trying to reposition itself as offering a nontraditional learning environment, some industry leaders exist that every potential nontraditional student should evaluate. These include the following:

- University of Phoenix
- Webster University
- Everest College
- Strayer University
- Grand Canyon University
- Capella University
- Walden University

FLUNK-PROOF FINANCES

It's crucial that students considering a nontraditional education for something that leads to any kind of licensure (nursing, counseling, teaching, and so on) check with their state's licensing board. The degrees offered nationwide by these schools might not necessarily meet the requirements for every state in which someone might want to work.

The primary advantage of these schools over some of the more recognized brick-and-mortar traditional and state schools offering nontraditional options is that schools like Capella University and Grand Canyon University really cater to the unique needs of nontraditional students. Whether it is their technology or how you interact with your academic advisor, these schools are not just going to be patient with nontraditional students—they're going to treat them like first-class citizens.

Nontraditional Educations Can Cost Less

Nontraditional degree programs can easily save you $5,000 to $10,000 annually over traditional schools. These savings don't necessarily come from a lower cost of tuition, though. In fact, many nontraditional schools have a higher per-unit rate than many state colleges and middle-priced private schools.

The savings comes, however, from the fact that most nontraditional students don't face an increased cost of room and board over their current situations. Just as with a student attending community college (more on the wisdom of this in Chapter 21), nontraditional students usually continue to live at home with their parents or their existing roommates. This can easily amount to saving $500 or more per month in housing costs for cash-strapped students and families. Throw in the additional savings of sharing and preparing meals for your student or with existing roommates, instead of shopping for one or eating at a school's dining hall, and you've found another $100 to $200 per month in savings.

In addition to the huge savings potentially reaped on room and board, nontraditional students typically save a good amount of money on transportation. These savings come from the fact that the student is either an online student, who doesn't have to commute at all, or a student attending intensive, time-compacted classes (4 to 5 hours once or twice per week), and thus only has to make one or two trips to campus each week. On top of all that, there is no need to buy airline tickets, rent a moving truck, or worry about whether a student should take his car to college.

Additional cost savings are also often experienced on the following things:

- **Textbooks**—Many nontraditional schools, especially those that are offered online, require fewer textbook purchases for each class. Some, like the University of Phoenix, even make slimmed-down versions of the textbooks available online for a reduced fee.

- **Student fees**—Most traditional schools charge their students a boatload of miscellaneous fees, ranging from student activity fees to a health-care fee. By contrast, many nontraditional schools do not require these because there is no expectation of the student using campus resources.

- **Student fun**—One of the drawbacks of nontraditional college degrees is that there are a lot less keggers at the local frat house (try none) and no late night road trips to Las Vegas or Atlantic City. But, for serious students who are more interested in a degree than college war stories, the absence of these temptation-filled adventures can easily save hundreds if not thousands of dollars.

One thing potential students need to be aware of is that many nontraditional schools are actually private companies who are attempting to make a profit. In many cases this can be good because it forces the schools to recognize that students are customers who can take their business elsewhere. But you do need to be aware that many of the employees of these schools, especially admissions advisors, are compensated in large part on whether they can talk you into enrolling.

Nontraditional Students Can Earn More

As I often tell the nontraditional students I work with and teach, they have a great opportunity to leapfrog both traditional students and their nondegreed peers when it comes to their standing in the workplace. That's because, in all my years of hiring people for various jobs, I never really much cared where or how they got their degrees, as long as they had one, as well as having substantial work experience.

Nontraditional educations give students of all ages the ability to obtain a degree *and* work at least part time simultaneously. Aside from the obvious financial benefits of earning an income to offset college costs, nontraditional students build their resumés and gain work experience before they graduate. This makes them strong contenders for jobs over traditional graduates who spent their four years living the college lifestyle.

For mid-career professionals looking to broaden their skills and get a leg up on the corporate ladder, nontraditional educations again give them a strong edge over those who take time off to go back and earn their undergraduate or graduate degrees. It makes for an intense few years of juggling work, family, and school, but it almost guarantees that you'll be better positioned to snag the cushy jobs down the road.

FLUNK-PROOF FINANCES

Just because nontraditional colleges might be a little easier on the wallet or your schedule doesn't mean the academic rigor is any less. In fact, because these schools are highly scrutinized by the Higher Learning Commission, you'll find that the workload is just as heavy as a traditional college—if not more so than.

Is a Nontraditional Education Right for You?

Before you or your student dives headlong into a nontraditional education, you need to consider a few things. Although I strongly believe that this is a great alternative to a traditional degree, you need to ask yourself some key questions. If you can't answer "Yes" to most of the following questions, you probably should steer clear of a nontraditional education and stick with a traditional two- or four-year degree:

- **Is your reading comprehension and retention strong?** Much of the nontraditional learning environment is based around the student absorbing the required material on her own, using class time and contact with her instructor to work on what she didn't grasp. For people who need a slower pace and get overwhelmed with large amounts of information, nontraditional might not be the right option.

- **Are you a highly motivated self-starter?** If you have a hard time getting it in gear, perpetually procrastinate, or get depressed easily, you can find yourself getting behind very quickly in a nontraditional environment.

- **Are you comfortable with technology?** Many of the nontraditional environments, even those that are not 100 percent online, require access to a reliable computer and proficiency with the Internet, e-mail, and Microsoft Office.

- **Do you prefer a professional, learning-focused environment?** Most nontraditional environments are designed to help people strapped for time and cash to squeeze their education in between other priorities. If you were hoping for wild spring breaks, crazy road trips, and making lifelong friends, you're going to be out of luck. Most students in these programs have no interest in the college lifestyle.

Types of Nontraditional Educations

The world of nontraditional education is evolving much more quickly than the world of traditional education. It seems that every year the schools pioneering this movement are inventing new flavors of nontraditional degree attainment. More and more, you can find schools that mix *asynchronous learning*, live online classes, intensive classroom experience, and destination learning. Although you'll need to shop around to find which mix is right for you, it's important to understand the basic variations of what is available.

> **DEFINITION**
>
> **Asynchronous learning** means that the teacher and the students do not have to be "in class" at the same time. If there are lectures, they're taped and the student watches them when it is convenient for him; class discussions that take place occur by people posting on a message board, when it fits into their schedules. This asynchronous format is one of the things that makes online degrees very attractive to busy students.

Online Programs

The number of students pursuing legitimate, fully accredited associate's, Bachelor's, and graduate degrees online is booming! These programs were initially confined to a few innovative schools, but more and more well-respected and long-established colleges are offering degrees that can be earned entirely online.

In my experience from both taking and teaching online classes at a variety of colleges and universities, these classes are every bit as rigorous as their classroom counterparts. The biggest reason for this is that active participation is required from every student during every week of the class (usually in the form of short posts on message boards). This requires students to both fully study the material, as well as actively engage their fellow classmates. In other words, there is no way to simply show up and hide in the back of the class for 16 weeks, like some students do in brick-and-mortar learning environments.

Online classes are like many other nontraditional settings in that students take only one or two classes at a time, focusing all their attention on these couple of classes. Often, due to the intensive nature of these classes, they are substantially shorter, ranging from 5 to 10 weeks.

Most of these classes are offered in an asynchronous format, meaning that there is no specific time the student has to be online, as long as she meets her minimum requirements for each week of the class. This means that there is usually not a live lecture or classroom discussion; instead, instructors and students exchange thoughts, ideas, and assignments by posting them to a secure online message board. However, more and more online classes are also being offered in a hybrid of flex format, where the students attend a few classroom sessions for each course, with the balance being done online.

Accelerated Programs

I was in my early thirties when I went back to a brick-and-mortar school to get my Master's degree and became a marriage and family therapist. As much as I would have liked to attend some of the traditional programs in my area, which took two to three years to complete, I had a family to raise and was interested in beginning my new career. All that led me to choose an accelerated program at National University, which had me in and out in 18 months.

In my accelerated program were all kinds of people with a similar need to get their schooling done sooner rather than later. Some of them were much older than me and had even less interest in wasting time before they began working in their new field. Others had a wedding coming up, were planning on moving to accommodate their or their spouse's job, or only had enough savings to make it through a shorter period of schooling.

Regardless of the reason, if you need to get schooling done as soon as possible, an accelerated program might be right up your alley. From a "paying for college" point of view, cutting six months to two years out of your undergraduate or graduate education can save you big bucks on room and board and other annual expenses associated with a traditional college, even if the tuition remains the same.

If you're considering an accelerated program, here are a few things to keep in mind:

- **You can't miss class**—In accelerated programs, missing even one class can mean missing 10 to 20 percent of the course materials. If you have a work or family schedule that is unpredictable, you'll need to pass on one of these programs.

- **You're on your own**—Most accelerated programs come with very little handholding from faculty and school personnel. You're expected to pull your own weight and often solve your own problems.

- **Financial aid might be limited**—Because the dollar amount of financial aid you can receive is limited by school year, accelerated programs can reduce your ability to fully use some of the juiciest programs (Pell Grants, forgivable loans, and so on) and can force you to rely more on unsubsidized loans or pay cash out of pocket.

- **Vacations cease to exist**—Part of what allows accelerated programs to get a student through at a faster pace than traditional schools is that they continue to hold class when the rest of the world is on vacation. Classes almost always go through summer, skip spring break and one-day holidays, and limit the holiday break to a week or two.

- **Students with subject matter experience do best**—When I went back for my Master's in counseling psychology, I had a strongly developed set of inter-personal and counseling skills because both my Wall Street and nonprofit experience required these. Students who did not have a similar background struggled much more with the basic concepts. In a similar fashion, people with a background in business will do best in accelerated business programs, people with a background in health care will do best in accelerated nursing programs, and so forth.

Evening and Weekend Programs

One of the easiest times for students with other commitments to go back to school is during the evenings or on weekends. Classes offered in this nontraditional format greatly reduce the conflicts students have with their ability to earn a living or find childcare. The downside, of course, is that these programs tend to cut into relation-ship time, even if the classes are only one or two nights per week.

The biggest thing to consider with night and weekend programs is your ability to run your body and life at a more frantic pace for an extended period of time. Not having your weekends or evenings to recoup from the workday and to devote to family life can lead to a serious case of exhaustion, substandard grades, and rocky relationships.

Vocational Schools

Although most people wouldn't lump in *vocational schools* with other forms of non-traditional education, I do. In part, that's because attendance of vocational schools dropped off during the 1980s and 1990s, with most of those students feeling the pressure to earn a college degree. However, as North America has become full of people with college degrees, fewer and fewer people are skilled in the trades necessary to keep basic industries running successfully.

> **DEFINITION**
>
> A **vocational school** is one that trains someone specifically to perform a certain job within a certain industry, such as welding or dental assisting. These schools do not typically require students to take general education classes such as English, math, or a foreign language. Because of this, they typically offer certificates to their graduates instead of degrees.

From welding to electronics repair, the job market is booming for people trained in certain hands-on professions. Entry-level people in these fields are earning more than ever, frequently exceeding what college graduates of the same age are earning. Further, many go on to own their own businesses in those fields, earning incomes well in excess of $100,000 annually.

Best of all, when it comes to paying for an education and the time that is required to earn it, many vocational programs last a year or less, do not cost nearly as much as a college degree, and are offered through nontraditional means that allow students to continue their current lives and control their costs.

Best-Paying Vocational Careers

Although plenty of careers can earn you good money with little or no formal training, they often take the right kind of personality and some luck to succeed. For example, it's not hard to get licensed as a real estate agent in many states and the potential income is unlimited. But, the number of people truly succeeding and making solid careers as Realtors is far less than the number of people who try and fail.

By contrast, many higher paid vocational careers don't take a major drive to conquer the world, extraordinary sales skills, or a huge dose of luck. They simply take mastering the required skills and acquiring the right certifications. Aside from that, all personality types are welcome and most will be destined to make a good living.

Here's a list of the top careers that take some formal vocational training, usually at a vocational college, that also pay handsomely ($50,000 to $100,000 per year) after someone graduates.

- Building inspector
- Court reporter
- Dental hygienist
- Electrician
- Emergency medical technician

- Interpreter
- Massage therapist
- Plumber
- Truck driver
- Welder

Selecting the Right Vocational School

As a kid growing up in Southern California, I distinctly remember commercial after commercial promising people big bucks for going back to school at places like Barbizon, Dootson Driving School, DeVry, and ITT Technical Institute. I remember, even as a kid, thinking that some of these operations looked kind of shady, especially the one that offered a home study course in gun repair!

Over time, it became clear that some of these organizations were very legitimate, with others being nothing more than diploma mills that siphoned off people's cash. Although the names might have changed somewhat, the challenge still remains: finding a legitimate vocational school that will really teach the skills needed to succeed in specific fields.

CHEAT SHEET

Many vocations require someone to be an apprentice or work under someone else for a certain amount of time prior to opening her own business. In selecting a vocational school, it's a huge plus to find one that helps students land apprenticeships or has a built-in career center to help you find employment after you graduate.

After you decide on a vocation that's right for you (as opposed to the one that just pays the most), it's essential that you do your homework on vocational schools. There are three primary ways to go about doing this, all of which are pretty darn easy.

First, you should call some local employers in your planned vocation and simply ask them which schools they'd recommend and hire from. If you explain why you are doing this, most people will be very happy to help. The call goes something like this:

> "Hi, my name is _____. I was thinking about going back to school to work in your field, and I was wondering if somebody there had five minutes to give me recommendations on schools to attend and avoid."

That's it. If you make 10 phone calls, you'll probably get 3 to 5 honest answers, which are more than enough to begin making an informed decision.

Second, as I've recommended so many times with so many different things, spend some time on the Internet searching for each school's name followed by the words "scam," "rip-off," or "complaints." Be sure to check with your local Better Business Bureau (BBB) as well. Just remember that even the best schools get some complaints, so focus on looking for common trends among the complaints. If people are consistently saying that "it was a waste of money" or "I couldn't get hired," then you should look elsewhere.

Lastly, find out if the school is accredited by one of the regional accrediting bodies for schools or is endorsed by your desired vocation's professional organizations. If it's not either accredited or endorsed, you should skip that school unless local employers strongly recommend the program.

Traditional Aid for Nontraditional Educations

Whether you're considering getting your college degree in a nontraditional manner or attending a vocational school, you can usually still count on many of the most popular forms of financial aid. In fact, due to the substantially lower cost of attending some of these schools, the financial aid you would receive either way might go a lot further. It's feasible that a lower-income student attending a vocational school costing $10,000 or less could have his entire education paid for through standard government programs.

All of the following financial aid programs can be used at traditional colleges offering nontraditional learning, 100 percent nontraditional schools, and trade/vocational schools, as long as they are legitimate schools eligible to receive Federal Title IV funding:

- Pell Grants
- Most state grants
- Federal student loans
- The American Opportunity Tax Credit
- The Lifetime Learning Credit

Unlike federal financial aid programs, scholarship programs might be a little more exclusive in where they let you use them. Many scholarship programs allow their awards to be used only at a four-year institution for a student who is actually working toward a degree. Again, this varies from scholarship to scholarship, so you should not give up applying, but just make sure you're only submitting applications that meet your choice of schools.

FLUNK-PROOF FINANCES

Be wary of schools that require the entire cost of attendance for their program to be paid upfront, even if you're using financial aid. If the program ends up being substandard and you drop out, you might have a tough time getting your money back and might end up owing Uncle Sam some dough.

As always, students should check for scholarship opportunities at their institution of choice, including trade and vocational schools. Further, if you or your student does attend a trade school to acquire a specific set of skills, you'll need to check for scholarship opportunities from both local and national professional organizations within that field.

The Least You Need to Know

- Nontraditional education is booming, and degrees from legitimate institutions are almost always held in the same regard as those earned through traditional methods.
- Nontraditional educations can save you big bucks on room, board, fees, transportation, and missed work opportunities.
- Each type of nontraditional education has its own pluses and minuses that you need to consider carefully.
- Vocational schools offer a great option for someone who wants a high-paying career but has minimal amounts of time and money to commit to an education.
- The vast majority of sources of financial aid are available for students who pursue nontraditional degrees.

Short–Term Savings Strategies

In This Chapter

- Trimming your budget to pay for college
- Best tips for earning some extra income
- Short-term investment strategies
- Choosing the right account structure

I'm probably going to date myself with this a bit, but as a kid, one of my favorite shows was *MacGyver*. In addition to the lead character sporting a mullet that just wouldn't quit, the show was wonderfully predictable. In the last 15 minutes, MacGyver would end up trapped, stranded, or surrounded by bad guys. Yet through sheer resource-fulness, he would manage to escape the situation every time, usually by building something like a helicopter out of a paperclip, a broom, and half of a ham sandwich.

Well, it's your turn to play MacGyver. But instead of building a nuclear reactor out a hair dryer and a Styrofoam cup, you're scrambling to scrape together as much cash from your monthly budget as you can. That's because every dollar you can pile up and every penny you can wring out of your budget will lower your ongoing need to beg and borrow. Even if you have just 3 or 6 months, you can begin making changes today that will arm you with more money when you start college, as well as free up cash flow during college that you can devote toward ongoing tuition expenses.

Revisiting Your Budget

Although most people reading this book probably wouldn't consider themselves rich, the reality is that a lot of money passes through your hands in your lifetime. Granted, a lot of money that comes into your household goes right back out, but it's still a lot of money nonetheless.

As I talked about in my book, *The Complete Idiot's Guide to Getting Out of Debt* (Alpha Books, 2009), the average American easily earns in excess of $1,000,000 during his working lifetime. Although I have no doubt that much of this goes toward nonnegotiable fixed expenses in many people's lives, I also know from years of experience that a whole lot of money just evaporates.

This is especially true when you stop to consider the money that comes into your household that you don't count as income, such as gifts or support from a former spouse or partner. In short, there is a lot you can do to free up a few thousand dollars per year, without having to wear burlap sacks or go Dumpster diving for your next meal.

FLUNK-PROOF FINANCES

I've said it before (in my other books), and I'll say it again: *budgets don't work.* For most people, a budget is a great attempt to rein in their spending, but it has no real teeth to it. To really get control of your spending, you need to create a spending plan that sets aside money for your hard-to-control expenses into a separate account each month. That way, you don't need to keep trying to remember how much you've budgeted for different expenses. When that account hits zero, you're done with those expenses until the next paycheck.

Redefining Necessity

At the heart of freeing up cash in your budget is a semi-painful discussion with yourself about the difference between *need* and *want.* In other words, what makes something a *necessity* versus just a *nicety.* By reexamining that fine line, you'll very likely find a substantial chunk of money.

To do this properly, you're going to need to do an honest analysis of all your household's expenses. This means that you can't just guess about what you spend where, but that you actually need to go pull out your credit card and bank statements, get your check register, and do the same for anyone else you share finances with.

When you have these in front of you, flip back to the College Cash Strategy Worksheet you've been working on in Appendix B. Under the "Spending and Savings Strategies" section, you'll notice a table with three columns that looks a bit like a budget. There are three columns: "Actual," "Compromise," and "Net Savings." You're going to use all your statements and go back and add up the amounts you're spending in each category under the "Actual" column. Then, you're going to go take a walk, work out, or do whatever you need to do to clear your mind.

After an hour, come back and look at those expenses and ask yourself, "Do I really *need* to spend that much on clothes, entertainment, or dining out? Or, do I just spend that much on those things without thinking about it?"

Then, for each item, if possible, write down a number in the "Compromise" column, which represents how much you think you can trim your household expenses for a few years. After that, figure out how much you could save annually by each new "Compromise" amount from the original "Actual" amount. Finally, multiply your savings amount for each line by 12 to see how much money you could truly free up over the course of one year of college and write the results in the "Net Savings" column.

Once you've done all of that and come up with an annual savings number, work your way down the worksheet, multiplying your annual savings amount by the number of years you're going to be paying for college, and subtracting this amount from the amount of money you still had to come up with after the first few sections. The result—what is left over after you subtract this out—tells you how much money you're going to have to come up with through scholarships, loans, and so on.

CHEAT SHEET

If there has ever been a time to push your ex for the child support or alimony owed you, this is it. If the relationship has not completely soured, put on your friendliest face and invite your ex to participate for the sake of your child. If there are concerns about giving you the money, provide instructions on how to make payments directly to the school. If your ex won't help out but is obligated, seek legal representation.

Save Thousands with Easy Budget Cuts

The following budget cuts can save you some big bucks, which you can immediately funnel into paying for college. But, they're only doable if you view them as luxuries (wants) not necessities (needs). In fact, I can almost guarantee you that if I could fast-forward to five years after college and ask you if you'd rather have thousands more in student loans to repay or have gotten rid of these "necessities" (even temporarily), you would choose the latter in a heartbeat.

- **Cancel your cable TV ($600 average annual savings)**—To this day, I'm utterly amazed by families who tell me they don't have money to reach their financial goals, yet have $100 to $200 per month in their budget for cable or satellite TV. Even at the low end for the most basic packages, it can run you

$50 per month. I'd suggest you ditch the cable TV for the next few years and pocket the savings. Heck, nowadays you can see most of your favorite shows online for free anyway through sites like Hulu.com.

- **Use coupons ($600 average annual savings)**—If you aren't already using coupons to do your grocery shopping, you're missing the boat. I know it feels like you don't have the time, but guess what? *You don't have the money, either.* A family of four using the coupons from their Sunday paper can easily save $100 per month, if not more, while a student living on her own should have no problem saving $50 per month.

  I'm addicted to coupon websites, especially TheGroceryGame.com and CouponMom.com. These websites help people strategize which coupons to use, when, and where to maximize their savings. On average, my wife can get $1,000 of groceries for between $500 and $600, saving our family over $5,000 per year!

- **Write letters ($250 average annual savings)**—One of the biggest financial black holes I find in people's budgets is gift giving. That's because most people do not actually include money in their monthly budgets for once-a-year gift-giving events like holidays, birthdays, anniversaries, and so on. Rather, they just spend on top of their already stretched budget. Ironically, speaking from my own experience, I've forgotten who gave me 90 percent of the gifts I've ever received and half of them don't even get used anymore. Instead of wasting money on this, consider writing a letter to your loved ones, telling them exactly why they matter to you. Chances are they'll keep that letter a lot longer than that new sweater.

- **Take your lunch ($780 average annual savings)**—I love eating out; it's just plain fun. Unfortunately, it can also be expensive. Although I'm not suggesting you and your loved ones don't occasionally treat yourself to a night at the local greasy spoon, I would suggest that regularly buying your meals at the sandwich shop next to your work or the cafeteria at your college can nickel and dime you to death. Every time you pack your own lunch or dinner, you're going to save roughly $5. If you do that three times per week, that's a savings of roughly $780 per year, per person!

- **Buy secondhand ($250 average annual savings)**—Although you might not want to buy the outfit you wear to your next job interview at your local secondhand store, you'd be surprised how nice much of the stuff is at these stores. I bought one of my favorite jackets almost 10 years ago for $1.50.

Especially if you have little ones who are going to grow (or rip) out of clothes, consider shopping secondhand. I can promise you that no one will ever know.

- **Quit smoking ($1,800 minimum savings per year)**—At an average cost of $5 per pack, you'll watch nearly $7,500 go up in smoke over a four-year period. That'd pay a lot of tuition. If there's ever been a time to quit, now is it.

- **Ditch your house phone ($250 average annual savings)**—In this day and age, a landline telephone can be one of the most redundant expenses in many people's budgets. The reality is that most people spend 90 percent of their phone time on their cell phones but continue to pay $20 per month for a landline phone. Ditch the landline phone, and pay for a few textbooks.

- **Cancel memberships and subscriptions ($250 average annual savings)**—Whether it is a newspaper in your driveway every morning or a membership to your local gym, many people have numerous recurring expenses that are automatically drafted from their bank accounts each month. If you are not using these on a frequent basis, get rid of them. Buy just the Sunday paper at your local grocer and go for a run or a hike instead of paying for a gym membership you never use.

- **Use your local library ($100 average annual savings)**—Whether you love movies, enjoy curling up with a good book, or pay exorbitant Internet fees to check your e-mail a couple times per week, consider using your local library. Aside from the obvious access to books, most libraries have a pretty good assortment of recently released movies and entire seasons of TV shows, all of which can be borrowed for free. Last year, my wife easily saved over $100 borrowing the books she needed for her book club, as opposed to buying them.

- **Adjust your thermostat by 3 degrees ($100 average annual savings)**—It's true, dialing your house's thermostat up or down 3 degrees during the summer or winter can save you roughly 10 percent of your heating and electrical bills. This can easily pencil out to $100 per year, even more if you live in an area with extreme temperatures.

- **Stop paying for your bank account ($100 average annual savings)**—If you're still paying a monthly fee for a bank account, you're missing the boat. Well over 100 FDIC-insured banks around the country offer free checking and savings accounts, on top of paying you interest on your money!

> **WORLD WIDE WISDOM**
>
> Some of the best bank accounts are from credit unions, small town banks, and Internet-based institutions, all of which are insured by the government. My local community bank offers a free checking account, with no minimums, that pays five times the national average interest rate for checking accounts. Check out BankDeals.Blogspot.com and Bankrate.com to find accounts that will minimize your cost and maximize your return.

Ten Sources of Extra Income

Although it might not be a pace that you want to keep the rest of your life, investing a few extra hours each week can lead to a few thousand dollars more that you can put toward college costs. Unlike cutting costs, I wouldn't try to embrace all of these strategies. But I'd pick at least one and run with it:

- **Rent out a room**—There are few things that can put more money in your pocket with less effort than renting out a room in your house or apartment. Whether you are a student with some space to spare or a parent whose student is off at school, an extra $200 to $600 per month will go a long way. Heck, in college we rented out our gardening shed to a guy for $200 per month!

- **Pick up an extra shift**—Become that guy or gal at work who is always hitting up people to take their extra shifts. Just taking one extra 8-hour shift per month at $10 per hour can put nearly $1,000 extra in your pocket each year.

- **Use your brain**—There's a lot of extra money to be made for people who have a gift for teaching. Substitute teaching at your local K–12 school can pay $50 to $120 per day, depending on where you live, while teaching a few hours per week at your local community college if you have a Master's degree can easily net you $1,000 per month. Even tutoring teenagers in the same area as your major can earn you $10 to $20 per hour part time. The great thing is that all these roles have very flexible hours, making them easy to fit around your existing job.

- **Become Santa's helper**—Your local shopping mall needs a lot of help starting around Thanksgiving of every year, with stores recruiting everything from seasonal gift-wrappers to nighttime shelf stockers. One stroll through the mall could help you or your student earn $500 to $1,000 in a short window of time.

- **Become a recycling pro**—I mentioned this in a previous book and have heard great feedback from families who've tried it. By simply being the person who rounds up all the cans and bottles at your kid's local Little League game or in your dorm, you can easily net $10 to $20 per week. To this day, I keep a few trash bags in my car in case I run across the mother lode of cans at some event.

- **Become a mystery shopper**—Although you should ignore all the cheesy classifieds and obvious e-mail spam you get, there are legitimate "secret shopper" jobs out there. The pay is not glamorous, but you often get to keep the items you buy, especially if it is food. I'm signed up with a service that literally begs me to eat at local restaurants and fill out a questionnaire. Check out National Shopping Service; Intellishop; and Service Intelligence, Inc.

- **Dust off your writing skills**—You know how I got my start as a full-time writer? I was trying to make some extra money by writing online over my holiday vacation. There are a number of great online writing communities out there, like Helium.com, where anyone can write and you're paid based on how many people read your articles.

- **Turn your hobby into gold**—Back when I used to do full-time youth work, my wife began making our Christmas gifts to help save some money. It didn't take long before she was selling her handmade jewelry to friends and family and earning a nice little side income. Check out *The Complete Idiot's Guide to Selling Your Crafts* by Chris Franchetti Michaels (Alpha Books, 2010) for more pointers on turning your hobbies into dollars.

- **Open a home daycare**—I've known a number of parents who have put their own adult children through school by watching other people's kids during the day. Home daycare providers are experiencing a steady demand for their services, especially with more and more parents having to go back to work in this rocky economy. Even a home daycare that only watches children on the weekends can easily net $1,000 to $2,000 per month.

- **Have an annual garage sale**—It's amazing how much junk you can accumulate in just one year. Consider timing your spring cleaning with an annual garage sale to help raise enough money to pay for your textbooks or other costs. Even better, send an e-mail to your friends and family telling them you're having a garage sale to raise tuition and see if they have any stuff they want to get rid of as well!

Say No to Gifts, Yes to Tuition

Before Grandma sticks you with another 12-pack of socks, let your closest friends and family know that you'd prefer tuition instead. Heck, they're probably agonizing over what to get you anyway, so you'll save them the trouble of driving around town by simply telling them that helping to fund an education would be the best gift they could give.

To make it easier for those wishing to contribute, as well as give them some level of comfort that their gift is going to be used for your child's education, consider opening a Section 529 account that others can contribute to. As the parent and the person who opened the account, you retain control of how the funds are invested and when they're paid out, but it helps (and may even encourage) people to feel like they're truly "setting money aside" for someone.

The Best Short-Term Investments

I used to love trying to build houses of playing cards as a kid. But I never got past the second or third story before I breathed on it wrong and the whole thing came tumbling down. Trying to get the most out of the savings that you're scraping together can be a little like that if you're not careful. If you get too aggressive or try to earn too much on it, you'll expose yourself to unnecessary risk. So here's the punch line: keep this money far away from the stock market or anything else where you can lose your *principal*.

The stock market is absolutely wonderful for long-term investments, returning an average of 10 percent per year since before the Great Depression. But that nice and neat 10 percent average is actually comprised of some ho-hum flat years, some incredible years, and some years that make stockbrokers jump out of windows. Because it'll always be easier for you to do better than a flat year in the stock market, and a 20 to 30 percent down year is definitely not something you should toy with, that really leaves you choosing between different *fixed-income investments* as a parking place for your savings.

DEFINITION

Principal refers to the original amount someone invests in something. The safest investments have no principal risk associated with them. Typically, these are **fixed-income investments,** whose return comes primarily from the fixed amount of interest they pay, as opposed to the value of the principal going up.

As any owner of junk bonds can tell you, though, not all fixed-income investments are created equal. In addition to making sure you get a good interest rate on whatever investment you park your money in, you need to ensure that the entity you're "loaning" your money to is going to stick around long enough to pay you your interest and principal. This means that loaning your money to the U.S. government at 3 percent is probably a lot smarter than loaning it to your third cousin Earl at 8 percent, even though the rate from the government isn't that great.

Money Market and Savings Accounts

Depending on the movement of interest rates at the time of you reading this book, money market and savings accounts might be one of the best short-term places to park your money, or one of the worst. As with every investment listed in this section, you'll need to compare both the rates you can earn on these accounts as well as their safety.

Safety, you ask? Aren't savings and money market accounts insured by the government?

Yes and no. Generally, savings accounts are *FDIC-insured* up to $250,000, which means that the U.S. government ultimately backs both your principal and the interest to which you're entitled. Money market accounts, on the other hand, usually have no guarantees associated with them, even though most professionals (including myself) consider them very safe. However, money market accounts can hypothetically lose some of their value, even if the money market fund invests only in government bonds. It's highly unlikely, but it's possible.

DEFINITION

FDIC insurance provides a guarantee to depositors at participating banks that their deposits are protected even if the bank goes out of business. It's important to note that brokerage firms are not covered by the FDIC (Federal Deposit Insurance Corporation), but by the SIPC (Securities Investor Protection Corporation), which is not directly backed by the government.

The primary advantage of using either a money market or savings account is that the money is highly liquid; in other words, it's easily accessible. These accounts are essentially bank accounts that pay interest, without any commitment to leave your money there for any length of time.

You should probably use a savings or money market account if:

- Rates on these accounts are the same or greater than CDs or Treasury instruments.

- You're going to college in less than a year.

- You're starting with a relatively small amount and adding to it on a regular basis.

- You cannot qualify for a prepaid tuition plan or your state's plan gives you limited flexibility on where you can attend school.

Certificates of Deposit

One of the classic trade-offs with fixed-income investing is that, generally, the longer you are willing to commit to not touching your money, the higher the interest rate you will earn. There are, of course, times where this is not true, but they are rare.

Certificates of deposit (CDs) are essentially a commitment on your part to a bank to deposit your money for a certain amount of time in exchange for a preset rate of interest. Typically, if you try to access your money prior to the maturity date of the CD, you'll pay a penalty or forfeit some of your interest.

CDs issued by a FDIC-insured bank are also FDIC-insured, so generally you have no risk to your nest egg if you buy them straight from a bank. However, some CDs are not FDIC-insured and are often sold by the fixed-income departments of Wall Street brokerages. You should avoid these for safety reasons, as well as another type of brokerage CD called "secondary CD's," which can be an accounting nightmare at tax time.

You should consider using a CD to park your short-term savings if:

- The CD is FDIC-insured.

- The rates are at least one-quarter of 1 percent higher than money market and savings account rates.

- There is no chance that you'll need to access that money prior to the date of the CD.

- Their rates are below 4 to 5 percent and you're not eligible for a prepaid tuition plan run by your state.

- Their rates are above 4 to 5 percent, if you're eligible for a prepaid tuition plan run by your state.

U.S. Treasury Bonds

If you're looking for a simple place to park the money and aren't worried about grinding out an extra quarter of a percent on your savings, then government bonds probably aren't for you. But if you have $1,000 or more—especially if you're sitting on $10,000 or more—you should give U.S. Treasury bonds a look.

WORLD WIDE WISDOM

The best place to get any type of government-issued bond, note, or bill is TreasuryDirect.gov. This is the official site of the U.S. Treasury, and it lets you purchase bonds with no fee and much smaller minimums than if you do so through secondary institutions or brokerage houses. That translates to a higher rate of return for you.

Several classes of government bonds are available, only a few of which are attractive to someone saving for the short-term:

- **Treasury bills (T-Bills)**—The shortest term of all government bonds, T-Bills can be bought to mature in 4, 13, 26, or 52 weeks. They don't actually pay interest separately but are issued at a discount to their maturity values. For example, a T-Bill that matures at $100 might be purchased for $97 today. That $3 increase at maturity represents the interest you've earned.

- **Treasury notes**—These are issued in increments as short as 2 years and as long as 10 years. They pay interest every 6 months, which most people deposit into a money market account until they have enough to buy another.

- **Zero coupon bonds**—Wall Street brokerage firms usually offer a large selection of quasi-Treasury bonds, known by funky names such as STRIPS, TINTS, or TIGERS. Though the discussion of how these bonds came to be is beyond the scope of this book, you should feel comfortable buying these as well, as long as they are based on U.S. Treasury securities. In a nutshell, these zero coupon bonds are issued at a discount compared to what they'll eventually pay out when they mature. Your return equals the difference between what you paid for and what it matures at, without the hassle of having to invest the small interest payments you might receive from things like a CD or other types of bonds.

One thing that makes U.S. Treasury bills and notes attractive is that their interest is not taxed by individual U.S. states as income tax. That means that a U.S. Treasury note paying 5 percent would actually leave you with a little more after taxes than a CD paying 5 percent because the interest on the CD is fully taxable by your state.

To decide if a CD or savings account is better than a government-issued bill, you need to do a simple computation known as the *tax-equivalent yield (TEY)*. The TEY essentially shows you what a fully taxable CD or savings account would have to earn to beat the tax-advantaged government bond.

DEFINITION

The **tax-equivalent yield (TEY)** shows what a fully taxable bond would have to earn to have the same after-tax yield as a bond that is not taxed by either your federal or state government.

To calculate the TEY, you divide the interest rate on a government bond by 1 minus your state income tax rate. For example, if a U.S. Treasury note was paying 5 percent and you expect to be taxed 8 percent by your state, you would calculate the TEY as .05/(1.00 – .08). This yields a TEY of 5.43 percent, meaning that if a CD or money market account was not paying above 5.43 percent, you'd be better off after taxes to stick with the U.S. Treasury note.

Short-term Treasury bills and notes are your best bet when:

- You have at least 3 to 6 months until you need the money.

- The other options can't beat the TEY on U.S. Treasury instruments, taking into account your state's income tax bracket.

- Their rates are below 4 to 5 percent and you're not eligible for a prepaid tuition plan run by your state.

- Their rates are above 4 to 5 percent, if you're eligible for a prepaid tuition plan run by your state.

Section 529 Prepaid Tuition Accounts

I saved the best (and my favorite) short-term savings option for the last. Unfortunately, not everyone will be able to use Section 529 Prepaid Tuition accounts for one reason or another. Specifically, these accounts must usually be opened no later than age 18, are only offered by some states, and might have minimum amounts of tuition that must be purchased (deposited).

These plans allow you to prepay tuition now, at today's rates, for your future education. Because tuition costs have been rising steadily at a rate of at least 4 to 5 percent per year, this will generally outperform most other short-term fixed income investments in most economies. Sweetening the pot is the fact that many states actually give income tax deductions or credits for contributing money to these plans as well.

Section 529 Prepaid Tuition plans are ideal when:

- A student is under age 18 with at least one year to go until the money is needed.

- Interest rates on other fixed incomes are under 4 to 5 percent.

- You live in a state where an income tax deduction or credit is offered for contributing to Section 529 plans.

- Your state's Section 529 plan allows students to go out of state or there is a high likelihood they'll go to school in state.

FLUNK-PROOF FINANCES

Due to the hoops that you have to jump through and the costs you might incur to liquidate certain types of investments, parents with less than a year or two until college should probably avoid sticking college funds in life insurance, annuities, retirement accounts, gold, collectibles, or ownership in a business.

The Best Accounts for Short-Term Savings

For first-time investors, the distinction between an account and an investment can be a little confusing. In basic terms, most of the investments previously mentioned in this chapter (CDs, bonds, and so on) can be owned in a variety of types of accounts, similar to how the same type of flower might be planted in a number of different pots.

Each type of account has different tax features, effects on financial aid, and withdrawal rules that need to be considered. Generally, if you've already filed your financial aid paperwork and you have less than 6 to 12 months until you are going to use the money, it's best just to own the assets in your own name and open a plain-old vanilla account. If they're for your child, it probably is not worth the hassle to try to create a special account just to avoid $10 to $20 in taxes.

However, if you have longer than 6 to 12 months; have not filed your FAFSA or CSS Profile yet; and have (or will have) significantly more than $1,000 by the time you start tapping it, you should consider some of these other account options.

Section 529 Accounts

In addition to using the Section 529 accounts discussed in Chapters 4 and 11 to purchase prepaid tuition, you can use them as a savings account. Depending on the state, they might or might not offer a fixed interest option or money market account that might fit your needs. The biggest advantage of Section 529 accounts, however, is that the earnings can be withdrawn tax-free when they're used for qualified college expenses. They might also qualify for a state income tax deduction, depending on your state's laws.

From a financial aid point of view, Section 529 plans owned by parents are treated as assets of the parents, meaning that 5.64 percent of the assets are expected to be used annually to fund college. This affects financial aid awards far less than accounts where the money is considered an asset of the child, which is expected to be used at a rate of 20 percent per year.

See Appendix F for a list of Section 529 plans organized by state.

Coverdell Educational Savings Accounts

Likewise, the Coverdell Educational Savings Accounts (ESAs) discussed in Chapters 4 and 11 function similarly to Section 529 plans, in that the assets can be withdrawn tax-free when they're used to pay for college and are considered a parental asset for financial aid purposes (5.64 percent versus 20 percent required usage). However, Coverdell ESAs do not offer a state income tax deduction and cannot be opened for someone over 18. Further, any unused money in the account must be distributed to the child by the time he reaches age 30, unless you have a family member under 30 to which the account can be rolled over.

In short, these accounts don't make sense for most people compared to a Section 529 plan. The one exception is that the money in Coverdell ESAs can be used for K–12 tuition at a private school as well. So if there is a chance that you won't use the money for college and might need it for private school tuition, this account might make sense.

Custodial Accounts

These were the original college savings account decades ago and have generally been replaced by Section 529 plans and Coverdell ESAs. These accounts essentially allow a parent to make a gift of cash or securities to a child, whose income and gains are taxed at a much lower rate than the parent's.

The problem is that these accounts are considered an asset of the child and count far more against financial aid than Section 529 plans, Coverdell ESAs, and savings accounts held just in a parent's name. The only time custodial accounts make sense is if a parent has stocks or mutual funds with built-in gains that she needs to sell to pay for college. If this is the case, you should pay a visit to your tax advisor to get expert guidance on transferring these to a custodial account and then selling them.

The Least You Need to Know

- Before you stress about financial aid and scholarships, take a hard look at your budget and see how much you can free up for the next few years.
- A little bit of creative extra income will go a long way toward knocking down your tall college bills.
- Don't get lured into risky short-term investments, even if they promise a much higher return.
- A high-yield, FDIC-insured money market or savings account might be the best option for parents with less than 12 months until college.
- Prepaid tuition plans can be the best savings option for parents with more than 12 months until college.

Working Your Way Through College

19

In This Chapter

- Creating your own financial aid
- Work-study and off-campus employment
- Making the most of summer jobs
- Pitching in around the house

A few years ago, there was a video floating around the Internet of a 16-year-old girl being led outside by her parents. Initially, you couldn't tell why one of the parents had his hands over her eyes, but then the new green Saab convertible came into the picture. When he uncovered her eyes, the daughter shrieked, began to cry, and couldn't speak for a few moments. Through the sobs, you could begin to make out her words. "It's the wrong color. It's the wrong color!"

For those of you who haven't figured it out, we live in an age of over-entitlement. Not only do kids (and many adults) think they deserve whatever it is their hearts desire, but they are also pretty sure they should have it right now. Sadly, just enough parents are caving to their kids' demands that those of us who take a stand often look like the bad guys.

When it comes to college, you need to take a stand. If you're putting someone else through college, you have every right to insist that he help foot the bill. Not only that, but if you're a student, working can be one of the single best things you can do to defray the costs of an education.

The Lost Art of Working Your Way Through College

You don't have to go back more than 30 or 40 years to find that many parents—even middle-class parents—saw college as a privilege, not a right. Many were willing to help their children pay for an education, but they very much expected them to help foot the bill. Often, these parents paid tuition but left the living expenses up to the student. This left many students slinging pizza, waiting tables, or parking cars to make ends meet.

WORLD WIDE WISDOM

The Internet is loaded with websites that help students find part-time and seasonal jobs. Two of the best are USAJobs.com/studentjobs, run by the Department of Labor, and CoolWorks.com.

Many of these young adults developed a true appreciation for both a hard day's work and how a college degree would change their employment options. Unlike many students today, who expect the world to beat a path to their doors, the students of yesteryear were simply thankful for a job and were committed to working their way up in a company.

I know that might seem like a bit of Grandpa's "I had to walk uphill both ways to school, barefoot and in the snow" lecture, but I sincerely believe that a student working at least part time during his college years makes as much or more sense than him sitting around playing videogames with his roommates. If you're the student, not only will you be taking pressure off yourself to land a juicy financial aid package or to take out larger loans, but you're a lot more likely to stay focused and out of trouble. If you're a parent, your student working a part-time job during school and a full-time job during the summer can easily shave $5,000 to $10,000 off the amount of money you need to come up with each year.

Working Part Time at School

Although holding down a full-time, 40-hour-per-week job is unrealistic for a full-time college student, working 10 to 15 hours a week is very reasonable. In fact, it helps create a set routine that you or your student must adhere to, making it all that much easier to also schedule regular times for study, rest, and play.

From a financial point of view, a student working 10 hours per week earning $8 per hour will earn roughly $1,200 pre-tax per semester. For a student attending only the fall and winter semesters each year, that is roughly $2,400 pre-tax, or $300 to $400 per month. That'll take a nice bite out of any unfunded tuition, room, and board. That's not counting the money a student can make working part or full time when he's home for the summer and holidays.

However, when it comes to working while enrolled, not all jobs and opportunities are created equal. In fact, some jobs can prove downright counterproductive to getting an education, while others can serve as a "double-dip," providing valuable benefits on top of a part-time paycheck. So perhaps the biggest question you'll need to answer if you or your student takes on a part-time job is whether it'll be through a work-study program or an unrelated outside employer.

Work-Study Programs

Work-study programs are a special type of financial aid that allows students to earn money for tuition by working in specially designated jobs. Usually these jobs, which are required to pay at least minimum wage, are offered on a student's campus or in partnership with a local nonprofit organization.

Most opportunities for work-study funds are offered through the Federal Work-Study (FWS) program administered by the Department of Education. The FWS program provides more than $1 billion annually to over 3,400 colleges and universities around the United States, with the average award in 2009 being approximately $1,500 per student. For anyone doing the math, at minimum wage, that works out to roughly 200 to 250 hours of work over the course of a school year, or 10 to 15 hours per week while school is in session.

In addition to the FWS program, many states provide their own work-study programs, as well as some schools having their own internally funded work-study programs.

Eligibility for work-study programs is primarily determined based on a student's demonstrated financial need. In other words, those who need it the most are the ones who tend to get it. Financial need is primarily determined through the calculation of someone's expected family contribution (EFC; see Chapter 8). The lower the EFC, the more likely someone is to qualify for work-study.

Unrelated Outside Employment

A work-study program might not be the best option for three main reasons. First, a student might simply not qualify based on her EFC to college. Second, the student might need to make substantially more than the few thousand dollars she can earn under a work-study program. Lastly, the student might be able to earn a much higher hourly rate doing something else besides work-study programs, especially if she has special training like being a lifeguard or childcare provider.

Here are some of the key things that a student and her family need to consider when evaluating off-campus, non–work-study employment:

- **The commute**—Having to walk or ride your bike a couple of blocks to your on-campus job is significantly cheaper and less time-consuming than having to drive or use public transportation to get to an off-campus job. This usage of time and money can be especially large if a student is living in a major metropolitan area like Los Angeles, New York, or Miami, as opposed to a small college town.

- **The fringe benefits**—Some companies such as Starbucks, Barnes & Noble, and Whole Foods Markets offer part-timers the ability to buy cheap group health insurance. Further, countless companies offer employees discounts on their purchases, which can help lower your direct and indirect college costs substantially, especially if you're working for a grocery store, travel provider, or clothing store.

- **Temptation**—Not all jobs are great for younger college students, no matter how noble their aspirations to work are. Whether it is tending bar or working at an establishment that offers a tempting discount on unnecessary purchases, the choices these jobs can lead to very quickly offset the monetary gain.

The Top Ten Paying Off-Campus Jobs

I've always figured that if you wanted to open a labor-intensive business, a college town is a heck of place to think about doing it. You have a ton of people with strong backs and low expectations who are willing to work for minimum wage. That doesn't mean that every student in a college town is earning the bare minimum, though. As many smart students have figured out, there are all kinds of jobs that break the $10-per-hour barrier, but you have to hustle to get them:

- **Lifeguard**—You don't have to look like David Hasselhoff or Pamela Anderson to make a double-digit hourly wage, nor do you have to have years of training. A short course at your local YMCA or Red Cross will get you certified as a lifeguard who can work at a local community pool. Because it does require some—albeit minimal—training, there'll be a lot fewer people fighting for these jobs.

- **Nanny**—Although the ideal candidate for a nanny position is usually female, I've known more than a few guys who served as a "manny" for a brood of rambunctious boys. Either way, if you're lucky enough to score a nanny position, it can easily pay $10 to $15 per hour or more than $100 for a day's work, plus meals. Again, a trip to your local YMCA or Red Cross for a first aid and CPR certification can greatly increase your marketability.

- **Bank teller**—It doesn't take a degree in accounting to cash checks or count out $20 bills. All it takes to land a job as a bank teller is a high school diploma and an attention to detail. Many teller jobs start off at $8 to $9 per hour, but raises often come quickly for those who do a good job.

- **Waiter or waitress**—There's no doubt that slinging hash browns, burgers, or coffee at a local restaurant can be exhausting, but many people don't realize that the pay can be five-star. The trick is to find someplace where the tips are good. If you're lucky, you can easily make $15 to $20 per hour on a busy night.

- **Swim instructor**—In college, my wife made $25 to $50 per hour giving private swim instructions to children. All it took was a couple hundred flyers and a bubbly attitude, and she was raking in the easy money. So if you or your student loves the water and will be going to school in a town where many of the residents have their own pools, don't hesitate to dive in.

- **Commissioned salesperson**—Although selling insurance or real estate might be out of the question for a college student, many local retailers hire part-time salespeople who earn both an hourly wage and a small commission. Especially if you or your student is a mini-expert on something, be it make-up or lawnmowers, you should look into these opportunities.

- **Construction**—Local contractors are always in need of part-time help. If you're willing to carry boxes, unload supplies, and cart away the trash, you can consistently earn $10 to $12 per hour without a problem.

- **Delivery person**—From pizza to flowers to legal documents, students with a reliable ride can rack up the dollars as they rack up the miles. If possible, try to find a position that reimburses your gas in addition to your time.

- **Anything night or graveyard**—If you or your student is going to be up late studying anyway, you might as well get paid to do it. If you're willing to burn the midnight oil for your local motel, gate-guarded community, or 24-hour call center, you'll typically get a substantial increase in pay over those who will only work the day shift.

- **Tutoring services**—With more and more students trying to claw their way into college, more parents than ever are hiring tutors to help coach their students through difficult subjects. This is especially true with math, science, and foreign language classes. By simply dropping off some flyers with the secretaries at your local high schools and posting them in local coffee shops, you can easily find a job that pays $10 to $20 per hour.

FLUNK-PROOF FINANCES

Many of the best jobs for college students are paid as if the student is an independent contractor. That means the student is on the hook for paying self-employment taxes (15.3 percent) on her income, on top of whatever income taxes she owes on those earnings. For the student not expecting this, it can leave her having to come up with a few hundred to a few thousand dollars in a hurry.

Making the Most of Your Summer Break

Using the summers wisely can dramatically change what it costs to put a student through school. In addition to taking low-cost classes at your local community college, which can save thousands, students can put in full workweeks and save up a lot of money.

How much money will vary depending on how long a student's summer break is, as well as what type of job he has. But even in the most conservative of scenarios, a summer job can go a long way toward meeting any remaining college costs. Consider a student working just 30 hours per week and earning only the federal minimum wage, from June 15 to August 15. Over that period, he'd earn nearly $2,000. If a student were to find a summer job that could pay him $10 per hour for a full 40-hour workweek and manage to work the typical 2½-month summer, he'd pile up nearly $5,000!

If you own a small business, having your student work for free over the summer can be a smart move. Having him pitch in around the shop, as part of your paying for his college, can save you paying wages and payroll taxes to someone else. Simply have him work for "free," keeping the money you would have paid in your bank account and later using it for college costs.

The whole summer job experience is usually a major financial bust for most students. It typically begins with them sleeping in for the first week they're home, with Mom or Dad reminding them daily that they need to find a job. When the job search actually starts, all the good jobs are taken, so it usually takes another 1 or 2 weeks to find a low-paying job that they'll spend all summer complaining about.

To make the most out of you or your student's summer, you have to have the right mindset and start planning well ahead of time. Most importantly, you have to make sure he's on board with the idea of using his summer to contribute financially to his college bills. If he's not, you need to have a heart-to-heart about how hard you're working and whether he should be chipping in.

Here are some tips to ensure that you or your student max out the summer earning potential:

- **Have a resumé ready**—Don't show up at a potential employer without a good cover letter and an error-free resumé. Be sure to highlight your academic track record, previous work experience, and pay history if it was more than a dollar or two above minimum wage.

- **Nail down concrete dates**—Before you're ever in front of a potential employer, you'll need to make sure you know when school ends, when you'll be home, and when you'll have to head back to school. Not knowing these in advance can give the wrong first impression to a potential employer.

- **Start looking during the holidays**—The time to look for summer employment is in the middle of winter. Although it is still technically a little too early for most businesses to begin hiring their summer and seasonal help, it's a great time to get your name on an employer's radar and get a feel for who's going to be hiring.

> **CHEAT SHEET**
>
> As with many other things, one of the best ways to find a juicy summer job is to ask the people you know. A month or two before summer starts, send an e-mail to your friends and family letting them know that you're hoping for a summer job that pays at least $10 per hour. You'll probably be surprised at the number of doors that open.

- **Pound the pavement at spring break**—March and April are the best times to seal the deal on summer employment opportunities. This is when employers are hiring for their key summer positions whose pay is not the bottom of the barrel. Further, if you're hoping to land an internship related to your studies, this is the window of time to do it.

- **Provide the right contact info**—If Mom or Dad has to play secretary for a student, a lot of good opportunities are going to be missed. So be sure potential employers are provided with a number and an e-mail where they can reach the student when he's back at school.

Say Hello to the New Maid

If your student (or you) can't land a summer job for one reason or another, don't hesitate to make her the family's personal assistant, maid, groundskeeper, and discount shopper for the summer. These are all roles that can cost a family big bucks, a lot of time, and a good amount of their sanity.

A parent with a student who is home for the summer shouldn't hesitate to mandate that the student absorb these roles, with the savings being put toward college expenses. Here are just a few ideas of how your student can contribute:

- **Lawn care**—Saves $50 to $100 per month minimum
- **Maid service**—Saves $100 to $200 per month
- **Daycare/childcare**—Saves $200+ per month, per child
- **Car washes**—Saves $20 to $40 per month, per car
- **Grocery shopping with coupons**—Saves $100 to $200 per month

In addition, by having a student run errands, act as the family taxi driver for younger siblings, and perform household duties or chores, Mom or Dad will be freed up to temporarily focus more time on their jobs. This naturally can result in higher productivity, a greater ability to earn overtime and expand their business, and so on.

The Least You Need to Know

- A part-time job during the semester can put thousands in your pocket and create a healthy routine for a student.
- Work-study programs are a special type of financial aid that helps students pay for college costs by giving them an on-campus employment option.
- Off-campus, non–work-study jobs can provide a substantially higher hourly rate and valuable benefits compared to work-study programs.
- Plan ahead to make the most of summer employment, being sure to send resumés no later than March or April.
- Students who cannot find summer employment should pitch in their time and energy around the house to lighten their parents' financial load.

Avoiding the
Biggest Mistakes

In This Chapter

- Dealing with denial and procrastination
- Recruiting help with the financial aid process
- Building a support system
- Creating a backup plan

Speaking as someone who has always considered eating to be my favorite sport and appetizers to be my specialty, I've found great wisdom in the old adage of "don't shop hungry." The few times I have, usually when my wife sends me to the store for a missing ingredient for that night's supper, I come home with a bag of beef jerky, some Cheez Whiz, jalapeño-flavored chips, and a slab of smoked salmon.

The same can be true when planning or paying for college. If you try to do it while you're stressed out, the results will probably be distressing. You'll make rash decisions, jump at the first available solutions, and throw good money after bad in the hopes of playing catch-up. In short, figuring out how to pay for college when both time and money are short takes a cool head and a methodical approach to solving your college funding problems.

Because I've touched on some of the specific mistakes to avoid in previous chapters (not hiring a scholarship guru, not using private lenders, and so on), in this chapter I talk about some big-picture stuff. These are as much problems in the way people go about their college planning as they are bad choices they make. Learn from these mistakes and you'll save yourself a lot of time and money.

Denial and Procrastination

Make no mistake about it, getting college paid for is not just about acquiring knowledge about programs and options. Getting college paid for is also a race to the finish, against both the calendar and other students and families. Just as there are only so many spots available at any given college, there is only so much money to go around for students in need.

CHEAT SHEET

When I do the orientation for new students at one of the colleges I teach at, I give them a fake check and have them make it out to themselves for $1,000,000 (the average increase in lifetime earnings for a graduate). I then have them post that on their fridge or next to their computer to help them overcome their procrastination and denial. What can you post somewhere visible to help you push through the difficult days? A check? A diploma with your name on it? A picture of graduating students?

So I bet you already know the punch line of this little lecture then, don't you? *Denial and procrastination are your enemies.* If you wait to begin thinking about what you need to do until after your vacation ends, the next holiday is over, or this current school year passes, you'll only be hurting your chances and exponentially increasing the amount of work you'll have to do later. As an antidote to these temptations, you have to truly embrace two things by the end of this book—working your plan and finding a partner in crime.

Mistake #1: Not Working Your Plan

Nike, perhaps as much as any company, is famous for its motto. What makes "Just do it" so catchy is not just what it says, but also what it doesn't say. It's a subtle jab at all those who dream big, think big, or make big commitments, but then for some reason fail to take action. It's a short reply to the long list of excuses: *shut up, and just do it.*

Hopefully, as this book draws to a close, you've begun to formulate a pretty solid action plan, whether you've used my College Cash Strategy Worksheet in Appendix B or formulated your own unique hit list of items. For that, I'm very proud of you and you should be proud of yourself. But, at the same time, I can guarantee you that there will be those who read this book and draw up a great strategy but never get around to the day-to-day action required to reach their funding goals.

Whether it is every day, every weekend, or once a month, you need to set aside time to perform the action steps on your College Cash Strategy Worksheet. If you don't, or don't consistently, I can guarantee that you will have nothing to show for it and your college dreams will slip through your fingers. If you can do it, if you can work your plan, slowly but surely things will begin to happen.

Mistake #2: Doing It Alone

Chances are that you're not the only person you know who is being terrorized by the ogre of tuition. If you're a student reading this book, there's no doubt that you have friends who are in the same boat financially. If you're a parent reading this book, chances are that your friends (or the parents of your kids' friends) are fighting the same battle. So before you charge off into the college funding wilderness all alone with a torch and a pitchfork, it might be wise to round up some of the local townsfolk.

CHEAT SHEET

Most colleges have newsletters, online forums, and support groups for parents and students. These can be great places to stay up-to-date on everything happening at your school, trade financial aid information and ideas, and learn cost-cutting tricks particular to your school. If you can't find one, consider starting one!

I suggest creating a group that meets regularly and whose goal is to get college paid for, whether it be for themselves or someone else. It's almost like a knitting group, except you're filling out scholarship applications instead of making a sweater for your dog.

The group could be as small as 2 people or as big as 10 to 12 (it gets a little chaotic with more than that) and would ideally meet once per month for 1 or 2 hours. You use the time to share your goals, progress, and ideas. You could even share research duties, spreading the workload around and having everyone report their findings on various funding opportunities. At the end of the meeting, you'll set a goal that everyone should accomplish by the following meeting, such as submitting four scholarship applications and finding four new ones.

Here's what a monthly, two-hour meeting might look like:

5:00–5:30 Potluck dinner

5:30–6:00 Update on each person's college funding strategy (goals, progress, and so on)

6:00–6:15 Share research

6:15–6:30 Assign research for next meeting

6:30–7:00 Fill out one application together

Recruiting Help

Whether you're a parent trying to put a child through college or an extraordinary student who has to shoulder paying for college yourself, you need to ask for some cheap labor from those who you're helping. That means that parents need to get their college-bound kids involved in helping to research, apply, and save for college. Likewise, students need to ask for help and delegate to their parents who cannot or will not otherwise shoulder the cost of college.

Mistake #3: Not Involving Your Kids

As a psychotherapist, I worked primarily with over-entitled teens and their parents (who usually did the over-entitling). These were kids who expected to have everything handed to them. They didn't necessarily come from wealthy families; in fact, many came from single-parent homes that were very tight on money. However, they all came from families where the parents took too much responsibility for their children's actions, consequences, futures, and so forth.

One of the biggest mistakes you can make in this process is figuring out how to pay for college while your child sits there staring at the computer or hanging out with friends. You need to involve him in the process and require him to contribute and make sacrifices. Although that might sound scary for some of you, the reality is that children who cannot pull it together to fill out a few applications will not likely pull it together enough to graduate from the college you're working so hard to pay for.

CHEAT SHEET

When working with teens and their parents on college finances, I always encourage the parents to come up with a transition plan that is loaded with incentives and contingencies. It outlines what they as parents will pay for in the way of college expenses, for how long, and under what behavioral circumstances. Ideally, they'd discuss this as a student goes off to his freshman year, so that everyone is on the same page and their student knows that a lack of responsibility will lead to him being on his own sooner rather than later.

On a related note, all this work you're doing to help ensure your child's future might be for a future that doesn't resemble anything he's remotely interested in. By involving him in the process, you'll be ensuring that all your hard work is for something he's truly interested in.

Here are my top tips and tasks for involving your college-bound student:

- **Show him the math**—Although you shouldn't try to make your child feel guilty about going to college, it is very healthy for him to understand the cost and the sacrifices being made. This will both motivate him in the financial aid process, as well as serve as a reminder to keep costs under control.

- **Have him research**—Introduce your student to one of the many scholarship databases or books (start with Appendix E in this book), and require him to begin identifying scholarships and grants for which he might qualify.

- **Have him prepare two essays per week**—Because most scholarships will require some type of essay from a student, commit him to preparing two essays a week that you can submit on his behalf (you do the proofreading, assemble the required documents, and mail it). Because many scholarship essays ask similar questions, your student will be able to reuse portions of essays for future applications, greatly cutting down on time.

- **Have him track the results**—Whether you create a fancy spreadsheet or simply track your scholarship submissions on a chart hanging on your fridge, have your student track the awards and denials.

Mistake #4: Not Involving Your Parents

Whether you're a student footing the bill yourself or a parent with parents of your own, you shouldn't hesitate to invite family into the process if your relationship is a healthy one. Remember, it is their child or grandchild who is trying to earn a college degree, something of which most people would be very proud of.

By involving parents in the financial aid process, you give them a way to be involved besides just contributing money, something that many cannot do. This gives them a dignified way of helping and is something that many parents or grandparents end up putting in massive overtime on.

Probably the single best activity for parents or grandparents willing to help is having them do scholarship research. With more than 100,000 scholarships available to students in the United States, there is just no way that one student or family can look at every opportunity. Simply instruct your parents on how to use one of the many scholarship databases and then ask them to e-mail or print anything that they think would be a good fit for you or your student. Be sure to share any success stories with them, as this will only inspire them to do more.

Mistake #5: Stopping After Freshman Year

If you've ever been in sales, there is a chance you've heard the term *pipeline*. The pipeline represents all of a salesperson's leads, deals that are about to close, and current customers. Good salespeople know that even when times are great, you need to be thinking 6 to 12 months down the road and filling up the pipeline. If you don't, it'll suddenly run dry on you and you'll be in deep trouble.

College funding is no different. You might be doing a great job of rounding up money for the upcoming year of college, but you need to always be thinking about the next year. If you don't, you're going to find yourself scrambling to catch up with financial aid applicants who didn't let down their guards. This is especially true if some of the awards or grants you received are nonrenewable or are given to a student for only one year before they're given to someone else.

FLUNK-PROOF FINANCES

The continued receipt of many financial aid awards is contingent on both grade point average (GPA) and behavioral expectations and will not be continued if students don't live up to certain conditions. This is especially true of scholarships granted by the college the student is attending because many other students in the vicinity would jump through flaming hoops for that money. Make sure you know the expectations for every award you receive and do everything in your power to protect that gift!

Mistake #6: Paying (or Paying Too Much) for Help

I know countless parents who have paid $1,000 or more for "expert" help in navigating the financial waters of college, only to have nothing to show for it. It turns out that the only thing many of these experts were truly an expert at was marketing themselves and pocketing people's money.

The reality is that you can effectively do 100 percent of the things that these college planning pros promise to do, with just a little bit of homework. If you find yourself stuck, your run-of-the-mill accountant or financial planner can generally answer any questions you have for less than a few hundred dollars.

Before you pay big money for help in any of these areas, you need to stop and consider a few things:

- **FAFSA applications**—There is no reason to pay someone to complete your *Free* Application for Federal Student Aid (FAFSA) for you. Although it can look intimidating, the required information is straightforward and requires straightforward answers. Any information you're unsure of can be found by calling your accountant or reading the tutorials and FAQs available online.

WORLD WIDE WEB

Starting in 2010, the IRS and the Department of Education will allow you to automatically transfer information from your tax return to your FAFSA form, when you complete your FAFSA online at fafsa.ed.gov. But, to complete the process once you're transferred from the Department of Education's website to the IRS website, you'll need to make sure you have your Social Security number, date of birth, and filing status from your last tax return. Without this info, the FAFSA-IRS link won't work.

- **Scholarship applications**—To a large degree, scholarships are a numbers game. Although you do need a polished scholarship essay, the reality is that the more applications you send out, the more likely you are to get an award. No hidden scholarships or application tricks exist that will magically put thousands in your pocket. Give yourself a scholarship, by keeping the $500 to $1,000 you'd pay one of these consultants in your pocket and spending it on your college education.

- **Investments and investment advice**—My general rule is that your investments and investment advice shouldn't cost you more than 1.5 percent of your assets' value each year. However, with college savings that will be used in a matter of months or years that is only a few years away, your need for advice is virtually nonexistent. Because you're simply comparing interest rates on different fixed-income securities, you can get all the advice you need from your accountant or tax preparer on which type of account to use for tax purposes. Aside from that, don't waste the precious little interest you're earning by paying someone to advise you on something that is straightforward.

Mistake #7: Not Having a Backup Plan

I've never understood the phrase about "life throwing you a curveball," mostly because that's all it seems to throw. Life rarely throws me anything right over the plate, except when I have my back turned.

Although I think that there is an extraordinarily good chance that you can get college paid for by following the steps in this book, so many factors are still outside your and my control. With that in mind, you have to have a Plan B in case everything goes haywire, the economy melts down, they change the financial aid rules, and so on.

> **CHEAT SHEET**
>
> Be sure to get a clear understanding of your college's withdrawal and refund procedures if your finances are hanging on by a thread. Often, there are a number of different dates that result in different levels of refunds, ranging from 100 percent down to 0 percent. Knowing these will help you to plan ahead should one of your major funding sources fall through.

One of the things I love about developing a worst-case scenario backup plan is that it keeps people from freaking out about the very intimidating goal of paying for a college education. They know in the back of their mind that they can still get a college education even if everything doesn't go as planned.

On the last page of your College Cash Strategy Worksheet, I've left three blank lines for you to fill in your back-up plans and free yourself from worrying about the ridiculous impossibility that *you won't* somehow get an education for yourself or your child. Look at the following options, consider what would be tolerable for you, and fill them in on the last page of that worksheet.

- **Go to a lower-cost school**—If the four-year college of your choice feels financially out of reach, think about a lower-priced four-year college in your local area, especially a state college. For added peace of mind, calculate the return on degree and return on major (which I talk about in Chapter 21) for that school. Chances are that the difference between that school and your dream school will be relatively small.

- **Take out loans**—Because the vast majority of people interested in going to college in the United States can get student loans (even if they earn a good amount of money), this should always be one of your top back-up plans. Of course, the idea of saddling yourself with thousands of dollars of student loan debt might not sound like fun and you might want to opt for a different fallback option. To fully understand the ramifications of taking out student loans, be sure to visit the Department of Education's Loan Repayment Calculator at www.ed.gov/DirectLoan/calc.html.

- **Go to community college**—Another attractive option, something that some savvy parents and students don't save for their backup plan, is attending a community college. Doing so allows you to earn a two-year associate's degree, as well as allowing you to later transfer to a four-year college for your remaining two years. All this allows you to work on your education at a much lower cost, simultaneously saving up funds for the final few years of your degree. (I talk more about community college in Chapter 21.)

- **Put off college for a few years**—The average age of college students in the United States has climbed substantially. This is the result of more and more young adults waiting a few years until attending college, as well as older adults returning to earn their degrees. Similar to attending community college, this allows someone to work, gain valuable experience, and save up funds to pay for a college degree.

- **Attend college part time**—One of the wisest decisions I ever made was earning my first Master's degree on a part-time basis. Doing so not only allowed me to continue to work and maintain the sanity of my family, but also allowed me to immediately apply what I was learning in my job. In hindsight, this proved to be a huge advantage over many of my peers who had to wait two or three years until graduation to apply what they were learning, if they could remember it at all.

- **Join the military**—Although many people have mixed feelings about the military, one thing is for sure: it's a great way to pay for college. Remember, in addition to being on the front lines, there are countless support and tactical roles that cater to people who wish to serve in other capacities. (See Chapter 15 for more about this option.)

The Least You Need to Know

- You have to be deliberate and work your plan on a regular basis to overcome procrastination and denial.

- Don't do all the work for your child; give her ownership by explaining the costs and delegating some of the workload.

- Form a group of people who meet on a regular basis to support each other and share college funding ideas.

- Avoid paying (much less overpaying) for college funding services that don't offer better results than what you could achieve on your own.

- Develop a backup plan to keep your education on track and your sanity in one piece.

Rethinking College

In This Chapter

- Calculating your "return on degree"
- Considering your opportunity costs
- Rethinking graduate school
- The amazing value of community colleges

Time for a pop quiz. What do Bill Gates (Microsoft), Michael Dell (Dell Computers), Steve Jobs (Apple), Simon Cowell (*American Idol*), Mary Kay Ash (Mary Kay Cosmetics), and food mogul Rachael Ray have in common? Surprisingly, these multi-millionaires and billionaires never graduated college!

There's no doubt that they are the extreme exceptions to the rule, and that going to college is still a very worthwhile investment for most people who aren't shooting for the stars. But, they and millions of others are living proof that college, especially a four-year traditional degree from a top 50 school, is not a requirement for obtaining the life you want.

In fact, after reading this book, you might be wondering if your college dreams might just not be worth it in their current form, in spite of all the resources I've provided you with. *That's okay!*

In this closing chapter, we finish nearly where this book started, by taking a look at college costs. Specifically, though, we take a look at what a degree is really worth, discuss whether brand-name colleges are worth the higher tuition, and knock around the merits of high-priced grad school.

Is Your College or Major Really Worth It?

Chances are, for every billionaire who dropped out of college, there are a hundred millionaires who went to some small college that didn't have a football team or a single building named after someone famous. The reality is, as I've said elsewhere in the book, a college degree is a door opener for people seeking success but by itself does not guarantee success.

In fact, the difference in lifetime earnings between an education at an Ivy League school and your local state school would probably be negligible for most of us. Although no studies on the matter have been performed to my knowledge, my guess is that many (if not most) Ivy League or top 50 school graduates who end up making a ton of money either inherited a family business or had some serious connections outside of their college experiences. In short, it's very possible that going to school is more important than where you go to school.

A Look at Return on Degree

The best use of your money might not be to spend as much as you can on the best school you can get into. In fact, studies have been done on students' *return on degree* and *return on major* to determine which schools and degrees result in the most financial bang for the buck. In other words, how does their investment of tuition dollars pay off in income after graduation?

> **DEFINITION**
>
> **Return on degree** and **return on major** are simple ratios that measure how much a graduate with a certain degree or from a certain school will earn at a certain point in his career. They're powerful tools when comparing the value of one college or major against another.

Although that might seem like a complex question to try to answer, the Internet is making it easier and easier. In fact, *SmartMoney Magazine* published a groundbreaking article in early 2009 that used readily available numbers on school tuition, as well as earnings surveys collected on PayScale.com from both recent and not-so-recent graduates. The findings were surprising. The Ivy League and highest-priced schools did not have nearly as good of a return on investment as many lower-priced public schools when tuition was compared against mid-career earnings for graduates from those schools.

For example, at the top of the list was Texas A&M, whose degree cost $18,297 in 1993, but whose graduates were earning an average of $96,100 15 years later. That yields a return on degree of 315 percent.

By comparison, the highest-listed Ivy League school was Princeton, with a total cost of degree of $64,150 and average earnings of $131,000 15 years later. In short, students at a school such as Texas A&M experienced a much higher level of future wages for every dollar they spent on tuition than those who went to a much more expensive school. For more information on this study, visit smartmoney.com.

> **WORLD WIDE WISDOM**
>
> You can spend a lot of money buying books and taking trips to try to decide which college is going to give you the most bang for your buck. Unfortunately, you might never get the questions you have answered. That's where CollegeConfidential.com comes in. Its message forums are one of the best resources I've found for getting a student's-eye view of what each campus and program is really like and whether a school lives up to its reputation.

Avoiding Useless Degrees

To be fair, no one's college experience is useless because college is usually an incredible time of self-discovery. But from the perspective of getting paid to use what you've learned, some degrees are pretty low on the get-job-when-you-graduate scale. Of course, I've known a few people (there are always exceptions) who got off-the-wall degrees and now are really important people at Fortune 500 companies, making a ton of money. But for the most part, people with degrees in film appreciation have ended up working in the local video store.

Perhaps the most important thing to realize is that there is no single degree that savvy students pursue. Every degree is slightly different. Some careers pay a lot of money for people with a standard undergraduate degree but don't really offer much advancement after the initial hire. Others don't pay a whole lot right out of the gates but can earn you a lot of money down the road. Still others are hard to build a career on, unless you go back and get a graduate degree to go with it.

Thankfully, there are a ton of studies out there on what graduates with certain degrees are likely to earn, such as those listed in the following table. It would be worth your time to look at these numbers and compare them to the amount of time and money you're going to put into your education to help you decide whether all this financial scraping and scrambling makes sense.

Degrees by Starting Salary (2008)

Degree	Starting Salary
Computer science	$56,921
Engineering	$56,336
Economics	$52,926
Nursing	$52,129
Chemistry	$52,125
Political science	$43,594
Marketing	$43,459
Human resources	$40,250
History	$35,956
Communications	$35,196
English/Literature	$34,757
Journalism	$32,250
Psychology	$30,877
Public relations	$30,677

Source: CNN/CareerBuilder.com

Calculating Your Return on Degree

Although I wouldn't advise trying to calculate the return on degree or return on major for every school and every degree in the nation, I do suggest using some basic calculations to evaluate the various programs you're considering.

Here are my top techniques for crunching the numbers on a chosen degree or field of study. You can go to the Internet or call the colleges you're considering to get the estimates you need to complete these calculations. If you're using Internet sources, try to stick with the same source all the way through your calculations to ensure your results are consistent:

- **Return on major (current)**—To compute this number, you'll need to divide the average *first-year* earnings for someone with a degree in your area of study by the total cost of you getting that degree. For example, for business majors, the National Association of Colleges and Employers (NACE) estimates that 2009 graduates will earn $44,607 in their first year after graduation. If your degree cost you $100,000, your current return on major would be 44.6 percent.

- **Return on major (future)**—This number can be a little harder to pinpoint, but it also means more. It gives you a sense of what someone with a certain degree is earning down the road, after he has built a career. The problem comes from finding estimates for careers 10 or 15 years out. Some of my favorite places to look for these income estimates are Payscale.com or the websites for the major financial magazines (for example, Forbes.com or Money.com). After you find the numbers, however, it's the same calculation as the previous one. For example, according to PayScale.com, someone with a business degree and between 10 and 20 years of experience commanded a median salary of $66,464. Comparing that against the same $100,000 education, his future return on major is 66.46 percent.

- **Return on degree (current and future)**—Whereas the return on major calculations we just did look at a broad profession's earning potential, the return on degree calculation looks at graduates from a particular school, regardless of their major. The calculation here is similar, except that you divide the current (first-year) salaries or the future (10, 15, or 20 years into their career) salaries for graduates from your school, instead of graduates with a certain degree. In a sense, this measures the value of a school's reputation or education quality relative to other schools.

The magic of return on degree or return on major numbers comes when you compare them against other schools with different costs or other professions with different potential earnings. Only then will you get a clearer picture of how your choice of a school or major will pay off comparatively. Although some websites do provide these numbers, many colleges diligently track these numbers, so talk to a school's enrollment counselor.

The Value of Skipping College

I won't waste too much of your time on this point, because I'm guessing that you're pretty intent on going to college since you bought this book. But many people, as they become hyper-focused on the college admissions and funding process, don't stop to consider the *opportunity costs* of going to college versus alternative career paths. In other words, instead of going to college, you could save or invest all that money and get a four-year head-start on building your resumé or starting the business you're dreaming of.

DEFINITION

Opportunity costs are the value of those things you give up when you choose one option over another. For example, the opportunity cost of choosing one job over another is the salary and benefits you won't be getting at the job you did not take.

The following table shows you how much money someone would accumulate over four years instead of paying out certain amounts. The interest rate used in this calculation is 5 percent, which is near the historical rate of return on CDs or bonds that mature in four to five years.

Opportunity Cost of College Tuition After Four Years

Annual Tuition	Future Value if Not Spent on Tuition*
$5,000	$22,628
$10,000	$45,256
$15,000	$67,884
$20,000	$90,512
$25,000	$113,140
$30,000	$135,768
$35,000	$158,397
$40,000	$181,025

Assumes the same tuition is invested at beginning of each year for four years, earning 5% compounded annually.

When you stop to think about it, that's a lot of money. That could go a long way toward purchasing a house (which in turn lowers your ongoing expenses) or starting a business (which could increase your income substantially).

Consider further that a whole lot of careers and vocations, such as those listed in the following table, can earn a ton of money without a college degree. Pair a career in one of these fields with accumulating (instead of spending) the money mentioned previously, and you might have a strong case for some people not going to college.

Top-Paying Jobs for Nongraduates

Career	Average Annual Pay
Air traffic controllers	$111,900
Law enforcement supervision	$79,000
Sales representatives	$75,500
Elevator installation/repair	$69,400
Gaming managers	$68,300
Firefighter supervision	$67,400
Ship captains	$62,000
Real estate brokers	$57,500
Transportation inspectors	$55,200
Electrical line repair	$55,100

Source: *Bureau of Labor Statistics (2008)*

Grad School Is No Guarantee of Success

It used to be that college was a *really* big deal, a way to set yourself apart from 90 percent of your peers in the workplace. In fact, according to the U.S. Census Bureau, in 1947 only about 5 percent of Americans had a college degree, making it a major ingredient for success through the end of the last century. By 2008, however, 28 percent of Americans had a college degree, up from 5 percent half a century ago. The result is more competition and less differentiation for holders of a four-year Bachelor's degree.

Not surprisingly, to keep or gain an edge in the workplace, many graduates began going back to graduate school starting in the early 1960s, especially for the coveted MBA degree. Since that time, the number of people holding MBA degrees has grown nearly 20-fold, from fewer than roughly 6,000 to more than 100,000, according to *BusinessWeek*. Of course, that means that graduate degrees, especially the more popular ones, are beginning to be so prevalent that they're not worth what they used to be.

The bottom line is that if you are planning to attend grad school—which can easily cost $50,000–$100,000—you might want to rethink it if your primary motivation is income potential. The return on degree and return on major for this huge expenditure is heading south. The one notable exception are degrees that are needed to qualify for licensure or certification of some kind. From practicing medicine to social work to law, graduate degrees in these areas tend to be holding steady as far as both job prospects and pay.

> **FLUNK-PROOF FINANCES**
>
> The explosion in grad school enrollment has led to a huge increase in the number of schools wanting to get in on the action. Unfortunately, many of these programs, especially those offered online, are not accredited by one of the seven regional accrediting bodies for colleges in the United States. Further, many do not meet the educational requirements to earn certain professional licenses in some states. Before you sign onto a graduate program, be sure to visit CHEA.org to learn more about the accreditation process.

The Amazing Value of Community College

More and more students and parents are realizing that *community college* (also called *junior college*) is one of the greatest untapped resources when it comes to getting an education in a cost-efficient manner. In fact, President Obama has made the community college system in America one of the cornerstones in his plan to expand access to higher education.

> **DEFINITION**
>
> **Community college** refers to a public, accredited school that offers college courses that can be transferred to a four-year college, as well as put toward a two-year degree known as an associate's degree.

What makes community college such an intriguing option is its unique combination of affordability, excellent instruction, increased acceptance rate to four-year schools, and an overall less risky transition from high school to college life. In fact, I find community college to be such an excellent option that I recommend that *all* students at least consider doing a year or two at a community college, even if they have more than enough money to go to a four-year school.

The Cost Savings of Community College

Right off the bat, the savings at a community college are jaw-dropping. Take the Los Angeles Community College District, which is the largest community college system in the United States. Students attending any community college within the system pay around $25 per unit for their undergraduate classes. By comparison, students at nearby UCLA pay more than $175 per unit, on top of higher registration and other fees. Over the course of just a couple of years, that can easily add up to $10,000 or more in savings.

But the costs don't stop there. Because most community college students typically live at home during those couple of years, the cost of room and board will not likely change from what a student or family is already used to paying for. This can result in an additional $5,000 to $10,000 in savings per year.

Granted, community colleges only offer a two-year associate's degree for those who do not transfer to a four-year school. However, this still results in an average increase of more than $400,000 in lifetime earnings compared to high school graduates.

All in all, a community college education can easily save a household roughly $10,000 to $20,000 in expenses, even if the student goes on to earn a four-year degree. In addition, at bare minimum, her income can be expected to rise nearly 50 percent over that of someone with just a high school diploma.

The Ability to Work and Save

There's a great double-benefit to students staying in their current living situations and attending a community college part time for two or three years: *they can work and continue to save money.* For students who cannot financially afford tuition at a four-year school, or who don't want to take out massive loans, working and going to community college part time solves a lot of problems.

Imagine that a high school student goes to work part time and community college part time, with the commitment of sticking half of his earnings into a savings account. With 20 hours of work per week, at roughly $10 per hour, he'd earn a little over $10,000 before taxes for the year. Because most students would continue to live and eat at home, they could easily save half of that, or $5,000 per year, to help pay for future college. After two or three years of bumping off general education classes at a much lower price, the student is now also ready to go off and finish at a four-year college, armed with an additional $15,000 in savings. Even adults with families working full time could take advantage of this, knocking out a couple of classes per semester online while continuing to work and fill up their financial war chest for their educational homestretch.

Higher Acceptance Rates at Many Schools

Although many four-year colleges want their students to attend their school for all four years, many other colleges actually welcome transfer students, granting a higher percentage of acceptances than to freshman applicants.

This occurs for a couple of reasons—primarily because community college students with strong grades are proven students who are highly likely to finish their studies (which is a stat that affects college rankings). Also, many of the larger state schools are maxed out when it comes to housing and facilities for their freshman and sophomore students, whereas transfers tend to live off-campus and not strain limited resources.

How significant is the change in acceptance rates? Although some private, liberal arts colleges may give only a slight edge to transfers, some state school acceptance rates go up by as much as 50 percent! If you have a particular school in mind, you should do some research and see if there is an advantage or disadvantage from an admissions point of view to attending a community college first and trying to transfer in later.

The Behavioral Benefits of Community College

I'm going to put all my expert hats on at one time here. As a financial planner, a family therapist, and someone who has worked with at-risk teens, one of the best things a parent can do for an out-of-control teen is to *not send her off to college*. Really, these kids don't need more freedom, less oversight, and a whole bunch of new influences.

Time and again, I've watched kids who graduate high school and go to community college get their heads on straight much more quickly than those who go to a four-year college and have a second adolescence (like yours truly). I'd go so far as to say that for teens who have been discipline cases in high school, there's a good chance your college tuition bills will drag on for longer than four years, if the students finish at all.

In my experience, kids who go on to a four-year school *after* doing a few years at community college and working a real job approach those last two years with a lot more seriousness. It's not that they don't have fun or indulge in the college experience, but they're just a tad more mature and tend to keep their eyes more focused on the finish line.

Presidential Game-Changers

Financial aid for college has come a long way in the last 30 to 40 years. College, which once was primarily the domain of the rich and privileged, has increasingly become available to the average family. It's likely that this process is going to continue under President Obama's administration and a Democratic majority in Congress.

> **WORLD WIDE WISDOM**
>
> One of the best features of Google is its "Alert" system. This system allows you to enter multiple search terms that matter to you, with Google e-mailing you whenever it finds something new on the Web that relates to that topic. This is especially helpful for staying on top of new and promised programs that you might be depending on, as well as programs that might be subject to budget cuts.

That has implications for all of us, both in the short term with the tuition bills you have to tackle now, as well as for your children and grandchildren and the educations they might or might not receive. You need to do your homework as a taxpayer and share your voice when it comes to the current programs paid for with taxpayer money. You also need to stay informed about the program changes as they come. I'm continually surprised by how many people are misinformed about the education funding promises that have been made, have been fulfilled, or are languishing by the latest batch of politicians. To stay informed, I strongly suggest signing up for a few of the good blogs and newsletters I've listed in Appendix C, beginning with my blog at CollegeSavings.About.com.

The Least You Need to Know

- Before you commit to a specific college or major, perform return on degree and return on major calculations to see how it matches up against your other options.

- The cost of grad school can be outrageous and isn't the instant ticket to success it used to be.

- A two-year associate's degree from a community college increases a worker's lifetime earnings by nearly 50 percent, while costing very little.

- Attending a community college for two years and then transferring to a four-year school for the final two years can save you tens of thousands of dollars.

- Politics can change the college funding landscape overnight, so you need to stay informed.

Glossary

accelerated program   A degree program that fits the class requirements for a college degree into a shortened period of time.

active-duty   Military personnel who serve on a full-time basis, even if not during a time of war or in combat.

Advanced Placement   Classes that can be taken during high school that can allow a student to skip certain general education courses later at the college level.

asynchronous learning   A classroom environment, usually online, that allows the student and the instructor to communicate with one another at different times.

blanket insurance   *See* group insurance.

board   Most commonly refers to the costs associated with feeding a student while enrolled at a college campus, usually through the school's cafeteria or dining facilities.

branches   Refers to the various arms of the U.S. military and includes the Army, Navy, Air Force, Marines, and Coast Guard.

challenge program   A program set up and run by a state, local community, or private corporation that offers to pay for some or all of the college expenses of all students who meet certain basic criteria. Such criteria might include residing in a certain area for a minimum amount of time, maintaining a minimum GPA, or attending a school within that state.

College Level Examination Program (CLEP)   Tests offered by the College Board that allow successful examinees to skip certain classes.

community college   An accredited school that offers college courses that can either be transferred to a four-year college or to a two-year degree known as an associate's degree.

consolidation   The process of combining all of a graduate's federal loans into a single loan.

contribution rate   In financial aid terms, this refers to the amount of an asset's worth that a parent or student is expected to use each year for funding their education.

Coverdell ESA   A special type of college savings account that allows a parent to save for a child's college education, paying no tax on the growth of the savings if it's eventually used for college costs.

Crummey trust   A rarely used type of education trust fund that has been replaced by newer and simpler college savings vehicles.

CSS Profile   A financial aid form used by many private colleges, in addition to the FAFSA form.

custodial account   *See* UTMA and UGMA accounts.

DANTES   A test that allows military personnel to receive partial college credit for their training and experience.

default   When a student has failed to make his required payments on a student loan and the loan has been turned over to a collections department.

deferment   A temporary suspension of loan payments under guidelines usually set by the government.

dependent student   A student who, for financial aid purposes, is still considered part of her parent's household.

direct costs   The costs directly related to attending school—namely tuition, room, board, and books.

expected family contribution (EFC)   A calculation from the FAFSA forms that determines the dollar amount that a family is expected to contribute in the current school year toward their child's education. Financial aid is awarded based on this amount.

FAFSA   *See* Free Application for Federal Student Aid.

FDIC insurance   Provides a guarantee to depositors at participating banks that their deposits are protected even if the bank goes out of business.

Federal Methodology   The formula used to calculate the expected family contribution for a student for federal financial aid purposes using information from the FAFSA form.

financial aid administrator   The person(s) at a college who is in charge of determining what financial aid is awarded to which students.

fixed-income investment   An investment whose return comes primarily from a preset rate of interest earned.

forbearance   A suspension or waiving of loan payments due, usually granted on a case-by-case basis by each lender.

forgivable loans   A type of student loan made to a student who intends to work in a certain field. If the student does in fact work in that field for a certain amount of time, then the loans are forgiven (erased). The primary difference between these loans and classic loan forgiveness programs is that these are unique loans made by state and local governments (as opposed to the U.S. Department of Education), with forgiveness promised in advance of graduation.

Free Application for Federal Student Aid (FAFSA)   The primary form used by the U.S. Department of Education for all students seeking governmental financial aid.

GI Bill   Military program that pays for a current or former soldier to receive a college education in return for a specified number of years of service.

grant   A type of financial award that is typically made from a government or state program and that does not need to be repaid if the student successfully completes the courses for which the grant money was used.

group insurance   An insurance policy that covers everyone who meets a certain classification or for everyone who is exposed to the same risk (for instance, physical injury).

half-time   A student's status, determined by each school, most often someone taking fewer than 12 semester hours per year.

income timing   The deliberate choosing of one tax year over another to receive income in, in order to lower one's potential expected family contribution.

independent student   A student who, for financial aid purposes, is considered financially separate from his parents.

indirect costs   Those costs incurred due to attending college but not directly related to the receipt of the education itself, such as travel, medical costs, and clothing.

inflation   The increase in the cost of a good or service over time.

Institutional Methodology   A formula used for private aid given by schools using information on the CSS Profile.

International Baccalaureate   Classes that can be taken during high school that might allow a student to skip certain general education courses at the college level.

junior college *See* community college.

loan forgiveness programs Government programs that forgive (erase) outstanding loans in return for working in certain fields.

loan repayment programs Government or private programs that repay outstanding loans in return for working in certain fields.

National Merit Scholarship Finalist One of approximately 15,000 students who demonstrate exceptional academic ability on the PSAT exam taken by high school students. With this title comes many offers for free or discounted educations around the country.

need based Financial aid that is awarded based on someone proving that her income and asset levels are below a certain benchmark.

nontraditional college A school that focuses primarily on educating students through an alternative format.

nontraditional education An education received in some manner other than attending face-to-face classes on a full-time basis.

nontraditional student Someone who attends a nontraditional school or receives a nontraditional education.

opportunity costs The value of those things you give up when you choose one option over another. For example, the opportunity cost of choosing one job over another is the salary and benefits you won't be getting at the job you did not take.

origination fee A fee charged at the time a new loan is issued, expressed in a percentage such as a "1% origination fee."

peer-to-peer lending (P2P) Loans made between private parties, as opposed to those made between a business or the government and a borrower.

Pell Grant A financial aid award made by the federal government to students who demonstrate financial need when compared to their cost of attendance at the school of their choice. Pell Grants do not need to be repaid if the student successfully completes his or her education.

Perkins loan A low-cost federal loan made to students demonstrating substantial financial need. Interest on Perkins loans is subsidized (paid for) during college by the government, with these loans also being subject to unique loan forgiveness programs for graduates choosing certain careers.

phase-out   Refers to tax benefits that are slowly decreased for a taxpayer after his income exceeds a certain amount.

principal   The original amount someone invests in an investment.

private student loans   A student loan issued by a corporation or bank without government backing or partnership and often subject to higher interest rates.

reservist   Part-time military personnel who serve on a limited basis each year but can be called up to active-duty (full-time) during times of war or crisis.

return on degree   A financial measure of how much someone earns for a degree from a specific school compared to what she paid to acquire it.

return on major   A financial measure of how much someone earns for a degree in a certain subject area compared to what he paid to acquire it.

room   The costs related to putting a roof over a student's head, whether on or off campus.

scholarship   A financial aid award made to a student, usually from a private organization or college, that does not need to be repaid.

Section 529 account   A special type of college savings account that allows a parent to save for a child's college education, paying no tax on the growth of the savings if it's eventually used for college costs.

Stafford loan   The most commonly used federal student loan, since it is available to students who demonstrate financial need, as well as many from middle- and upper-class families. Stafford loans are available to both undergraduate and graduate students and may be eligible for certain loan forgiveness programs.

subsidized loan   A type of student loan on which all the interest is paid by the government until the student graduates.

tax credit   A tax benefit that directly reduces the amount of taxes someone owes on a dollar-for-dollar basis.

tax deduction   A tax benefit that lowers the amount of income on which someone's tax liability is calculated.

tax-equivalent yield (TEY)   A calculation that shows what a fully taxable bond would have to earn to have the same after-tax yield as a bond that is not taxed by either the federal or state government.

term life insurance   Life insurance that covers someone for only a specified number of years; it's much cheaper than whole life insurance.

total cost of attendance   An estimate provided by a school of the total annual expense of attending that school, including all the direct and indirect costs.

tuition   The direct costs for the education received, usually expressed in a per-unit or per-semester format.

tuition reimbursement   An employer-sponsored plan where an employee receives financial assistance in earning his degree. Some programs require the employee to pay his costs and then submit a request for reimbursement, while others simply pay the employee's tuition and expenses.

tuition reward programs   Programs that set aside money into a separate account for future students every time a participating parent uses a credit or debit card or shops at a participating retailer.

tuition waiver   When a college waives tuition for a certain class of students, such as National Merit Scholarship Finalists or people with incomes below a certain dollar amount.

tuition-free college   A college at which all students in attendance receive a free education (as opposed to just certain students receiving scholarships), usually in exchange for a commitment to work at the college as they earn their degree. After being accepted to a tuition-free college, a student can rest assured that the majority of her education expenses will be paid for as long as she meets the school's academic standards.

unsubsidized loan   A type of student loan on which interest accumulates even prior to a student's graduation.

UTMA and UGMA accounts   Increasingly outdated accounts that allow parents to make an irrevocable gift to a child of cash or other assets, with the income on those assets receiving preferential tax treatment.

vocational school   A specialized type of school that trains students for the skills required to work in certain skilled-labor professions.

whole life insurance   Life insurance that has a built-in savings component that is occasionally recommended as a college savings vehicle; it's much more expensive than term life insurance.

work-study   A specialized type of financial aid that provides certain students with money to pay their living expenses by providing jobs.

College Cash Strategy Worksheet

This worksheet is meant to be a companion to the chapters in the book, but it has also been designed so you can complete it without having to read the book in sequential order. It is broken into three primary sections, which should be done in order.

The first section, "Unique Costs and Resources," takes into account what college will actually cost by the time you get there and what you already have piled up. It provides you with a *Total Unmet College Cost* number, which is what this book is going to try to whittle away at.

The second section, "Spending and Savings Strategies," helps you chip away at your *Total Unmet Need* from the first page by primarily focusing on how money flows in and out of your household.

The third and last section, "Funding Strategies," focuses on solutions you can use to eliminate the rest of the *Unfunded College Need*.

Unique Costs and Resources

Step 1: Calculate Your Unique College Costs

$_____ Annual tuition for college (in today's dollars)

+ $_____ Room costs (enter on-campus annual cost or off-campus monthly costs × 12)

+ $_____ Board costs (enter annual cost of dining plan or monthly food costs × 9)

+ $_____ Book costs (enter one semester's estimate of costs × 2)

Line A: Subtotal of annual direct costs = $_____

$_____ Annual travel costs (airfare for holidays, hotel for parents' weekend, costs of moving)

+ $_____ Leisure travel costs (spring break, road trips, and so on)

+ $_____ Medical costs (enter only *new* costs such as insurance or student health fees)

+ $_____ Campus and student activity fees (flat fee charged by campus)

+ $_____ Greek life or club expenses or dues

+ $_____ Technology

+ $_____ Furnishings

+ $_____ Clothes

+ $_____ Lost income

Line B: Subtotal of annual indirect costs = $_____

Line C: Total of annual costs (Lines A + B) = $_____

Step 2: Calculate Estimated Direct and Indirect Cost Savings

$ _____ Tuition negotiation and discounts

+ $ _____ Discount for being college employee

+ $ _____ AP/IB classes (cost of classes opted out of)

+ $ _____ CLEP and other exams (cost of classes opted out of)

+ $ _____ Alternative classes (total difference between primary college's cost for classes and cost of alternative classes that will be taken)

+ $ _____ Off-campus or residential advisor housing savings

+ $ _____ Savings on board (meals)

+ $ _____ Savings by renting texts/purchasing used books

+ $ _____ Savings on technology purchases (divide by expected years until graduation for purposes of estimating an annual cost)

+ $ _____ Travel savings (10 percent of your estimated travel costs)

Line D: Subtotal of annual cost savings = $_____

Line E: Annual costs after savings (Line C – Line D) = $_____

Step 3: Adjust Your Annual Costs for Inflation

To correctly adjust the cost of each year of college for inflation, insert your total annual costs from Line E for each year below where college costs will occur. If no costs will occur, put a "0" on the total cost line. The total of all these years are added up to determine your inflation-adjusted college costs.

Years from Today	Annual College Expenses (Line E)		Inflation Multiplier		Total Cost for Year
1	$_____	×	1.050	=	$_____
2	$_____	×	1.050	=	$_____
3	$_____	×	1.153	=	$_____
4	$_____	×	1.216	=	$_____
5	$_____	×	1.276	=	$_____
6	$_____	×	1.340	=	$_____
7	$_____	×	1.407	=	$_____
8	$_____	×	1.477	=	$_____
9	$_____	×	1.551	=	$_____
10	$_____	×	1.629	=	$_____

Line F: Total inflation-adjusted cost for all years of college = $_____

Step 4: Calculate Your Unmet Need

$_____ Line F: Your unique inflation-adjusted college costs (total of all years)

– $_____ Money saved specifically for that student

– $_____ Total financial help expected from others for all years of college

– $_____ Total expected scholarships for all years of college

– $_____ Any previous amounts figured into your budget to pay for college (totaled for all years)

Line G: Your total unmet college cost = $_____

Spending and Savings Strategies

Calculate Annual Budget Savings Potential

Expense	Actual	Compromise	Net Savings
Entertainment	$_____	$_____	$_____
Dining out	$_____	$_____	$_____
Gifts	$_____	$_____	$_____
Memberships	$_____	$_____	$_____
Subscriptions	$_____	$_____	$_____
Clothes	$_____	$_____	$_____
Cable TV	$_____	$_____	$_____
Vacations	$_____	$_____	$_____
Hobbies	$_____	$_____	$_____
Groceries	$_____	$_____	$_____
Hair and beauty	$_____	$_____	$_____
Home phone	$_____	$_____	$_____
Cell phone	$_____	$_____	$_____
Other	$_____	$_____	$_____
Total monthly savings potential =			$_____
Multiplied by 12 months =			$_____
Total annual savings potential =			$_____
Line H: Annual savings potential multiplied by years in college =			$_____
Line J: Savings adjusted need (Line G – Line H) =			$_____
– Additional income earned from 2nd job, etc. (years in college × annual amount) =			$_____
Line K: Total estimated financial aid required (your bottom line) =			$_____
Line L: Annual estimated aid need (Line K ÷ estimated years in college) =			$_____

Funding Strategies

At this point, you've calculated what college is going to cost you, what you can do to trim those costs, the value of assets you'll have at your disposal, and your ability to trim your household budget to free up additional funds. If there's anything besides a 0 on Line K, this is the amount you'll need to pull together through financial aid over the course of paying for a degree. Line L breaks this down even further into what you'll need in financial aid for each year of college. Everything from Chapter 5 on in the book deals with tackling this number, whether it be through scholarships, loans, or innovative programs that you might not have heard of. That means that you've got some decisions to make and some actions you need to take:

1. Decide if you want to try to meet the estimated financial aid required (Line K) or opt for an alternative college experience (community college, distance education, military, and so on).

2. If you still plan on attending the college of your choice, visit the Student Loan Calculators at www.ed.gov/DirectLoan/calc.html. Plug in your total Unfunded College Need and see if the monthly payment for a student loan of that size is something you can live with, in a worst-case scenario where no other aid becomes available.

3. If you can live with the payments, visit fafsa.ed.gov and submit your FAFSA form to start the ball rolling.

4. At the same time as you're applying for loans, make a hit list of at least five different college funding techniques besides applying for scholarships that you will try to use to lower your college costs or increase your financial aid packages. List them below:

_____

_____

_____

_____

_____

5. Commit to submitting five scholarship applications for every $1,000 in annual estimated aid need (Line L) you have. If you need $10,000 per year, you should submit 50 well-researched scholarship applications to have a shot at covering your costs.

   $_____ (total amount needed) ÷ $1,000 × 5 = _____ applications

6. Set your daily and weekly activity goals:

   Daily: Research scholarship/aid opportunities ____

   Weekly: Complete and mail aid application ____

7. Decide on three backup plans just in case (military, community college, vocational school, delaying the start of college, and so on):

   _____

   _____

   _____

Resources

Appendix C

The following are organizations and websites that might be useful to you in your journey as you tackle the high cost of a college education.

General Resources

General Information Websites About College Planning

CollegeSavings.About.com

FinAid.com

SavingForCollege.com

Professionals to Help with College Planning

American Institute of Certified Public Accountants
www.aicpa.org

Certified Financial Planners
www.cfp.net/search
1-800-487-1497

National Institute of Certified College Planners
www.niccp.com
1-800-811-0159

Resources for Lowering Your College Costs

Finding a Job at a College:

www.higheredjobs.com

www.universityjobs.com

Skipping Classes with the AP/IB Programs:

Advanced Placement—www.collegeboard.com

International Baccalaureate—www.ibo.org

Testing Out of Classes:

CLEP Exams for all students—www.collegeboard.com

DANTES for military personnel—dantes.doded.mil

Textbook Discounts

www.amazon.com

www.bigwords.com

www.ecampus.com

www.half.ebay.com

Textbook Rentals

www.campusbookrentals.com

www.chegg.com

Travel Discounts

The Student Advantage Discount Card:

www.studentadvantage.com

Travel Discount Websites:

www.kayak.com

www.orbitz.com

www.priceline.com

www.travelocity.com

Alternative Travel Websites:

www.amtrak.com

www.greyhound.com

Saving Money on Food

www.couponmom.com

www.thegrocerygame.com

Overseas Travel

www.TeachAbroad.com

www.TravelAbroad.com

Student Health Insurance

Aetna Student Health—www.aetnastudenthealth.com

eHealthInsurance—www.eHealthInsurance.com

United Healthcare Student Insurance—www.uhcsr.com

Staying in Touch

www.skype.com

Assets and Investments

Check the Value of Your Savings Bonds:

www.treasurydirect.gov

Section 529 Plans Ratings and Reviews:

www.SavingForCollege.com

IRS Information at www.IRS.gov

Publication 503—Child and Dependent Care Expenses

Publication 550—Investment Income and Expenses

Publication 590—IRA's and Retirement Plans

Publication 910—IRS Guide to Free Tax Services

Publication 970—Tax Benefits for Education

Financial Aid and Student Loans

CSS Profile for Private Schools—profileonline.collegeboard.com

Federal Student Aid—studentaid.ed.gov

Financial Aid Estimator—www.fafsa4caster.com

Free Federal Aid Application—www.fafsa.ed.gov

Loan Forgiveness

AmeriCorps—www.americorps.gov

Directory for Lawyers—www.equaljusticeworks.org

Directory for Medical Professionals—www.aamc.org

Directory for Teachers—www.aft.org

Peace Corps—www.peacecorps.gov

Scholarship Resources

Books

Cassidy, Daniel. *The Scholarship Book*. Prentice Hall, 2008.

College Board. *College Board Scholarship Handbook*. College Board, 2009.

Schlachter, Gail, and David Weber. *The Kaplan Scholarship Book*. Kaplan Publishing, 2009.

Tanabe, Kelly, and Gen Tanabe. *The Ultimate Scholarship Book*. Supercollege, LLC, 2010.

Scholarship Search Websites

www.CollegeBoard.com

www.FastWeb.com

www.SallieMae.com/scholarships

Tuition Reward Programs

www.babymint.com

www.futuretrust.com

www.sagescholars.com

www.upromise.com

Military Benefits for Education

Forum for Health Professionals Using HPSP:

Forums.studentdoctor.net

The Montgomery and Post-9/11 GI Bills:

www.GIBill.va.gov

Nontraditional Educations

Largest Nontraditional Schools:

DeVry University—www.devry.edu

Everest University—www.everest.edu

Grand Canyon University—www.gcu.edu

ITT Tech—www.itt.edu

Kaplan University—www.kaplan.com

Strayer College—www.strayer.edu

The University of Phoenix—www.phoenix.edu

Webster University—www.webster.edu

Directory for State Financial Aid

This appendix is meant to be a guide to the state-run commissions that offer financial assistance to students in each state. It is not meant to be an exhaustive guide of the various programs offered in each state, but rather a springboard for you to do more research.

Alabama

Alabama Commission on Higher
Education
Main programs:
Alabama Student Assistance Program
Alabama Education Grant Program
Telephone: 334-242-1998
Web: www.ache.state.al.us

Alaska

Alaska Commission on Postsecondary
Education
Main program:
AlaskAdvantage Education Grant
Telephone: 1-800-441-2962
Web: akadvantage.alaska.gov

Arizona

Arizona Commission for
Postsecondary Education
Main programs:
Arizona Private Postsecondary
Education Student Assistance Program
(PFAP)
Special Leveraging Educational
Assistance Partnership (SLEAP)
Telephone: 602-258-2435
Web: azhighered.gov/

Arkansas

Arkansas Department of Higher
Education
Main programs:
GO! Opportunities Grant
Academic Challenge Scholarship
Telephone: 501-371-2000
Web: www.adhe.edu

California

California Student Aid Commission
Main program:
Cal Grant
Telephone: 1-888-224-7268
Web: www.Calgrants.org

Colorado

Colorado Department of Higher
Education
Main program:
Colorado Student Grant
Telephone: 303-866-2723
Web: highered.colorado.gov

Connecticut

State of Connecticut Department of
Higher Education
Main programs:
Capitol Scholarship
CT Aid for Public College Students
CT Independent College Student
Grant Program
Telephone: 860-947-1855
Web: www.ctdhe.org

Delaware

Delaware Higher Education
Commission
Main program:
Scholarship Incentive Program (ScIP)
Telephone: 302-577-5240
Web: www.doe.k12.de.us/dhec/

District of Columbia

DC Office of the State Superintendent
of Education
Main program:
DC Tuition Assistance Program
(DCTAG)
Telephone: 1-877-485-6751
Web: osse.dc.gov

Florida

Florida Office of Student Financial
Assistance
Main program:
Florida Student Assistance Grant
(FSAG)
Telephone: 1-888-827-2004
Web: www.floridastudentfinancialaid.
org/

Georgia

Georgia Student Finance Commission
Main programs:
HOPE Grant
Georgia Tuition Equalization Grant
Telephone: 1-800-505-GSFC
Web: www.gsfc.org

Hawaii

Hawaii Postsecondary Education
Commission
Main programs:
Hawaii Student Incentive Grant
(HSIG)
State Higher Education Loan
Telephone: 808-956-8213
Web: www.hawaii.edu/offices/bor/

Idaho

Idaho State Board of Education
Main programs:
Idaho Opportunity Scholarship
Leveraging Educational Assistance
State Partnership Program (LEAP)
Telephone: 208-332-1574
Web: www.boardofed.idaho.gov

Illinois

Illinois Student Assistance
Commission
Main programs:
Illinois Incentive for Access (IIA)
Monetary Award Program (MAP)
Telephone: 1-800-899-4722
Web: www.collegezone.com

Indiana

State Student Assistance Commission
of Indiana
Main program:
Higher Education Awards and
Freedom of Choice Grants
Telephone: 1-888-528-4719
Web: www.in.gov/ssaci

Iowa

Iowa College Student Aid Commission
Main programs:
Iowa Grant
Iowa Tuition Grant
Telephone: 1-877-272-4456
Web: www.iowacollegeaid.gov

Kansas

State of Kansas Board of Regents
Main programs:
Kansas Comprehensive Grants
State Scholarship
Telephone: 785-296-3421
Web: www.kansasregents.org

Kentucky

Kentucky Higher Education
Assistance Authority
Main programs:
Academic Common Market (ACM)
College Access Program (CAP)
Kentucky Educational Excellence
Scholarship
Kentucky Tuition Grant (KTG)
Telephone: 1-800-928-8926
Web: www.kheaa.com

Louisiana

Louisiana Office of Student Financial
Assistance
Main programs:
Go Grant
Leveraging Education Assistance
Partnership (LEAP)
Taylor Opportunity Program for
Students (TOPS)
Telephone: 1-800-259-LOAN ext.
1012
Web: www.osfa.state.la.us

Finance Authority of Maine
Main program:
State of Maine Grant Program
Telephone: 1-800-228-3734
Web: www.famemaine.com

Maryland

Maryland Higher Education
Commission
Major programs:
Educational Assistance Grant
Part Time Grant
Telephone: 1-800-974-1024
Web: www.mhec.state.md.us

Massachusetts

Massachusetts Department of Higher
Education
Main programs:
Cash Grant
MASSGrant
Telephone: 617-727-9420
Web: www.osfa.mass.edu

Michigan

Michigan Higher Education
Assistance Authority
Main program:
Michigan Tuition Grant
Telephone: 1-800-642-5626
Web: www.michigan.gov/mistudentaid

Minnesota

Minnesota Office of Higher
Education
Main program:
Minnesota State Grant
Telephone: 1-800-657-3866
Web: www.getreadyforcollege.org

Mississippi

Mississippi Office of Student Financial
Aid
Main programs:
Higher Education Legislative Plan
(HELP)
Mississippi Tuition Assistance Grant
(MTAG)
Telephone: 1-800-327-2980
Web: www.ihl.state.ms.us/

Missouri

Missouri Department of Higher
Education
Main programs:
Access Missouri Financial Assistance
Program
Bright Flight Program
Telephone: 1-800-473-6757
Web: www.dhe.mo.gov

Montana

Montana Guaranteed Student Loan
Program
Main programs:
Montana Higher Education Grant
(MHEG)
Montana Tuition Assistance Program
(MTAP) – Baker Grant
Telephone: 1-800-537-7508
Web: www.mgslp.state.mt.us

Nebraska

Nebraska's Coordinating Commission
for Postsecondary Education
Main program:
Nebraska State Grant (NSG)
Telephone: 402-471-2847
Web: www.ccpe.state.ne.us

Nevada

Nevada State Treasurer
Main programs:
Access Grant
Millennium Scholarship
Nevada Student Incentive Grant
Telephone: 1-888-477-2667
Web: http://nevadatreasurer.gov

New Hampshire

NH Postsecondary Education
Commission
Main programs:
Leveraged Incentive Grant Program
NH Incentive Program
Telephone: 603-271-2555
Web: www.nh.gov/postsecondary/
financial

New Jersey

State of New Jersey Commission on
Higher Education
Main programs:
College Bound Grant Program
Educational Opportunity Fund
Telephone: 1-800-792-8670
Web: www.state.nj.us/highereducation

New Mexico

New Mexico Higher Education
Department
Main programs:
College Affordability Grant
New Mexico Student Incentive Grant
Student Choice Grant
Telephone: 1-800-279-9777
Web: hed.state.nm.us

New York

New York State Higher Education
Services Corporation
Main programs:
Part-Time TAP
Tuition Assistance Program (TAP)
Telephone: 1-888-697-4372
Web: www.hesc.com

North Carolina

North Carolina State Education
Assistance Authority
Main programs:
EARN Scholarship
North Carolina Education Lottery
Scholarship (ELS)
North Carolina's Community College
Grant and Loan Program
Telephone: 1-866-866-CFNC
Web: www.cfnc.org

North Dakota

North Dakota University System
Main program:
North Dakota State Student Incentive
Grant (SSIG)
Telephone: 701-328-4114
Web: www.ndus.edu

Ohio

Ohio Board of Regents
Main program:
Ohio College Opportunity Grant
Program (OCOG)
Telephone: 1-888-833-1133
Web: regents.ohio.gov

Oklahoma

Oklahoma State Regents for Higher
Education
Main programs:
Oklahoma Tuition Aid Grant Program
(OTAG)
Oklahoma Tuition Equalization Grant
(OTEG)
Telephone: 1-800-858-1840
Web: www.okhighered.org

Oregon

Oregon Student Assistance
Commission
Main program:
Oregon Opportunity Grant (OOG)
(formerly called the State Need Grant)
Telephone: 1-800-452-8807
Web: www.osac.state.or.us

Pennsylvania

Pennsylvania Higher Education
Assistance Agency
Main program:
PA State Grant
Telephone: 1-800-692-7392
Web: www.pheaa.org

Rhode Island

RI Higher Education Assistance
Authority
Main programs:
Academic Promise Scholarship
Rhode Island State Grate Program
Telephone: 1-800-922-9855
Web: www.riheaa.org

South Carolina

South Carolina Commission on
Higher Education
Main program:
SC Tuition Grants Program
Telephone: 803-896-1120
Web: www.che.sc.gov

South Dakota

South Dakota Board of Regents
Main program:
South Dakota Opportunity
Scholarship
Telephone: 605-773-3455
Web: www.sdbor.edu

Tennessee

Tennessee Student Assistance
Corporation
Main programs:
Tennessee Student Assistance Award
Program (TSAA)
Tennessee Hope Access Grant
Tennessee Hope Scholarship
Telephone: 1-800-342-1663
Web: www.tennessee.gov/tsac

Texas

Texas Higher Education Coordinating
Board
Main programs:
Texas Educational Opportunity Grant
Program (TEOG)
TEXAS (Towards EXcellence, Access
and Success) Grant
Telephone: 1-888-311-8881
Web: www.collegeforalltexans.com

Utah

Utah Higher Education Assistance
Authority
Main program:
Utah Centennial Opportunity
Program for Education (UCOPE)
Grant
Telephone: 1-877-336-7378
Web: www.uheaa.org

Vermont

Vermont Student Assistance
Corporation
Main programs:
Vermont Incentive Grants
Vermont Non-Degree Grants
Vermont Part-Time Grants
Telephone: 1-800-882-4166
Web: services.vsac.org

Virginia

State Council of Higher Education for Virginia
Main programs:
College Scholarship Assistance Program
Tuition Assistance Grant Program (VTAG)
Virginia Commonwealth Award
Virginia Guaranteed Assistance Program (VGAP)
Telephone: 804-225-2600
Web: www.schev.virginia.gov

Washington

Washington Higher Education Coordinating Board
Main programs:
College Bound Scholarship
State Need Grant (SNG)
Telephone: 1-888-535-0747
Web: www.hecb.wa.gov

West Virginia

West Virginia Higher Education Policy Commission
Main programs:
West Virginia Higher Education Grant
West Virginia PROMISE (Providing Real Opportunities for Maximizing In-State Student Excellence)
Telephone: 304-558-4614
Web: www.hepc.wvnet.edu

Wisconsin

State of Wisconsin Higher Educational Aids Board
Main programs:
Talent Incentive Program (TIP) Grant
Wisconsin Higher Education Grant (WHEG)
Wisconsin Tuition Grant (WTG)
Telephone: 608-267-2206
Web: heab.state.wi.us

Wyoming

The Wyoming Student Loan Corporation (WyoLoan)
Main program:
WyoLoan Low-Interest Loans
Telephone: 1-800-999-6541
Web: www.wyoloan.org

The Best Scholarship Programs

In this appendix I've put together a list of some of the best scholarships available for a wide variety of students. Although there are literally thousands upon thousands of different scholarship and grant programs, the ones you'll find here are all given to multiple recipients. This, of course, significantly raises your chances of winning because you don't have to beat out every other applicant.

The scholarships are arranged according to some common themes, such as Heritage, Academic/Subject-Related, Geographic, and so on. I've also included a section containing scholarships for people with certain health conditions and family members of military personnel. I've included the website for each program as well, since it'll be the place to find the most up-to-date details on each scholarship program, which can change from year to year.

I suggest that you carve out some time and browse through this entire appendix, highlighting any scholarship that might be of interest. Then, when you're done, go back and visit the website of each scholarship program to find out the specifics of applying, such as deadline, eligibility details, and so forth.

Heritage and Gender-Related Scholarships

Name: **Adelante Hispanic Fund**
Type: Heritage, 3.0 GPA minimum
Number of Scholarships: 20+
Scholarship Amount: $2,000
Website: www.adelantefund.org

Name: **American Indian Education Foundation**
Type: Heritage, 2.0 GPA minimum
Number of Scholarships: 100+
Scholarship Amount: $2,000
Website: www.nrcprograms.org

Name: **Armenian Association Scholarship Program**
Type: Heritage
Number of Scholarships: 150
Scholarship Amount: $2,000
Website: www.amaa.org

Name: **Asian & Pacific Islander Scholarship Fund**
Type: Heritage, 2.5 GPA minimum
Number of Scholarships: 200+
Scholarship Amount: $2,500
Website: www.apiasf.org

Name: **Bobby Sox Scholarship Program**
Type: Gender, Athletic
Number of Scholarships: 50+
Scholarship Amount: $100–$2,500
Website: www.bobbysoxsoftball.org

Name: **Carl's Jr. La Estrella Latina Scholarship**
Type: Heritage, Geographic (California, Arizona, Nevada, Oklahoma, Texas)
Number of Scholarships: 50+
Scholarship Amount: $1,000
Website: www.carlsjr.com

Name: **Chinese American Citizens Scholarship**
Type: Heritage
Number of Scholarships: 15+
Scholarship Amount: $100–$1,000
Website: www.cacanational.org

Name: **College Assistance Migrant Program (CAMP)**
Type: Heritage, Migrant Workers
Number of Scholarships: 2,500+
Scholarship Amount: $750–$5,000
Website: www.migrantstudents.org

Name: **Ford Motor Minority Dealers Scholarship**
Type: Heritage (any minority), 2.5 GPA minimum
Number of Scholarships: 10
Scholarship Amount: $2,500
Website: www.fmmda.org

Name: **Frankel Trust to Empower Jewish Youth**
Type: Heritage
Number of Scholarships: 10+
Scholarship Amount: $6,500
Website: www.azfoundation.org

Name: **General Motors Minority Dealers Scholarship**
Type: Academic, 3.0 GPA minimum
Number of Scholarships: 20+
Scholarship Amount: $2,500
Website: www.gmmda.org

Name: **Girls Going Places Scholarship**
Type: Gender
Number of Scholarships: 15
Scholarship Amount: $1,000–$10,000
Website: www.guardianlife.com

Name: **Iranian Scholarship Foundation**
Type: Heritage
Number of Scholarships: 10+
Scholarship Amount: Up to $10,000
Website: www.iranianscholarships.org

Name: **La Unidad Latina Scholarships**
Type: Heritage
Number of Scholarships: 25+
Scholarship Amount: $500–$1,000
Website: www.launidadlatine.org

Name: **LULAC General Scholarship Program**
Type: Heritage
Number of Scholarships: 500+
Scholarship Amount: $250–$1,000
Website: www.lnesc.org

Name: **Mexican American Grocers Scholarship**
Type: Heritage
Number of Scholarships: 50+
Scholarship Amount: $750–$1,500
Website: www.maga.org

Name: **Midwest Region Korean Scholarships**
Type: Heritage, Regional
Number of Scholarships: 50+
Scholarship Amount: $1,000–$2,000
Website: www.kasf.org

Name: **Morris Udall Scholarship**
Type: Heritage (Native American, Alaskan native)
Number of Scholarships: 125+
Scholarship Amount: $350–$5,000
Website: www.udall.gov

Name: **P.E.O Sisterhood Scholarship Program**
Type: Gender (women going back to school)
Number of Scholarships: 3,000+
Scholarship Amount: $500–$2,000
Website: www.peointernational.org

Name: **Point Foundation Scholarship**
Type: Lesbian, gay, bisexual, and transgender
Number of Scholarships: 25+
Scholarship Amount: $10,000+
Website: www.pointfoundation.org

Name: **Turkish American Scholarship**
Type: Heritage, Subject Matter (communications related)
Number of Scholarships: 10+
Scholarship Amount: $5,000
Website: www.turkishcoalitionforamerica.org

Name: **United Negro College Fund**
Type: Heritage, 2.5 GPA minimum
Number of Scholarships: 1,000+
Scholarship Amount: $750–$7,500
Website: www.uncf.org

Name: **Verizon Asian-Pacific American Scholarship**
Type: Heritage
Number of Scholarships: 25+
Scholarship Amount: $2,000
Website: www.ocanatl.org

Name: **Women's Opportunity Scholarship Program**
Type: Gender (returning to school)
Number of Scholarships: 25+
Scholarship Amount: $5,000+
Website: www.soroptomist.org

Name: **Xerox Minority Scholarship**
Type: Heritage, Subject (technology)
Number of Scholarships: 100+
Scholarship Amount: $1,000–$10,000
Website: www.xerox.com

Academic or Subject-Related Scholarships

Name: **ADDC Education Scholarships**
Type: Subject (petroleum industry)
Number of Scholarships: 15+
Scholarship Amount: $1,000–$1,500
Website: www.addc.org

Name: **Alice Halton Scholarship**
Type: Subject (information management)
Number of Scholarships: 20+
Scholarship Amount: $1,000–$2,000
Website: www.alhef.org

Name: **American Board of Funeral Service Scholarship**
Type: Subject (funeral service)
Number of Scholarships: 25+
Scholarship Amount: $500–$2,500
Website: www.abfse.org

Name: **American Chemical Society Scholarship**
Type: Subject (chemistry), Heritage (minority)
Number of Scholarships: 100+
Scholarship Amount: Up to $3,000
Website: www.acs.org

Name: **American Dental Hygienist Association Scholarship**
Type: Subject (dental hygienics)
Number of Scholarships: 25+
Scholarship Amount: $1,500
Website: www.adha.net

Name: **American Hotel & Lodging Foundation Scholarship**
Type: Subject (hospitality management)
Number of Scholarships: 200+
Scholarship Amount: $3,000
Website: www.ahlef.org

Name: **American Nuclear Science Society Scholarship**
Type: Subject (nuclear science)
Number of Scholarships: 30+
Scholarship Amount: $2,000
Website: www.ans.org

Name: **American Meteorological Society Scholarship**
Type: Subject (meteorology)
Number of Scholarships: 10+
Scholarship Amount: $2,500
Website: www.ametsoc.org

Name: **American Society of Mechanical Engineers Scholarship**
Type: Subject (mechanical engineering)
Number of Scholarships: 15+
Scholarship Amount: $1,500
Website: www.asme.org

Name: **American Welding Society Scholarship**
Type: Subject (welding)
Number of Scholarships: 100+
Scholarship Amount: $500–$1,000
Website: www.aws.org

Name: **Anita Borg Scholarship Fund**
Type: Gender, Subject (computer science)
Number of Scholarships: 20+
Scholarship Amount: $1,000–$10,000
Website: www.google.com/anitaborg

Name: **Bank of America Achievement Scholarships**
Type: Academic
Number of Scholarships: 300+
Scholarship Amount: $500–$2,000
Website: www.bankofamerica.com/foundation

Name: **California Parks and Recreation Scholarship**
Type: Subject (related to parks, recreation, and so on)
Number of Scholarships: 20+
Scholarship Amount: $1,000–$2,000
Website: www.cprs.org

Name: **Centex Build Your Future Scholarship**
Type: Subject (architecture or construction related)
Scholarship Amount: $1,500–$3,000
Website: www.nationalhousingendowment.com

Name: **CFA Institute 9/11 Scholarship**
Type: Subject (economics, finance, or accounting)
Number of Scholarships: 10+
Scholarship Amount: $1,000–$25,000
Website: www.cfainstitute.org

Name: **Coca-Cola Scholarships**
Type: Academic, 3.0 GPA minimum
Number of Scholarships: 500+
Scholarship Amount: $2,500–$5,000
Website: www.coca-colascholarships.org

Name: **Colorado Nurses Scholarships**
Type: Subject (nursing), State (Colorado)
Number of Scholarships: 20+
Scholarship Amount: $1,000
Website: www.coloradonursesfoundation.org

Name: **Commitment to Agriculture Scholarship**
Type: Subject (agriculture)
Number of Scholarships: 100+
Scholarship Amount: $1,500
Website: www.ffa.org

Name: **Dade Behring Medical Technician Scholarship**
Type: Subject (laboratory technician)
Number of Scholarships: 50+
Scholarship Amount: $1,000
Website: www.ascls.org

Name: **Davidson Fellows Scholarship Program**
Type: Academic
Number of Scholarships: 25+
Scholarship Amount: $10,000–$50,000
Website: www.davidsongifted.org

Name: **Delta Mu Delta Scholarship**
Type: Subject (business)
Number of Scholarships: 25+
Scholarship Amount: $100–$2,000
Website: www.dmd-ntl.org

Name: **Department of Homeland Security Scholarship**
Type: Career (homeland security)
Number of Scholarships: 50+
Scholarship Amount: $1,000–$5,000
Website: www.orau.org

Name: **Ecolab Scholarship**
Type: Subject (hospitality)
Number of Scholarships: 10+
Scholarship Amount: $1,000–$2,000
Website: www.ahlef.org

Name: **Elizabeth Davis Scholarship**
Type: Subject (home health care)
Number of Scholarships: 10+
Scholarship Amount: $500–$3,000
Website: www.vsac.org

Name: **Epsilon Sigma Alpha Scholarship**
Type: Academic, 3.0 GPA minimum
Number of Scholarships: 10+
Scholarship Amount: $1,000
Website: www.esaintl.com

Name: **FORE Merit Scholarships**
Type: Subject (health administration)
Number of Scholarships: 75+
Scholarship Amount: $1,000–$5,000
Website: www.ahima.org

Name: **Herman Smith Scholarship**
Type: Subject (construction)
Number of Scholarships: 10+
Scholarship Amount: $2,000
Website: www.nahb.com

Name: **Humane Studies Fellowships**
Type: Subject (humanities)
Number of Scholarships: 100+
Scholarship Amount: $500–$10,000+
Website: www.theihs.org

Name: **Jewell Taylor Scholarship**
Type: Subject (consumer and family science)
Number of Scholarships: 15+
Scholarship Amount: $5,000
Website: www.aafcs.org

Name: **John A. Wickham Scholarship**
Type: Subject (engineering or science)
Number of Scholarships: 10+
Scholarship Amount: $2,000
Website: www.afcea.org

Name: **L & E Marmet Scholarship**
Type: Subject (energy or science), State (West Virginia)
Number of Scholarships: 25+
Scholarship Amount: $2,000–$3,000
Website: www.tgkvf.org

Name: **Leroy Collins Memorial Scholarship**
Type: Subject (journalism), Geographic (Florida)
Number of Scholarships: 20+
Scholarship Amount: $3,000
Website: www.ficf.org

Name: **Mary McMillan Scholarship**
Type: Subject (physical therapy)
Number of Scholarships: 10+
Scholarship Amount: $3,000–$5,000
Website: www.apta.org

Name: **McKesson Scholarship**
Type: Subject (nursing)
Number of Scholarships: 25+
Scholarship Amount: $1,000–$5,000
Website: www.nsna.org

Name: **Mu Alpha Theta Scholarship**
Type: Subject (math)
Number of Scholarships: 10+
Scholarship Amount: $4,000
Website: www.mualphatheta.org

Name: **National FFA Undergraduate Scholarship**
Type: Subject (agriculture and related subjects)
Number of Scholarships: 1,000+
Scholarship Amount: $1,000
Website: www.ffa.org

Name: **Physician Assistant Foundation Scholarship**
Type: Subject (physician's assistant)
Number of Scholarships: 40+
Scholarship Amount: $2,000–$5,000
Website: www.aapa.org

Name: **Plastics Pioneers Association Scholarship**
Type: Subject (plastics industry)
Number of Scholarships: 10+
Scholarship Amount: $3,000
Website: www.4spe.org

Name: **Wildlife Leadership Award**
Type: Subject (wildlife studies)
Number of Scholarships: 10+
Scholarship Amount: $2,000
Website: www.rmef.org

State, Regional, and Geographic Scholarships

Name: **Arkansas Governor's Scholarship**
Type: State, Academic
Number of Scholarships: 200+
Scholarship Amount: $500–$10,000
Website: www.arkansasgovernorsscholarship.com

Name: **Barnett Memorial Scholarship**
Type: State (Missouri), Academic
Number of Scholarships: 300+
Scholarship Amount: Up to full cost of tuition
Website: www.dhe.mo.gov

Name: **Big 33 Academic Scholarship Program**
Type: State (Ohio and Pennsylvania), Academic
Number of Scholarships: 150+
Scholarship Amount: $500–$4,000
Website: www.big33.org

Name: **Buster Bynum Scholarship**
Type: Geographic (southeastern U.S.)
Number of Scholarships: 25+
Scholarship Amount: $1,000
Website: www.sesptc.com

Name: **CalGrant Program**
Type: State (California)
Number of Scholarships: 200,000+
Scholarship Amount: $1,500–$9,700
Website: www.csac.ca.gov

Name: **Champions for Children Scholarships**
Type: State (Michigan), Volunteerism
Number of Scholarships: 100+
Scholarship Amount: $1,000
Website: www.msmentoring.org

Name: **Comcast Leaders Scholarships**
Type: Geographic (any area Comcast Cable TV serves)
Number of Scholarships: 1,500+
Scholarship Amount: $1,000
Website: www.comcast.com

Name: **ConocoPhilips Scholarship**
Type: State (Alaska)
Number of Scholarships: 20
Scholarship Amount: $3,000–$5,000
Website: www.conocophillipsalska.com/scholarships

Name: **COSTCO Stores Scholarship**
Type: State (Washington)
Number of Scholarships: 20+
Scholarship Amount: $250–$1,000
Website: www.icwashington.org

Name: **DC Adoptions Scholarships**
Type: State (Washington, D.C.)
Number of Scholarships: 2,000+
Scholarship Amount: $10,000
Website: www.dc.gov

Name: **Delaware Legislative Essay Contest**
Type: Regional, Essay
Number of Scholarships: 50+
Scholarship Amount: $1,000–$5,000
Website: www.doe.state.de.us

Name: **Delaware Scholarship Incentive Program**
Type: Geographic, 2.5 GPA minimum
Number of Scholarships: 1,000+
Scholarship Amount: $700–$2,000
Website: www.doe.state.de.us

Name: **District 1 Family Scholarship**
Type: Geographic (southeastern U.S.)
Number of Scholarships: 20
Scholarship Amount: $500–$1,500
Website: www.ahepadistrict1.org

Name: **Florida Association of Post-Secondary Schools Scholarship**
Type: State, Subject (vocational)
Number of Scholarships: 500+
Scholarship Amount: $1,000–Full Tuition
Website: www.fapsc.org

Name: **Florida Association of Realtors Essay Contest**
Type: Geographic, Essay
Number of Scholarships: 25+
Scholarship Amount: $500–$5,000
Website: www.floridarealtors.org

Name: **Flying J Scholarships**
Type: Geographic (communities with Flying J travel plazas)
Number of Scholarships: 100+
Scholarship Amount: $2,000
Website: www.flyingj.com

Name: **Ford Foundation Truck Scholarship**
Type: Geographic (towns with Ford dealerships)
Number of Scholarships: 500+
Scholarship Amount: $1,000
Website: www.ffa.org

Name: **Gromet Foundation**
Type: Geographic (Hawaii)
Number of Scholarships: 25+
Scholarship Amount: $1,500–$5,000
Website: www.gromet.org

Name: **Harry Gregg Foundation Scholarship**
Type: State (New Hampshire), Health (disabilities)
Number of Scholarships: 150+
Scholarship Amount: $1,000
Website: www.crotchedmountain.org

Name: **Illinois Odd Fellows Scholarship**
Type: State
Number of Scholarships: 20+
Scholarship Amount: $500–$1,000
Website: www.ioof-il.org

Name: **Iowa Grand Lodge Masonic Scholarship**
Type: State
Number of Scholarships: 50+
Scholarship Amount: $2,000
Website: www.gl-iowa.org

Name: **Kansas State Scholarships**
Type: Geographic
Number of Scholarships: 1,000+
Scholarship Amount: $500–$1,000
Website: www.kansasregents.org

Name: **Kentucky Educational Excellence Scholarship**
Type: State, 2.5 GPA minimum
Number of Scholarships: 50,000+
Scholarship Amount: $500–$2,500
Website: www.kheaa.com

Name: **Laura Settle Scholarship**
Type: State (California), Subject (education)
Number of Scholarships: 25+
Scholarship Amount: $2,000
Website: www.calrta.org

Name: **Lily Foundation Community Scholarship**
Type: State (Indiana)
Number of Scholarships: 75+
Scholarship Amount: Up to full tuition
Website: www.icindiana.org

Name: **Lowe's Scholarship Program**
Type: Geographic (communities with Lowe's home improvement stores)
Number of Scholarships: 350+
Scholarship Amount: $1,000–$15,000
Website: www.lowes.com/scholarships

Name: **McWherter Scholarship**
Type: State (Tennessee), Academic (3.5 GPA minimum)
Number of Scholarships: 50+
Scholarship Amount: $500–$6,000
Website: www.collegepaystn.com

Name: **Meyerhoff Scholarships for Maryland**
Type: State (Maryland), 3.0 GPA minimum
Number of Scholarships: 10+
Scholarship Amount: $7,000
Website: www.centralsb.org

Name: **Michigan Community Caring Scholarships**
Type: State
Number of Scholarships: 75+
Scholarship Amount: $1,000
Website: www.communitycaring.org

Name: **New Hampshire Incentive Program**
Type: State
Number of Scholarships: 4,000+
Scholarship Amount: $125–$1,000
Website: www.nh.gov

Name: **One Family Scholarship**
Type: State (Massachusetts), must be homeless or formerly homeless
Number of Scholarships: 100+
Scholarship Amount: Up to $10,000 per year
Website: www.onefamilyinc.org

Name: **Palmetto Scholarship**
Type: State (South Carolina), Academic
Number of Scholarships: 5,000+
Scholarship Amount: $6,700–$10,000
Website: www.che.sc.gov

Name: **People Helping People Scholarship**
Type: State (North Carolina)
Number of Scholarships: 100+
Scholarship Amount: $2,500
Website: www.ncccs.cc.nc.us

Name: **Ruth Johnson Fund**
Type: State (West Virginia)
Number of Scholarships: 50+
Scholarship Amount: $1,000
Website: www.tgkvf.org

Name: **Tennessee Aspire Scholarship**
Type: State
Number of Scholarships: 10,000+
Scholarship Amount: $1,500
Website: www.collegepaystn.com

Name: **What Drives You Scholarship**
Type: Essay, Regional (Utah, New Mexico, Oregon, and Washington)
Number of Scholarships: 20+
Scholarship Amount: $1,000–$3,500
Website: www.yourturn2apply.com

Name: **World Class Scholarships**
Type: Regional (anywhere serviced by Mediacom)
Number of Scholarships: 50+
Scholarship Amount: $1,000
Website: www.mediacomworldclass.com

Health-Related Scholarships

Name: **Asthma Award of Excellence Scholarship**
Type: Health (asthma)
Number of Scholarships: 25+
Scholarship Amount: $1,000
Website: www.aaaai.org

Name: **Beth Carew Scholarship**
Type: Health (bleeding disorders)
Number of Scholarships: 10
Scholarship Amount: $2,000
Website: www.colburn-keenanfoundation.org

Name: **Chairscholars Foundation Scholarship**
Type: Health (physically challenged)
Number of Scholarships: 20+
Scholarship Amount: $2,500–$5,000
Website: www.chairscholars.org

Name: **Creon/Solvay Pharmaceuticals Scholarships**
Type: Health (cystic fibrosis)
Number of Scholarships: 40
Scholarship Amount: $2,000
Website: www.solvay-pharmaceuticals-us.com

Name: **Keppra Family Epilepsy Scholarship**
Type: Health (epilepsy)
Number of Scholarships: 30+
Scholarship Amount: $5,000
Website: www.keppra.com

Name: **Lilly Reintegration Scholarships**
Type: Health (schizophrenia)
Number of Scholarships: 100+
Scholarship Amount: $500+
Website: www.reintegration.com

Name: **Little People of America**
Type: Health (4'10" height or shorter)
Number of Scholarships: 10
Scholarship Amount: $250–$1,000
Website: www.lpaonline.org

Name: **MaryEllen Locher Scholarship**
Type: Health (children of breast cancer victims)
Number of Scholarships: 30+
Scholarship Amount: $1,500–$3,000
Website: www.maryellenlocherfoundation.org

Name: **National Federation of the Blind Scholarship**
Type: Health (blindness)
Number of Scholarships: 15+
Scholarship Amount: $3,000–$5,000
Website: www.nfb.org

Name: **National Multiple Sclerosis Program**
Type: Health
Number of Scholarships: 300+
Scholarship Amount: $1,000–$3,000
Website: www.nationalmssociety.org

Name: **Optimist International Deaf Scholarship**
Type: Health (deaf or hard of hearing)
Number of Scholarships: 250+
Scholarship Amount: $500–$1,500
Website: www.optimist.org

Name: **Pfizer Epilepsy Scholarship**
Type: Health
Number of Scholarships: 25
Scholarship Amount: $3,000
Website: www.epilepsy-scholarship.com

Military-Related Scholarships (Family)

Name: **Freedom Alliance Scholarships**
Type: Military (children of deceased personnel)
Number of Scholarships: 100+
Scholarship Amount: $100–$1,000
Website: www.freedomalliance.org

Name: **Hanscom Spouses' Club Scholarship**
Type: Military (spouse), Regional (New England)
Number of Scholarships: 15+
Scholarship Amount: $1,000–$3,000
Website: www.hanscomsc.org

Name: **Joanne Holbrook Patton Military Spouse Scholarship**
Type: Military (spouse of military personnel)
Number of Scholarships: 50+
Scholarship Amount: $1,000
Website: www.nmfa.org

Name: **Marine Scholarships**
Type: Military (children)
Number of Scholarships: 1,000+
Scholarship Amount: $500–$2,000
Website: www.mcsf.org

Name: **Military Officers Association Scholarship**
Type: Military (children)
Number of Scholarships: 25+
Scholarship Amount: $1,000
Website: www.moaa.org

Name: **Purple Heart Scholarship Program**
Type: Military (recipients of Purple Heart or their descendants)
Number of Scholarships: 50+
Scholarship Amount: $3,000
Website: www.purpleheart.org

Name: **ROTC Civilian Marksmanship Scholarship**
Type: Military
Number of Scholarships: 100
Scholarship Amount: $1,000
Website: www.odcmp.org

Name: **ThankUSA Scholarship**
Type: Military (children of active-duty personnel)
Number of Scholarships: 1,000+
Scholarship Amount: $1,000
Website: www.thankusa.org

Name: **Wings Over America**
Type: Military (children of Navy pilots)
Number of Scholarships: 30+
Scholarship Amount: $3,000
Website: www.wingsoveramerica.us

Essay Scholarships

Name: **America in Solidarity Scholarship**
Type: Essay
Number of Scholarships: 10+
Scholarship Amount: $200–$1,000
Website: www.americasolidarity.org

Name: **Appalachian College Association Scholarships**
Type: Essay
Number of Scholarships: 25+
Scholarship Amount: $6,000
Website: www.acaweb.org

Name: **Bill Dickey Golf Scholarships**
Type: Essay, Golf
Number of Scholarships: 75+
Scholarship Amount: $1,000–$6,000
Website: www.nmjgsa.org

Name: **Earl Woods Scholarship**
Type: Essay
Number of Scholarships: 10+
Scholarship Amount: $5,000
Website: www.tigerwoodsfoundation.org

Name: **Horatio Alger Scholarship Program**
Type: Essay
Number of Scholarships: 100
Scholarship Amount: $20,000
Website: www.horatioalger.com

Name: **Life Lessons Scholarship**
Type: Essay (children who have lost a parent)
Number of Scholarships: 20+
Scholarship Amount: $500–$5,000
Website: www.lifehappens.org

Name: **Newsweek and Kaplan "My Turn" Scholarship**
Type: Essay
Number of Scholarships: 10
Scholarship Amount: $1,000–$5,000
Website: www.kaptest.com

Name: **Oklahoma Young Farmers and Ranchers Scholarship**
Type: Essay (speech), State
Number of Scholarships: 25+
Scholarship Amount: $100–$1,000
Website: www.okfarmbureau.org

Name: **Prudential Community Spirit Awards**
Type: Essay
Number of Scholarships: 100+
Scholarship Amount: $1,000–$5,000
Website: www.principals.org

Name: **Sweet 16 Magazine Scholarships**
Type: Essay
Number of Scholarships: 15+
Scholarship Amount: $500–$16,000
Website: www.guidepostmag.com

Name: **Tuskegee Airmen Scholarship**
Type: Essay
Number of Scholarships: 40+
Scholarship Amount: $1,500
Website: www.taisf.org

Name: **Voice of Democracy Scholarship**
Type: Essay
Number of Scholarships: 50+
Scholarship Amount: $1,000–$5,000
Website: www.vfw.org

Other Scholarships

Name: **American Quarterhorse Foundation**
Type: Organizational
Number of Scholarships: 20+
Scholarship Amount: $2,000
Website: www.aqha.com

Name: **Beta Club Scholarship**
Type: Organization
Number of Scholarships: 200+
Scholarship Amount: $1,000–$15,000
Website: www.betaclub.org

Name: **Datatel Scholarship Program**
Type: Institution (schools using Datatel services)
Number of Scholarships: 150+
Scholarship Amount: $1,000–$2,400
Website: www.datatelscholars.org

Name: **Division II Degree Completion Program**
Type: Athletic (D-II schools), 2.5 GPA minimum
Number of Scholarships: 100+
Scholarship Amount: $5,000–full cost of tuition
Website: www.ncaa.org

Name: **Education Is Freedom Scholarship Program**
Type: Need-Based
Number of Scholarships: 200+
Scholarship Amount: $2,000
Website: www.educationisfreedom.com

Name: **Elks Most Valuable Student Scholarship**
Type: Need-Based
Number of Scholarships: 500+
Scholarship Amount: $1,000–$15,000
Website: www.elks.org

Name: **Houston Livestock Show Scholarship**
Type: Organization (FFA, 4-H)
Number of Scholarships: 300+
Scholarship Amount: $1,000–$3,750
Website: www.texasffa.org

Name: **Key Club Scholarships**
Type: Organization (Key Club)
Number of Scholarships: 50+
Scholarship Amount: $1,000
Website: www.keyclub.org

Name: **Miss Cheerleader of America Scholarship**
Type: Athletic (cheerleading)
Number of Scholarships: 100+
Scholarship Amount: $500–$1,000
Website: www.misscheerleaderofamerica.com

Name: **Quarter Century Wireless Association**
Type: Hobby (amateur radio)
Number of Scholarships: 15+
Scholarship Amount: $1,000–$1,600
Website: www.farweb.org

Name: **Sallie Mae Scholarships**
Type: Variety of scholarships available
Number of Scholarships: 500+
Scholarship Amount: $500–$5,000
Website: www.thesalliemaefund.org

Name: **U.S. Junior Chamber of Commerce Scholarship**
Type: Need-Based
Number of Scholarships: 10+
Scholarship Amount: $1,000
Website: www.usjaycees.org

Name: **Wallrath 4-H Scholarship**
Type: Organizational (4-H), Regional (Texas)
Number of Scholarships: 200+
Scholarship Amount: $1,000–$15,000
Website: www.texas4-h.tamu.edu

Name: **Wells Fargo CollegeSTEPS Scholarship**
Type: Organizational (join free CollegeSTEPS program)
Number of Scholarships: 20
Scholarship Amount: $1,000
Website: www.wellsfargo.com/collegesteps

Directory of State Section 529 Plans

Section 529 plans may be one of the most advantageous ways to save money for college, even for a short period of time. That's because Section 529 plans might allow you to avoid all taxation on the growth of your savings, as well as provide you with a state income tax deduction for amounts you deposited. While it is generally recommended that you choose the plan managed by the state you live in, some states' plans may offer substandard benefits or above-average costs. Prior to selecting a plan, be sure to contact your tax advisor and check out the Section 529 reviews on Morningstar.com.

Alabama

Plan Name: Prepaid Affordable College Tuition (PACT)
Type: Prepaid Tuition
Investment Manager: State Treasurer/Trust Fund
Available Through: State of Alabama
Minimum Investment: $6,408 in 2009–2010
Deductible Contributions for Residents?: Yes
Telephone: 1-800-252-7228
Website: www.treasury.alabama.gov/pact/

Plan Name: CollegeCounts
Type: Savings
Investment Manager: Van Kampen Mutual Funds
Available Through: Direct from investment manager
Minimum Investment: $250 one-time or $25 per month
Deductible Contributions for Residents?: Yes
Telephone: 1-866-529-2228
Website: www.alabama529.com

Plan Name: Higher Education Fund
Type: Savings
Investment Manager: Van Kampen Mutual Funds
Available Through: Stockbrokers
Minimum Investment: $1,000 one-time or $25 per month
Deductible Contributions for Residents?: Yes
Telephone: 1-866-529-2228
Website: www.vankampen.com

Alaska

Plan Name: University of Alaska College Savings Plan
Type: Savings
Investment Manager: T. Rowe Price Mutual Funds
Available Through: Direct from investment manager
Minimum Investment: $250 one-time or $50 per month
Deductible Contributions for Residents?: No
Telephone: 1-866-277-1005
Website: www.uacollegesavings.com

Plan Name: T. Rowe Price College Savings Plan
Type: Savings
Investment Manager: T. Rowe Price Mutual Funds
Available Through: Direct from investment manager
Minimum Investment: $250 one-time or $50 per month
Deductible Contributions for Residents?: No
Telephone: 1-800-369-3641
Website: www.price529.com

Plan Name: John Hancock Freedom 529 Plan
Type: Savings
Investment Manager: John Hancock Mutual Funds
Available Through: Stockbrokers
Minimum Investment: $1,000 one-time or $50 per month
Deductible Contributions for Residents?: No
Telephone: 1-866-222-7498
Website: www.johnhancockfreedom529.com

Arizona

Note: Arizona offers deductions to residents who invest in any state's plan, not just those set up by the state of Arizona.

Plan Name: InvestEd
Type: Savings
Investment Manager: Waddell & Reed
Available Through: Directly with investment manager
Minimum Investment: $500 one-time or $50 per month
Deductible Contributions for Residents?: Yes
Telephone: 1-888-923-3355
Website: www.invested529.com

Plan Name: CollegeSure 529 Plan
Type: Savings
Investment Manager: College Savings Bank
Available Through: Stockbrokers
Minimum Investment: $250 one-time or $100 per month
Deductible Contributions for Residents?: Yes
Telephone: 1-800-888-2723
Website: arizona.collegesavings.com

Plan Name: Fidelity Arizona 529
Type: Savings
Investment Manager: Fidelity Investments
Available Through: Direct from investment manager
Minimum Investment: $50 one-time or $25 per month
Deductible Contributions for Residents?: Yes
Telephone: 1-800-544-1262
Website: www.fidelity.com/arizona

Arkansas

Note: Arkansas may match parent contributions up to $500 per child, based on a family's income.

Plan Name: GIFT Plan
Type: Savings
Investment Manager: UPromise Investments
Available Through: Direct from investment manager
Minimum Investment: $25 one-time or $10 per month
Deductible Contributions for Residents?: Yes
Telephone: 1-800-587-7301
Website: www.thegiftplan.com

Plan Name: iShares 529 Plan
Type: Savings
Investment Manager: UPromise Investments and Blackrock
Available Through: Direct from investment manager
Minimum Investment: $500 one-time or $50 per month
Deductible Contributions for Residents?: Yes
Telephone: 1-888-529-9552
Website: ishares529.s.upromise.com

California

Plan Name: Scholarshare 529 Plan
Type: Savings
Investment Manager: Fidelity Investments
Available Through: Direct from investment manager or through an advisor
Minimum Investment: $50 one-time or $25 per month
Deductible Contributions for Residents?: No
Telephone: 1-800-522-7297
Website: www.scholarshare.com

Colorado

Note: Colorado may match parent contributions up to $500 per child, based on a family's income.

Plan Name: Stable Value College Savings Program
Type: Savings
Investment Manager: MetLife
Available Through: Direct from investment manager
Minimum Investment: $25
Deductible Contributions for Residents?: Yes
Telephone: 1-800-448-2424
Website: www.collegeinvest.org

Plan Name: Direct Portfolio College Savings Program
Type: Savings
Investment Manager: UPromise and Vanguard Investments
Available Through: Direct from investment manager
Minimum Investment: $25
Deductible Contributions for Residents?: Yes
Telephone: 1-800-997-4295
Website: www.collegeinvest.org

Plan Name: Scholars Choice 529 Plan
Type: Savings
Investment Manager: Legg Mason Investments
Available Through: Stockbrokers
Minimum Investment: $250 one-time or $50 per month
Deductible Contributions for Residents?: Yes
Telephone: 1-888-572-4652
Website: www.scholars-choice.com

Plan Name: Smart Choice Savings Plan
Type: Savings
Investment Manager: FirstBank Holding Company
Available Through: Direct from investment manager
Minimum Investment: No minimum
Deductible Contributions for Residents?: Yes
Telephone: 1-800-964-3444
Website: www.collegeinvest.org

Connecticut

Plan Name: Connecticut Higher Education Trust (CHET)
Type: Savings
Investment Manager: TIAA-CREF
Available Through: Direct from investment manager
Minimum Investment: $50 one-time or $25 per month
Deductible Contributions for Residents?: Yes
Telephone: 1-888-799-2438
Website: www.aboutchet.com

Delaware

Plan Name: Delaware College Investment Plan
Type: Savings
Investment Manager: Fidelity Investments
Available Through: Direct from investment manager
Minimum Investment: $50 one-time or $25 per month
Deductible Contributions for Residents?: No
Telephone: 1-800-544-1655
Website: www.fidelity.com/delaware

District of Columbia

Plan Name: DC 529 College Savings Plan
Type: Savings
Investment Manager: Calvert Mutual Funds
Available Through: Direct from investment manager or through an advisor
Minimum Investment: $100 one-time or $25 per month
Deductible Contributions for Residents?: Yes
Telephone: 1-800-987-4859
Website: www.DCCollegeSavings.com

Florida

Plan Name: Florida College Investment Plan
Type: Savings
Investment Manager: Florida College Board
Available Through: Direct from investment manager
Minimum Investment: $250 one-time or $25 per month
Deductible Contributions for Residents?: No
Telephone: 1-800-552-4723
Website: www.myfloridaprepaid.com

Plan Name: Florida Prepaid College Fund
Type: Prepaid Tuition
Investment Manager: Florida College Board
Available Through: Direct from investment manager
Minimum Investment: $5,735 for 2009–2010
Deductible Contributions for Residents?: No
Telephone: 1-800-552-4723
Website: www.myfloridaprepaid.com

Georgia

Plan Name: Florida College Investment Plan
Type: Savings
Investment Manager: TIAA-CREF
Available Through: Direct from investment manager
Minimum Investment: $25
Deductible Contributions for Residents?: Yes
Telephone: 1-877-424-4377
Website: www.path2college529.com

Hawaii

Plan Name: Hawaii College Savings Plan
Type: Savings
Investment Manager: UPromise and Vanguard Investments
Available Through: Direct from investment manager
Minimum Investment: $15
Deductible Contributions for Residents?: No
Telephone: 1-866-529-3343
Website: www.hi529.com

Idaho

Plan Name: Idaho College Savings Plan (Ideal)
Type: Savings
Investment Manager: UPromise Investments
Available Through: Direct from investment manager
Minimum Investment: $25
Deductible Contributions for Residents?: Yes
Telephone: 1-866-433-2533
Website: www.idsaves.org

Illinois

Plan Name: Bright Directions Plan
Type: Savings
Investment Manager: Union Bank and Trust of Nebraska
Available Through: Stockbroker
Minimum Investment: No minimum
Deductible Contributions for Residents?: Yes
Telephone: 1-866-722-7283
Website: www.brightdirections.com

Plan Name: Bright Start College Savings Plan
Type: Savings
Investment Manager: Oppenheimer Funds
Available Through: Direct from investment manager or through an advisor
Minimum Investment: $25 one-time or $15 per month
Deductible Contributions for Residents?: Yes
Telephone: 1-877-432-7444
Website: www.brightstartsavings.com

Plan Name: College Illinois Prepaid Tuition
Type: Prepaid Tuition
Investment Manager: Illinois Student Assistance Commission
Available Through: Direct from investment manager
Minimum Investment: $1,583 for 2009–2010
Deductible Contributions for Residents?: Yes
Telephone: 1-877-877-3724
Website: www.collegeillinois.com

Indiana

Plan Name: CollegeChoice 529 Plan
Type: Savings
Investment Manager: UPromise Investments
Available Through: Direct from investment manager or through an advisor
Minimum Investment: $25
Deductible Contributions for Residents?: Yes
Telephone: 1-866-485-9415
Website: collegechoicedirect.s.upromise.com

Iowa

Plan Name: College Savings Iowa
Type: Savings
Investment Manager: UPromise and Vanguard Investments
Available Through: Direct from investment manager
Minimum Investment: $50
Deductible Contributions for Residents?: Yes
Telephone: 1-888-672-9116
Website: collegesavingsiowa.s.upromise.com

Plan Name: Iowa Advisor 529 Plan
Type: Savings
Investment Manager: UPromise Investments
Available Through: Stockbroker
Minimum Investment: $25
Deductible Contributions for Residents?: Yes
Telephone: 1-800-774-5127
Website: iowaadvisor529.s.upromise.com

Kansas

Plan Name: Iowa Schwab 529 Plan
Type: Savings
Investment Manager: Schwab Investments
Available Through: Direct from investment manager or through an advisor
Minimum Investment: $250 one-time or $50 per month
Deductible Contributions for Residents?: Yes
Telephone: 1-866-663-5247
Website: www.schwab.com/529

Plan Name: Learning Quest 529 Education Savings Program
Type: Savings
Investment Manager: American Century Mutual Funds
Available Through: Direct from investment manager or through an advisor
Minimum Investment: $250 one-time or $50 per month
Deductible Contributions for Residents?: Yes
Telephone: 1-800-579-2203
Website: www.learningquestsavings.com

Kentucky

Plan Name: Kentucky Education Savings Trust
Type: Savings
Investment Manager: TIAA-CREF
Available Through: Direct from investment manager
Minimum Investment: $25
Deductible Contributions for Residents?: No
Telephone: 1-877-598-7878
Website: www.kysaves.com

Louisiana

Note: The state of Louisiana may provide a percentage match (up to 14 percent) on contributions, depending on household income.

Plan Name: START Savings Program
Type: Savings
Investment Manager: Louisiana State Treasurer
Available Through: Direct from investment manager
Minimum Investment: $10
Deductible Contributions for Residents?: Yes
Telephone: 1-800-259-5626
Website: www.startsaving.la.gov

Maine

Note: The state of Maine may provide a $200 contribution to any new account opened with more than $50, depending on household income. Additionally, the Alfond College Challenge donates up to $500 for all accounts opened on behalf of a Maine baby.

Plan Name: NextGen College Savings Plan
Type: Savings
Investment Manager: Merrill Lynch
Available Through: Direct from investment manager or through an advisor
Minimum Investment: $250 one-time or $25 per month
Deductible Contributions for Residents?: Yes
Telephone: 1-877-463-9843
Website: www.nextgenplan.com

Maryland

Plan Name: Maryland College Investment Plan
Type: Savings
Investment Manager: T. Rowe Price Mutual Funds
Available Through: Direct from investment manager
Minimum Investment: $250 one-time or $50 per month
Deductible Contributions for Residents?: Yes
Telephone: 1-888-463-4723
Website: www.collegesavingsmd.org

Plan Name: Maryland Prepaid College Trust
Type: Prepaid Tuition
Investment Manager: College Savings Plan of Maryland
Available Through: Direct from investment manager
Minimum Investment: $3,841 for 2009–2010
Deductible Contributions for Residents?: Yes
Telephone: 1-888-463-4723
Website: www.collegesavingsmd.org

Massachusetts

Plan Name: U.Fund College Plan
Type: Savings
Investment Manager: Fidelity Investments
Available Through: Direct from investment manager
Minimum Investment: $50 one-time or $15 per month
Deductible Contributions for Residents?: No
Telephone: 1-800-544-2776
Website: www.fidelity.com/ufund

Michigan

Plan Name: Michigan 529 Advisor Plan
Type: Savings
Investment Manager: TIAA-CREF & Allianz Investments
Available Through: Stockbroker
Minimum Investment: $25
Deductible Contributions for Residents?: Yes
Telephone: 1-866-529-8818
Website: www.mi529advisor.com

Plan Name: Michigan Education Savings Trust (MEST)
Type: Savings
Investment Manager: TIAA-CREF
Available Through: Direct from investment manager
Minimum Investment: $25
Deductible Contributions for Residents?: Yes
Telephone: 1-877-861-6377
Website: www.misaves.com

Plan Name: Michigan Education Trust (MET)
Type: Prepaid Tuition
Investment Manager: Michigan Department of the Treasury
Available Through: Direct from investment manager
Minimum Investment: $1,340 for 2009–2010
Deductible Contributions for Residents?: Yes
Telephone: 1-800-638-4543
Website: www.michigan.gov/setwithmet

Minnesota

Note: The state of Minnesota may provide a percentage match (up to 15 percent) on contributions, depending on household income.

Plan Name: Minnesota College Savings Plan
Type: Savings
Investment Manager: TIAA-CREF
Available Through: Direct from investment manager
Minimum Investment: $25
Deductible Contributions for Residents?: No
Telephone: 1-877-338-4646
Website: www.mnsaves.org

Mississippi

Plan Name: Mississippi Affordable College Savings (MACS)
Type: Savings
Investment Manager: TIAA-CREF
Available Through: Direct from investment manager or through an advisor
Minimum Investment: $25
Deductible Contributions for Residents?: Yes
Telephone: 1-800-486-3670
Website: www.collegesavingsms.com

Plan Name: Mississippi Prepaid Affordable College Tuition (MPACT)
Type: Prepaid Tuition
Investment Manager: Mississippi Department of the Treasury
Available Through: Direct from investment manager
Minimum Investment: $1,622 for 2009–2010
Deductible Contributions for Residents?: Yes
Telephone: 1-800-987-4450
Website: www.treasury.state.ms.us

Missouri

Note: Missouri offers deductions to residents who invest in any state's plan, not just those set up by the state of Missouri.

Plan Name: Missouri 529 Plan (MOST)
Type: Savings
Investment Manager: UPromise Investments
Available Through: Direct from investment manager or through an advisor
Minimum Investment: $25
Deductible Contributions for Residents?: No
Telephone: 1-888-414-6678
Website: www.missourimost.org

Montana

Plan Name: Pacific Life Montana 529 Plan
Type: Savings
Investment Manager: Pacific Life
Available Through: Direct from investment manager or through an advisor
Minimum Investment: $500 one-time or $50 per month
Deductible Contributions for Residents?: Yes
Telephone: 1-800-722-2333
Website: collegesavings.pacificlife.com

Plan Name: Montana Family Education Savings Program
Type: Savings
Investment Manager: College Savings Bank
Available Through: Direct from investment manager
Minimum Investment: $250 or $100 per month
Deductible Contributions for Residents?: Yes
Telephone: 1-800-888-2723
Website: montana.collegesavings.com

Nebraska

Plan Name: TD Ameritrade 529 Account
Type: Savings
Investment Manager: TD Ameritrade
Available Through: Direct from investment manager
Minimum Investment: No minimum
Deductible Contributions for Residents?: Yes
Telephone: 1-877-408-4644
Website: collegesavings.tdameritrade.com

Plan Name: College Savings Plan of Nebraska
Type: Savings
Investment Manager: Union Bank and Trust of Nebraska
Available Through: Direct from investment manager or through an advisor
Minimum Investment: No minimum
Deductible Contributions for Residents?: Yes
Telephone: 1-888-993-3746
Website: www.PlanForCollegeNow.com

Plan Name: State Farm 529 Plan
Type: Savings
Investment Manager: Oppenheimer Funds
Available Through: Stockbroker
Minimum Investment: $250 one-time or $50 per month
Deductible Contributions for Residents?: Yes
Telephone: 1-800-321-7520
Website: www.statefarm.com

New Hampshire

Plan Name: UNIQUE College Savings Plan
Type: Savings
Investment Manager: Fidelity Investments
Available Through: Direct from investment manager
Minimum Investment: $50 one-time or $15 per month
Deductible Contributions for Residents?: No
Telephone: 1-888-993-3746
Website: www.PlanForCollegeNow.com

Plan Name: Fidelity Advisor 529 Plan
Type: Savings
Investment Manager: Fidelity Investments
Available Through: Stockbroker
Minimum Investment: $1,000 one-time or $50 per month
Deductible Contributions for Residents?: No
Telephone: 1-800-544-1914
Website: www.fidelity.com/unique

New Jersey

Plan Name: NJBEST College Savings Plan
Type: Savings
Investment Manager: Franklin Templeton Funds
Available Through: Direct from investment manager or through an advisor
Minimum Investment: $250 one-time or $25 per month
Deductible Contributions for Residents?: Yes
Telephone: 1-877-337-5268
Website: www.njbest.com

New Mexico

Plan Name: Education Plan's College Savings Program/Scholar's Edge
Type: Savings
Investment Manager: Oppenheimer Funds
Available Through: Direct from investment manager or through an advisor
Minimum Investment: $25
Deductible Contributions for Residents?: No
Telephone: 1-877-465-2378
Website: www.theeducationplan.com

New York

Plan Name: New York 529 College Plan
Type: Savings
Investment Manager: UPromise and Vanguard Investments
Available Through: Direct from investment manager or through an advisor
Minimum Investment: $25
Deductible Contributions for Residents?: Yes
Telephone: 1-877-697-2837
Website: www.nysaves.org

North Carolina

Plan Name: National College Savings Program
Type: Savings
Investment Manager: College Foundation
Available Through: Direct from investment manager
Minimum Investment: $25
Deductible Contributions for Residents?: Yes
Telephone: 1-800-600-3453
Website: www.nc529.org

North Dakota

Note: The state of North Dakota may provide a dollar match on contributions, depending on household income.

Plan Name: The College SAVE Program
Type: Savings
Investment Manager: UPromise Investments
Available Through: Direct from investment manager
Minimum Investment: $25
Deductible Contributions for Residents?: Yes
Telephone: 1-866-728-3529
Website: www.collegesave4u.com

Ohio

Plan Name: Ohio CollegeAdvantage
Type: Savings
Investment Manager: Blackrock Investments
Available Through: Direct from investment manager or through an advisor
Minimum Investment: $25
Deductible Contributions for Residents?: Yes
Telephone: 1-800-233-6734
Website: www.collegeadvantage.com

Oklahoma

Note: The state of Oklahoma may provide a dollar match on contributions, depending on household income.

Plan Name: Oklahoma College Savings Plan
Type: Savings
Investment Manager: TIAA-CREF
Available Through: Direct from investment manager
Minimum Investment: $100
Deductible Contributions for Residents?: Yes
Telephone: 1-877-654-7284
Website: www.ok4saving.org

Plan Name: Oklahoma Dream 529 Plan
Type: Savings
Investment Manager: TIAA-CREF
Available Through: Stockbroker
Minimum Investment: $1,000 one-time or $50 per month
Deductible Contributions for Residents?: Yes
Telephone: 1-877-529-9299
Website: www.okdream529.com

Oregon

Plan Name: Oregon College Savings Plan
Type: Savings
Investment Manager: TIAA-CREF
Available Through: Direct from investment manager
Minimum Investment: $25
Deductible Contributions for Residents?: Yes
Telephone: 1-866-772-8464
Website: www.oregoncollegesavings.com

Plan Name: Oregon MFS 529 Savings Plan
Type: Savings
Investment Manager: MFS Mutual Funds
Available Through: Stockbroker
Minimum Investment: $250
Deductible Contributions for Residents?: Yes
Telephone: 1-866-637-7526
Website: www.mfs.com

Pennsylvania

Plan Name: Pennsylvania 529 Plan
Type: Savings
Investment Manager: UPromise and Vanguard Investments
Available Through: Direct from investment manager
Minimum Investment: $25
Deductible Contributions for Residents?: Yes
Telephone: 1-800-294-6195
Website: www.makecollegepossible.com

Rhode Island

Note: Rhode Island residents may receive a matching contribution up to $500, subject to available funds.

Plan Name: CollegeBound Fund
Type: Savings
Investment Manager: Alliance Bernstein Funds
Available Through: Direct from investment manager or through an advisor
Minimum Investment: $250
Deductible Contributions for Residents?: Yes
Telephone: 1-888-324-5057
Website: www.collegeboundfund.com

South Carolina

Plan Name: FutureScholar 529 Program
Type: Savings
Investment Manager: Columbia Management
Available Through: Direct from investment manager or through an advisor
Minimum Investment: $250 one-time or $50 per month
Deductible Contributions for Residents?: Yes
Telephone: 1-888-244-5674
Website: www.futurescholar.com

Plan Name: South Carolina Prepaid Tuition Program
Type: Prepaid Tuition
Investment Manager: South Carolina Department of the Treasury
Available Through: Direct from investment manager
Minimum Investment: $17,088 for 2009–2010, with payment plans
Deductible Contributions for Residents?: Yes
Telephone: 1-888-772-4723
Website: www.scgrad.org

South Dakota

Plan Name: CollegeAccess 529 Plan
Type: Savings
Investment Manager: Allianz Investments
Available Through: Direct from investment manager or through an advisor
Minimum Investment: $250 one-time or $50 per month
Deductible Contributions for Residents?: No
Telephone: 1-866-529-7462
Website: www.CollegeAccess529.com

Tennessee

Plan Name: BEST Prepaid Tuition Program
Type: Prepaid Tuition
Investment Manager: Tennessee Department of the Treasury
Available Through: Direct from investment manager
Minimum Investment: $1,766 in 2009–2010
Deductible Contributions for Residents?: No
Telephone: 1-888-772-4723
Website: treasury.tn.gov/best

Texas

Plan Name: Texas Tuition Promise Fund
Type: Prepaid Tuition
Investment Manager: Texas Higher Education Board
Available Through: Direct from investment manager
Minimum Investment: One unit of tuition
Deductible Contributions for Residents?: No
Telephone: 1-800-445-4723
Website: www.texastuitionpromisefund.com

Plan Name: Lonestar 529 Plan/Texas College Savings Plan
Type: Savings
Investment Manager: Oppenheimer Mutual Funds
Available Through: Stockbroker
Minimum Investment: $25
Deductible Contributions for Residents?: No
Telephone: 1-800-445-4723
Website: www.lonestar529.com

Utah

Note: Utah residents may receive a matching contribution, based on household income levels.

Plan Name: Utah Educational Savings Plan
Type: Savings
Investment Manager: Utah Higher Education Assistance Authority
Available Through: Direct from investment manager
Minimum Investment: No minimum
Deductible Contributions for Residents?: Yes
Telephone: 1-800-418-2551
Website: www.uesp.org

Virginia

Plan Name: CollegeAmerica 529 Plan
Type: Savings
Investment Manager: American Funds
Available Through: Stockbroker
Minimum Investment: $250
Deductible Contributions for Residents?: Yes
Telephone: 1-800-421-0180
Website: www.americanfunds.com

Plan Name: CollegeWealth 529 Plan
Type: Savings
Investment Manager: Virginia College Savings Plan
Available Through: Participating banks
Minimum Investment: Varies by institution
Deductible Contributions for Residents?: Yes
Telephone: 1-888-567-0540
Website: www.virginia529.com

Plan Name: Virginia Education Savings Trust (VEST)
Type: Savings
Investment Manager: Virginia College Savings Plan
Available Through: Direct from investment manager
Minimum Investment: $250
Deductible Contributions for Residents?: Yes
Telephone: 1-888-567-0540
Website: www.virginia529.com

Plan Name: Virginia Prepaid Education Plan (VPEP)
Type: Prepaid Tuition
Investment Manager: Virginia College Savings Plan
Available Through: Direct from investment manager
Minimum Investment: $3,620 for 2009–2010
Deductible Contributions for Residents?: Yes
Telephone: 1-888-567-0540
Website: www.virginia529.com

Washington

Plan Name: Guaranteed Education Tuition
Type: Prepaid Tuition
Investment Manager: Washington State Higher Education Board
Available Through: Direct from investment manager
Minimum Investment: One unit of tuition ($117 for 2010)
Deductible Contributions for Residents?: No
Telephone: 1-800-955-2318
Website: www.get.wa.gov

West Virginia

Plan Name: SMART529 College Savings Plan
Type: Savings
Investment Manager: Hartford Life Insurance
Available Through: Direct from investment manager or through an advisor
Minimum Investment: $250 one-time or $25 per month
Deductible Contributions for Residents?: Yes
Telephone: 1-866-574-3542
Website: www.smart529select.com

Wisconsin

Plan Name: EDVEST
Type: Savings
Investment Manager: Wells Fargo Investments
Available Through: Direct from investment manager or through an advisor
Minimum Investment: $250 one-time or $15 per month
Deductible Contributions for Residents?: Yes
Telephone: 1-888-338-3789
Website: www.edvest.com

Wyoming

Plan Name: Direct Portfolio College Savings Plan
Type: Savings
Investment Manager: UPromise and Vanguard Investments
Available Through: Direct from investment manager
Minimum Investment: $25
Deductible Contributions for Residents?: No
Telephone: 1-800-448-2424
Website: www.collegeinvestwyoming.org

Plan Name: Stable Value Plus Plan
Type: Savings
Investment Manager: MetLife
Available Through: Direct from investment manager
Minimum Investment: $25
Deductible Contributions for Residents?: No
Telephone: 1-800-448-2424
Website: www.collegeinvestwyoming.org

Index

Numbers

401k loans, asset liquidation strategies, 51

A

Academic Competitiveness Grant. *See* ACG
academic scholarships, 111
accelerated programs (nontraditional educations), 197-198
acceptance rates, community colleges, 248
accounts
  asset liquidation strategies
    Coverdell ESAs, 47
    Crummey Trusts, 47
    other children's college accounts, 48-49
    savings bonds, 46
    Section 529 plan, 48
    UTMA accounts, 47
  short-term savings, 215-217
    Coverdell Educational Savings Accounts, 216-217
    custodial accounts, 217
    Section 529 accounts, 216

ACG (Academic Competitiveness Grant), 127-128
activity fees, hidden costs, 10
advanced placement classes, 16-17
AFT (American Federation of Teachers), 88
aid (financial aid)
  aid-reducing assets, 45
  CSS Profile (College Scholarship Profile), 102
  EFC (expected family contribution)
    calculation, 94-101
    dependent versus independent students, 95-96
    legalities, 98
    shifting assets, 98-101
    simplifying, 97-98
    tactics to lower, 96-97
  income timing, 101
  Institutional Methodology formula, 102
  non-nuclear families, 103
  nontraditional educations, 201-202
  taxability, 141-142
airfare, cost-cutting strategies, 32-33
Alice Lloyd College, 145

alternative classes, tuition discounts, 17-18
American Federation of Teachers. *See* AFT
American Opportunity Tax Credit. *See* AOTC
AmeriCorps Segal Education Award, 91
AOTC (American Opportunity Tax Credit), 133-134
application process
  scholarships, 114-122
  student loans, 60-61
  tuition-free colleges, 150-151
asset liquidation strategies
  calculations, 43-44
  college accounts, 46-49
  first assets to use, 45-46
  home equity loans, 52-53
  nonfinancial assets, 49-50
  retirement accounts, 50-51
  unclaimed assets, 48
  whole life insurance, 53-54
assets
  aid-reducing assets, 45
  contribution rates, 47
  income timing, 101
  low tax, 45

U

U.S. Air Force Academy, 148

U.S. Coast Guard Academy, 148

U.S. Merchant Marine Academy, 148

U.S. Naval Academy, 148

U.S. Treasury bonds (short-term investments), 213-214

unclaimed assets, asset liquidation strategies, 48

undergraduate tuition-free colleges, 144-147

Uniform Transfer to Minors' Act. *See* UTMA accounts

unique trait scholarships, 113

University of Pennsylvania, 146

unsubsidized student loans, 59-60

upfront costs
Perkins loans, 64
Stafford loans, 62

UPromise program, 158-159

UTMA (Uniform Transfer to Minors' Act) accounts, asset liquidation strategies, 47

V

vocational schools (nontraditional educations), 198-201
best-paying careers, 199-200
selection process, 200-201

volunteers, loan forgiveness programs, 91

vouchers, employer tuition reimbursement, 167

W-X-Y-Z

waivers, tuition waiver programs, 146-147

warnings
employer tuition programs, 167
peer-to-peer lending, 184-185
student loans
drug-related incidents, 68-69
private loans, 67-68
refund checks, 66-67

Webb Institute, 145

websites
College Board, 111
Equal Justice Works, 92
Fafsa4caster, 126
Fast Web, 111
Sallie Mae, 111

weekend programs (nontraditional educations), 198

West Point, 148

whole life insurance, asset liquidation strategies, 53-54

withdrawal penalties (retirement accounts), 50-51

work opportunities, 219
community colleges, 247-248
household jobs, 226-227

part-time options, 220-224
off-campus employment, 222-223
top ten jobs, 223-224
work-study, 221-222
summer jobs, 225-226

work-study programs, 221-222

workplace earnings, nontraditional educations, 194-195

worksheets, College Cash Strategy, 4